We The People's
Guide to
Bankruptcy

Due

We The People's GUIDE TO Bankruptcy

A Do-It-Yourself Plan for Getting Out of Debt

Ira Distenfield and Linda Distenfield

WILEY

John Wiley & Sons, Inc.

Published by John Wiley & Sons, Inc., Hoboken, New Jersey.
Published simultaneously in Canada.

For general information on our other products and services please contact our Customer Care Department within the United States at (800) 762-2974, outside the United States at (317) 572-3993 or fax (317) 572-4002.

Wiley also publishes its books in a variety of electronic formats. Some content that appears in print may not be available in electronic books. For more information about Wiley products, visit our web site at www.Wiley.com.

Library of Congress Cataloging-in-Publication Data:

Distenfield, Ira, 1956–
  We the People's guide to bankruptcy : a do-it-yourself plan for getting out of debt / Ira and Linda Distenfield.
    p. cm.
  Includes index.
    ISBN 0-471-71589-1 (paper : alk. paper)
    1. Bankruptcy—United States—Popular works.   I. Title: Guide to bankruptcy.
II. Distenfield, Linda, 1942–   III. Title.

KF1524.6.D57 2004
346.7307'8—dc22   2004058898

Printed in the United States of America

10 9 8 7 6 5 4 3 2 1

CONTENTS

FOREWORD

Bill Lockyer
California Attorney General

Access to information is essential to life. Access to the legal system often supports a *successful* life. As Attorney General of California, I am a great admirer of We The People and the progress this enterprise has made to significantly improve access to the legal system for all Americans. We The People has led the way by being dedicated to arming people with the information to understand difficult legal situations and the role that certain legal documents can play in their lives.

My ability to access quality information has allowed me to make good decisions throughout my personal and professional life. That's the whole point of information: It permits you to solve problems and be a smart and confident decision-maker. Information educates, trains, prepares, and opens new doors. It imparts knowledge; and it can also console, warn, and advise. I like to think of access to information as a basic necessity alongside food and water, and therefore it should be easy, inexpensive, and inviting. Unfortunately, it's not always that way. When it comes to the legal system, the gap between those "privileged" to access and use the law to their advantage and those who cannot is real for many Americans. And for the 1.6 million Americans who need to file for bankruptcy each year, facing the courts can be an overwhelming task.

As Attorney General I have witnessed the law's positive impact on people's lives, but I've also watched the legal system grow more complex and expensive every day. For too many Americans, the legal system is an 800-pound gorilla that sits on the other side of the table. One can have all the technology that money can buy and yet still feel completely cut off from the legal system, or the opportunity to utilize desperately needed benefits that only the legal system can provide, such as a bankruptcy filing.

Every day, millions of Americans need to complete and file basic legal documents with the courts. Many of these documents don't require an attorney or a fancy degree to complete. I understand the need for competent independent counsel when necessary, but I also support the right to manage one's own legal affairs. Ira and Linda Distenfield founded We The People with a simple mission: to serve people who need to make uncontested legal transactions but who don't know how to approach the legal system and who neither have the resources nor desire to hire a lawyer. What I like best is seeing people served regardless of wealth or privilege.

This book helps you navigate the complex and daunting bankruptcy courts while providing do-it-yourself assistance to clerical preparation and court filing. Whether you can afford legal representation or not, this book equips you with knowledge and skills required by the courts for understanding and completing your own bankruptcy filing, a transaction that more and more individuals must consider every year.

Twenty years ago few people had personal computers; no one had heard of the Internet; no one had e-mail, or a way to carry a library of information on a computer chip that you keep in a hand-held device the size of your wallet. Fast-moving technology has given us ever more access to more information; has changed our expectations; and has changed our way of thinking. The impact that widespread information has had on Americans is evident: Americans feel better equipped and comfortable making pivotal life decisions, such as entering the housing market, changing careers, or starting a small business. Why? Information empowers people to change their lives for the better and make hard decisions. It is the ultimate equalizer.

My experiences have taught me about responsibility, leadership, and the value of being an independent thinker. I prepare relentlessly and always encourage others to do the same through studying, reading, and learning independently. My advice for anyone thinking about bankruptcy or going through a bankruptcy is to gather as much information as you can before, during, and after the process. Only then can you be assured that you're doing your absolute best to plan for and safeguard your future.

Success is not measured by status or wealth, but by how we deal with the challenges we face, by how we overcome those challenges through the decisions we make, and by the steps we take to move forward in our lives. This book allows you not only to access and gain information, but to use its information to make sense of a difficult situation and take control of your life. You are entitled to the law's help in re-starting your financial life as much as anyone else. Be prepared for whatever course you take—with or without a lawyer by your side—and you'll welcome the rewards that await you in your future.

ABOUT THE AUTHORS

Ira Distenfield is the Cofounder, Chairman of the Board, and Chief Executive Officer of *We The People Forms And Service Centers USA, Inc.,* a company he started with his wife in 1993. We The People is presently the largest independent paralegal company in the nation with offices in more than 150 cities and 31 states. Before his involvement with *We The People,* Mr. Distenfield was a Senior Vice President with Gruntal & Co., Inc., and a First Vice President with Smith Barney. He is a former President of the Port of Los Angeles, which, under his leadership, became the largest revenue producing port in the United States. He is an active member in his community and was named among the Outstanding Young Men of America by the U.S. Chamber of Commerce. He presently serves on the Santa Barbara County Sheriff's Council and is a member of the Santa Barbara County Parole Board.

Linda Distenfield is the Cofounder, President and Chief Operating Officer of *We The People Forms And Service Centers USA, Inc.* Before her involvement with *We The People,* Mrs. Distenfield served as Santa Barbara County's first full-time Film Commissioner. She also served as the Scheduling Director to the Honorable Tom Bradley, former Mayor of Los Angeles and gubernatorial candidate for the State of California. Mrs. Distenfield is active in several Santa Barbara organizations, and is a founding member of the Santa Barbara Firefighters Alliance.

The Distenfields live in Santa Barbara, California, but travel extensively throughout the country as they expand their company and support the franchise's growth. They enjoy seven children and three grandchildren.

ACKNOWLEDGMENTS

We owe our success to the thousands of customers we have helped through the years regain control of their lives or simply access the information they need to move forward and plan smartly. They continue to inspire, teach, and challenge us. Without them, this book would not have been possible.

Thanks to our supervising attorneys for their guidance and support of We The People, and especially Jason Sears, Esq. and Brant Jackson, Esq., who graciously reviewed the manuscript and offered their own expertise. Also to Bonnie Solow and Kristin Loberg for their direction and help through the writing and publishing process.

Finally, we'd like to dedicate this book to the millions of people out there who seek sound knowledge and have the courage to take charge of their own legal affairs—with or without the support of attorneys and professionals—and use what they learn to enhance their lives.

Introduction

If you're not a lawyer, and don't have access to one through family, friends, colleagues, or coworkers, facing a legal dilemma is a challenge—and mightily intimidating. Many transactions in life require legal documents, from a blissful marriage to an ugly divorce; from the birth of your children to the death of your parents. In fact, most all transactions in life that we experience at some point involve legal documents. *What's a legal document?* you ask. Legal documents are nothing more than papers that state a contractual relationship (example: marriage) or grant a right (example: trademark). Some are filed in a court, while others are kept between two agreeing people. All legal documents provide information of an official nature, and they are as prevalent as the air you breathe and the water you drink.

Life Is a Series of Transactions

The most significant transitions in life are punctuated by legal documents. You can think of life as a series of transactions, for which you leave a paper trail of official and unofficial records: birth (certificate), education (degrees), work (employment permit or contract), marriage (certificate), major purchases (titles, deeds), minor purchases (receipts), travels (passport), maybe divorce (agreement), retirement (investment portfolios), and death (certificate). Dozens more also come to mind. If you gathered up all the legal documents that you have amassed since birth, your collection would impress you. And you'd wonder how you managed to accumulate so many importance pieces of information (about you!) without really thinking about it along the way.

Some transactions are easier to make than others. Some require sticking to specific laws and the approval of courts or government agencies. Examples include agreements, guardianships, child custodies, prenuptials, small claims, incorporations, trademarks, copyrights, evictions, and so on. But even the more common transactions of everyday life often involve legal documents. When you buy a house, secure a loan, finance a car, obtain your baby's birth certificate, purchase insurance, rent an apartment, hire a general contractor for home improvements, renew your drivers' license, get a new credit card, or even accept the risk of parking your car in the mall lot, you deal with special legal documents without even realizing it.

Why Some Transactions Are Easy, Others Are Not

The difference between the seemingly mindless transactions and the complicated ones is clear: Someone else does most of the work in executing the simple transactions, and those transactions frequently don't involve the courts or a remote agency. For example, the document you sign when you lease a car is a legal document—a contract—that is between you and the car dealer, which will be upheld in a court of law (if you don't live by the contract's rules, such as making those monthly payments). You don't think so much about this contract as being a legal document, though, because the car dealer does all the work (and sometimes manages to squeeze more money from you in the form of document prep and dealer fees). Such a contract does not involve attorneys or filing with the courts, either, so the process is much less intimidating. You fill in the blanks, sign or initial your name on dozens of lines, and eventually drive off in a new car.

But for other, bigger transactions in life, such as filing for bankruptcy or getting a family business incorporated, it's hard to find someone to do the work for you at a low cost. The process seems more complicated, more remote—more people, more filing, more knowledge in areas you don't know—and sometimes engages the courts or other entities to complete. Moreover, these complex transactions typically necessitate specific sets of documents you don't find in your corner market (or that are not handed to you without asking), and they incur certain fees that are unavoidable. Where do you find these documents? How do you fill them out and pay for these transactions? Who can tell you what to expect?

Help! I Don't Know How to Do This

In an information age, you start by educating yourself about your particular need, and research ways of getting what you want for the least amount of money (and you ponder over hiring that big, expensive attorney if you can't figure out how to do it on your own). Trouble is, because these transactions do entail unavoidable fees, attorneys jump at the chance to maximize profits based on those fees—and based on making you believe that you can't execute those transactions on your own. Truth is, you can. And you don't need a fancy degree or legal background to do so.

Welcome to We The People. We are a company that specializes in legal document preparation without the high costs related to lawyers. We are the first and only nationwide legal document preparation service in the country. Over the past decade, we have successfully served more than 500,000 consumers, including 20,000 bankruptcies in the last year alone. With 150 offices nationwide and growing every month, we have researched the requirements of most local jurisdictions, down to the color of paper and exact wording preferred.

By the time a publisher approached us to put our valuable information into a book, we were the nation's number one expert in the ins and outs of legal document preparation. And as founders of We The People, we felt exceedingly equipped to share our knowledge and experience. We've empowered hundreds of thousands of people over the past 10 years and we hope to empower millions more by sharing with you all the information that we've gathered. As you'll soon find out in the next few pages, knowledge is power.

This book is the first in that series, which gives you the information you need to complete the trickier transactions in life that make most people cringe. They make people cringe because people don't know the how-tos to these complicated transactions, and the guidance they need is not so obvious in the real world. So you are not alone if you are reading this book and searching for help.

We start with bankruptcy, because sometimes you need a fresh start and there's just no other way to go about it.

Bankruptcy: A Blessing in Disguise?

Filing for bankruptcy doesn't make you a bad person, nor does it ruin your chance of having a happy and productive life. To the contrary, filing for bankruptcy might give you the right beginnings for ultimately achieving all that you've dreamed for your future. It can be a blessing in disguise.

If you know you're dealing with a transaction like bankruptcy that must involve the courts, you might feel like you are on one side of the table and the legal community (that is, your bankruptcy court) is on the other—untouchable and impossible to penetrate without money and an attorney. It doesn't have to be this way. Although the mailman, who sees how many past due and collections notices he delivers to you, isn't going to drop the proper documents for bankruptcy filing into his stash of mail for you, filing for bankruptcy is easier than you think. The documents and procedures are not a secret.

Facing a personal bankruptcy is scary on two fronts: It's a transaction that involves court filings (thus fees), and it's usually a deeply emotional experience. You're not driving off in a new car or getting ready to marry your soulmate. To the contrary, you're surrendering to either a series of financial challenges in life or a lot of bad luck, or both. And a bankruptcy can't cost you more than you already can't afford.

So you've scanned the selection of self-help legal software and books at your local bookseller or online. Perhaps you've found some too simplified, others by authors with questionable credentials, while the vast majority prove as dry and complex as the legal documents you're trying to fill out!

In This Book

This book explains the process of filing for bankruptcy in simple, practical language. As unique as your particular situation might be, we have heard a version of your story walk into one of our offices, and we know how to treat each and every case successfully. We know how daunting the task of filing for bankruptcy can be. And we know the relief customers feel once we guide them through the paperwork and proper filings. We see it every day with smiles, gifts, notes of thanks, and grand sighs of relief from our customers. We hope this book becomes your friend, a lifeline similar to the way our offices become lifelines to the people courageous enough to walk in and ask for help.

Throughout the book, we answer questions you have about the kinds of dilemmas you are facing: Is bankruptcy the right course of action to take? If so, what kind is appropriate? How will it impact my future employment, credit and current assets?

In addition to stories that will encourage, uplift, and hopefully inspire you, we provide step-by-step instructions on how to fill out all the official forms. For any local requirements, we tell you where you need to go and detail any complications you may encounter. We are your guiding light through this difficult, sometimes painful process.

The Story Behind *We The People*

Before we begin, let us explain how We The People came to be. We are Ira and Linda Distenfield, the founders of We The People, who both came from different experiences that, conjoined, made for a perfect union in our new venture. It all began in the early 1990s. As senior vice president of a major New York Stock Exchange member firm and president of the Los Angeles Port Authority, Ira frequently hired attorneys to handle his affairs. But something always struck him as odd. Why was he charged the same hourly rate for document preparation—primarily a clerical function—as for high-level legal advice?

Considering a career change, Ira began to research the paralegal field. He uncovered some surprising facts: The legal industry is a $100 billion business. At least half of a typical attorney's practice involves the processing of simple legal documents, often performed by nonattorneys. And if consumers hired independent paralegals rather than attorneys, their legal bills can be cut by as much as 90 percent.

While the marketplace offered an array of alternatives to attorneys, such as do-it-yourself legal software and court-run Internet web sites, Ira saw an untapped niche. He believed that legal forms were designed to confuse, created for lawyers and not the average consumer. Even though people can pick up legal forms at a drive-through courthouse kiosk or download them from the Internet, they still needed help filling them out.

We knew we needed marketing and organizational and legal expertise to succeed in our venture. As far as marketing, Ira capitalized on his 25 years as a stockbroker and experience traveling around the world encouraging countries to export their goods via Los Angeles Harbor as president of the L.A. Port Authority. Linda took advantage of her administrative skills honed during her tenure as scheduling director for former Los Angeles mayor Tom Bradley. Together we attended paralegal school for a year to learn how to process legal documents and hired an attorney to supervise our work.

In 1994, we opened our first We The People office in Santa Barbara, California. We knew this kind of service made sense in our lives, but we wondered if it would make sense for others. Was there a market for this type of service? Within three months, we got our answer.

Gifts started appearing at our door. "You got me through this bankruptcy for $199, and my lawyer wanted $3,000. Here, we bought a little box of candy for you," read a typical note. In Ira's 25 years of business experience, he had never witnessed such a personal gesture.

Our tiny one-room office in an executive suite filled a huge consumer need. For prices as much as 90 percent less than lawyer fees, customers who didn't require the advice of an attorney got help with more than 80 kinds of legal documents, such as divorce, bankruptcy, incorporation, living trusts, and wills. Customers provided information in simple workbooks. That information was then typed into the appropriate forms.

The Future of *We The People*

Ten years later, customer enthusiasm has fueled the launch of 150 offices in 30 states. In 2003, our company handled approximately 20,000 bankruptcies, 13,000 wills, and 38,000 divorces, more than any single law firm in the United States. We The People's multi-million-dollar revenues continue to rise as more stores open and meet the needs of more people. Under the guidance of former New York City Mayor Rudolph Giuliani's consulting firm, Giuliani Partners, we plan to open 31 stores throughout the five boroughs of the city of New York this year and expand into additional markets nationwide. As testament to our careful research of the rules of each local jurisdiction, We The People has helped more than half a million people to successfully complete their legal matters. What makes us exceptional: We The People not only has become experts in the preparation of documents, but we know what many local courts require. Our company's expanding markets continue to afford us greater power in getting more information for fulfilling our customers' needs. An attorney can have only so much information. A robust company operating in more than half of the United States, however, can supply a wealth of information from the broadest of help to the most localized.

No Lawyers Means You Save Money

More and more people are seeking alternatives to the high cost of attorneys. According to an American Bar Association study in 1996, each year half of all low- and moderate-income households need legal help but must forgo it—in part because they can't afford a lawyer. As attorney fees rise to an average of $200 per hour, the number of people forced to navigate the system on their own has also climbed. In fact, fees have risen to such a point that even some lawyers privately say that, should they need it, they might be priced out of the legal market!

> According to the U.S. Bureau of Labor Statistics, the legal forms business is the largest growth industry in the nation, second only to home health care.

Whether it's buying bulk at Costco or trolling the Internet for the best deal on a printer, consumers are driven now more than ever to get the most for their money. Legal services are not immune.

The simple truth is that lawyers are not necessary for many legal services. The head of one non-profit that provides legal help for low-income folks has estimated that only about five percent of its typical clients actually require a full-range, high-cost lawyer. As a result, a growing number of Americans are choosing to represent themselves in legal matters. In California, for instance, more than 50 percent of bankruptcies and 60 percent of divorces are now filed without an attorney. Our entry into the self-help legal industry has made a major impact in people's ability to access the legal system, and as we continue to open more stores nationwide, those statistics will change.

You have three choices for getting legal documents completed:

1. Type them yourself.
2. Go to a reputable legal document assistant (such as We The People).
3. Go to a lawyer.

> In its March 1991 issue, the American Bar Association *Journal* reported a study in which it was estimated that consumers can save more than $1.3 billion annually by representing themselves in just four routine legal transactions: uncontested divorces, wills, bankruptcies, and incorporations. When you represent yourself in a legal matter, it's referred to as doing it *pro se* (for yourself).

This book is useful for any of the above options. Even if you decide to hire a lawyer to help you through your bankruptcy, you still need to educate yourself about the process and be as knowledgeable and prepared as possible. The more you know, the better your outcome, the more successful you will be. In fact, you have a chance of outperforming other lawyers who are representing other debtors at their 341 meeting (a mandatory meeting you'll attend as part of your bankruptcy process)!

While some do-it-yourself legal resources provide general information, few provide guidance at the local level. By reading this book, you set yourself up for completing your entire bankruptcy transaction. You can use the worksheets contained in this book to prepare for filling out the official forms, which you can easily download at www.wethepeopleforms .com. You'll know how to find local forms you may have to obtain from your jurisdiction, and you'll be able to approach the courts with confidence and a good base of knowledge. You won't need to navigate the maze of Internet research—or call your mother to cry for help. Should you need further assistance, one of our offices can also assist you in understanding the specific requirements of your local bankruptcy court (see Appendix C for a listing of We The People stores by state); and we can help you type your paperwork if you choose to use our services.

None of this book's contents can substitute the person-to-person contact you can get when you walk into one of our offices, but this book is an excellent companion for those who don't have access to one of our locations, or who prefer to complete the process as independently as possible. Backed by We The People's expertise, this book reflects years of experience and stands at the top of the self-help legal document market. No organization can claim that they have assisted 500,000 people over the past decade in filling out and filing basic legal documents. Having We The People's information in one comprehensive book that won't become outdated anytime soon is like having a universal tool tucked away in your pocket. You can draw on this reference for years to come. And it will add to your peace of mind, too.

Your Future

When you're considering a bankruptcy, the first questions that rush through your mind are: *How will this affect my credit and buying power in the future? Will I ever qualify for a loan again? What are the steps I have to take? How much is it going to cost? How long will it take? What is expected of me?* The following page contains a summary of these answers, which will be detailed later in the book.

Two types of bankruptcy apply to individuals: Chapter 7 and Chapter 13. This book will concentrate on Chapter 7. Under this Chapter, most of your debts are eliminated, save for certain exceptions. We will, however, explain other types of bankruptcies (in chapter 3) and give you other options in lieu of filing for bankruptcy. If you haven't decided whether or not to file for bankruptcy, this book provides the insights and information you need to make that crucial decision. Bankruptcy is not a transaction to take lightly. It has far-reaching effects on your life that are both financial and emotional. By now, you've already begun a financial and emotional journey that likely makes you uncomfortable and uneasy. Just considering bankruptcy is a serious matter. But it doesn't have to be so terrifying as to paralyze you and prevent you from making good choices. That's what this book is about.

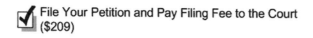

Chapter 7 Order of Events

☑ File Your Petition and Pay Filing Fee to the Court ($209)

☑ Automatic Stay Goes Into Effect, Stopping All Creditors from Contacting and Collecting from You

☑ Court Appoints a Trustee to Administer Your Case to the Bankruptcy Court

☑ Attend Meeting of the Creditors Before Your Trustee in Noncourtroom Setting to Confirm Paperwork

☑ Await Court's Discharge of Your Debts and Closure of Your Case

☑ Move On With Your Life and Re-establish Good Credit!

Average Total Time for Bankruptcy Case to Close from Day 1 of Filing: 4 to 6 months.

In Most Cases,
You:

☑ Never go before a judge.

☑ Can stay in your home and keep most of your assets.

☑ Become released of most burdensome debts and begin to rebuild your credit and life right away.

Finally, having a greater sense of control over your situation by doing most of the work yourself as you move through this transaction in your life is a liberating experience. With this book, and the knowledge you gain from it, you will succeed in a difficult transaction and move forward in your life. You will become a smart and empowered individual able to base decisions on what you've learned.

So let's begin.

CHAPTER 1

What Is Bankruptcy?

First and foremost, filing for bankruptcy is taking charge of your financial affairs once they've spun out of control to the point you cannot get through your day without thinking about your situation. You may feel stuck and unable to plan for your future because you owe so much money. Bankruptcy is a way of erasing certain debts that prohibit you from moving forward and pursuing the American dream. Do you know what's involved when your debts become overwhelming?

The decision about whether to file for bankruptcy is a difficult one. Knowing what is involved and how simple the process is can make the decision a little easier. Knowledge in this topic is power—and it's not just for the lawyers! Regardless of your skills, job, or IQ, you can learn everything you need to know, from the basics to the intricacies of bankruptcy, and take charge of your life. In turn, you can open your own door to a fresh start and welcome a new beginning.

You're Not Alone

Personal bankruptcies are at an all-time high following the 1990s when consumers did a lot of, well, consuming. In fact, the economic boom of the 1990s was driven largely by consumer spending, as people tended to save less and spend more on goods and services. Lower interest rates spurred a housing boom and urged people to spend even more and think less about the

Personal bankruptcy filings in 2003 rose 5.3 percent in just a year. Whether debt problems were the result of losing a job, a divorce, an illness, or simply overspending, more than 1.6 million Americans chose bankruptcy as the way to solve their financial problems. Household debts sat at a record high of $8.9 trillion nationwide. By early April 2004, the American Bankruptcy Institute, which compiles per capita bankruptcy statistics every three months based on figures from the Census Bureau and U.S. Bankruptcy Courts, estimated that for the previous year (ending March 31st) there was one filing for every 72.9 households.

financial consequences. By the early 2000s, the scales were tipping and bankruptcy filings were beginning to add up. Filings have doubled nationwide in the past decade, increasing from 813,000 filings in 1993 to 1,625,200 in 2003, according to federal bankruptcy court records.

That's a lot of household debt, and a lot of bankruptcies. In fact, the statistics translate to a rate of 185 per hour! Like we said above, you're not alone in this transaction.

Knowledge Is Power

We will repeat this truth throughout this book: Knowledge is power! Repeat this statement out loud to yourself and feel the confidence it gives you. Facing a bankruptcy might make you feel crippled, but don't let that happen. Use the information in this book to empower yourself and to make good decisions for your future. Keep this statement in the back of your mind as you move through these chapters. It will fuel you with the energy you need to conquer your fears related to a bankruptcy, to get done what you need to get done, and to move on.

It's Your Constitutional Right

Filing for bankruptcy is a constitutional right of protection against creditors (people to whom you owe money). It allows people to make a fresh start after experiencing financial difficulties so severe that creditors' demands can no longer be reasonably satisfied.

Most people who file for bankruptcy are insolvent, which is defined by the Federal Bankruptcy Code as a financial condition such that what you owe is more than what you have.

Do you qualify for filing for bankruptcy? Are you insolvent? Filing for bankruptcy is a personal choice you have to make. Ask yourself:

- Do I owe more than what I have?
- Do I lack the means to pay off rising debt?

If you said yes to these two questions, then you probably qualify for bankruptcy. From a legal standpoint, you don't even have to be insolvent to qualify for bankruptcy. Relief is available irrespective of the amount of your debts or whether you are solvent or insolvent. The exact qualifications for bankruptcy will be discussed in the next chapter. But if you carry an enormous amount of personal debt in the form of credit cards, medical bills, or fallout of a divorce or job loss and you are unable to pay for basic living expenses, then you likely qualify for relief.

Being insolvent is also referred to as being upside down, which makes sense if you think of being physically upside down and unable to upright yourself without the fresh start that bankruptcy can provide. If you won the lottery today and suddenly came into a ton of money, you wouldn't feel upside down anymore. And you wouldn't be thinking about bankruptcy. You'd be paying your creditors back quickly and promising yourself never to return to the state of being in so much debt.

But chances are, you're not going to hit the jackpot (and we don't suggest you travel to Las Vegas to waste any last resources of money you've got trying to beat the odds). You need to begin to look at yourself and your finances realistically and to take charge of your situation before you lose your mind. We know how mentally draining and troublesome a bankruptcy can be. Imagine getting that clean slate, that ability to start over and rebuild your life for the better. Imagine closing the door to years of financial hardship and struggle, angry creditors, and threatening letters that reduce your quality of life.

You may know that bankruptcy will help you, but you still struggle with the decision to take action. If you are like most individuals, you have spent a lifetime trying to do the right thing. You have sacrificed in order to meet your obligations. Sometimes you have paid creditors when you really could not afford to do so. You may have ignored medical needs or sacrificed the comfort and well-being of your loved ones in order to satisfy a financial obligation. If you pay only the minimum balance on your credit cards, you will never see that huge balance owed move downward. (In chapter 2 we'll give you other options to filing for bankruptcy that might be more suitable for your current needs.)

But there comes a time when, regardless of your sacrifices, there is simply not enough money to meet your obligations. Your creditors are not happy because you cannot pay them the way they expect to be paid. You are not happy because as hard as you try and continue to sacrifice, you are not able to solve your financial problems. If anything, they get worse. Even when you stop using credit cards, their balance totals haunt you with so much interest that you cannot begin to pay down the actual principal amount because all you can afford is the interest payment. Bankruptcy begins to look like the solution to your problems.

Examples of Common Exemptions (Things You Can Keep) in Most States

- House (to protect a certain amount of the equity in your home)
- Household appliances
- Personal clothing and furniture
- Personal automobile
- Business vehicle
- Tools of trade
- Retirement funds

Note that each state will vary, so the above list may not match your particular situation. In this chapter, we give you the overview of what bankruptcy entails, from the law to the actual process of filing for bankruptcy. You'll learn about all the people involved in the process, what you stand to gain when filing for bankruptcy, and what you stand to lose.

Bankruptcy is defined and recognized on the federal level, but filing for bankruptcy requires attention to the details given by your particular state and sometimes your particular district. In this book, we strive to give general information that pertains to all bankruptcy filings no matter the state in which you reside. When necessary, we use examples from specific states and direct you to resources where you can find information about your specific state. The biggest differences among the states are the exemptions involved with a bankruptcy. Exemptions are the rules that allow you to keep some of your assets in your bankruptcy. You are allowed to keep certain necessities of life, such as your personal clothing and car to get to work. These items are exempt from your bankruptcy. In other words, you don't have to worry about losing them. Lists of exemptions by state can be found at www.wethepeopleforms.com. (More on this later.)

MIRANDA'S STORY

I feel like I've followed the rules all my life. I graduated from college with a 3.4 grade point average. I found a job in my field at the local school district. I earn $30 an hour, more than many of my former classmates. And I pay off all my bills each month. That is, until recently, when a series of unexpected events turned my financial life upside down.

It all started when my baby was born. A medical problem racked up hospital bills that far exceeded my health coverage. Then a bitter divorce left me with $20,000 in attorney fees. I began to pay what I could each month toward both bills. But that wasn't good enough. The hospital and attorney arranged to garnish (take money out of) my wages, to the tune of $500 each month!

I borrowed $8,000 from my family. I turned off my telephone, Internet and cable services. I started charging food and gas on my credit cards. But nothing I did seemed to make up for the fact that nearly one-third of my income was now gone. As the bills mounted, I found myself falling behind on rent and unable to make even the minimum due on my credit cards. With 18% interest rates and penalties for missed payments, my debt doubled and then tripled!

Creditors began calling me at work. (They couldn't reach me at home—my phone was turned off!) My boss wondered what was going on. Then a third creditor notified me of their intention to garnish my wages. I decided I needed to take action, and fast. There was no way I was going to hire another attorney. I couldn't risk another $20,000 bill. So I researched the possibility of filing for bankruptcy.

I downloaded the appropriate documents off of my local court's Web site. The information required wasn't as hard as I thought: basically, how much I owed; my living expenses; and my assets, like car, computer, furniture, etc. I admit, it took me a little while to get my financial paperwork in order and dig out some documents that were buried in my home office, but it felt good getting my financial papers organized. It was time to get organized and know exactly where my money (or lack of it) was located. And once I filed the papers with the Bankruptcy Court, I felt this great sense of relief. When creditors called, I simply gave them my case number and they were not allowed to call again. The Automatic Stay is wonderful. It stopped the garnishment of my wages the moment I filed.

Within three months, the court had discharged all my debt and I had full use of my income again. I felt this sense of empowerment, that I had taken control of the situation without an expensive attorney. On my own initiative, I had started to rebuild my financial security.

I opened a savings account and began putting away a set amount each month. I took out a better health insurance plan for my baby girl. And I enrolled in graduate school to increase my future earning potential. Bankruptcy has definitely given me a shot at getting my life back together. And I did it on my own!

The Law

The laws of bankruptcy go back hundreds of years to our forefathers, who shared a concern enough to specifically make room for laws regarding bankruptcy in our Constitution. While the laws have changed through the years, the purpose of bankruptcy remains the same: to give people a certain right of protection against creditors. Filing for bankruptcy protection solves financial problems by wiping out debt; in exchange for this, one gets a new beginning. Article I, Section 8, of the United States Constitution authorizes Congress to enact "uniform Laws on the subject of Bankruptcies." Under this grant of authority, the United States Congress adopted the first national bankruptcy law in 1800. It has been amended somewhat throughout the years and present law is based on the Bankruptcy Act of 1978. Bankruptcy law has been modified to some degree since 1978, but it essentially remains the same.

> Remember the ultimate rights outlined in our Constitution: the right to life, liberty, and the pursuit of happiness. Well, if you're full of fear and trepidation now that you're experiencing a financial crisis and cannot enjoy life, find liberty, nor pursue happiness, rest assured that there are solutions to your problems.

If you are finding it very difficult to enjoy life because of financial pressures, understand that our forefathers made sure that our Constitution gave Congress the power to enact a law to give you the relief from such financial difficulties. This is how we came to have the Bankruptcy Code.

The Bankruptcy Code, which is codified as Title 11 of the United States Code, is the uniform federal law that governs all bankruptcy cases. This may look cold and confusing, but here's what the Section 342(b) of that code states:

> Prior to the commencement of a case under this title by an individual whose debts are primarily consumer debts, the clerk shall give written notice to such individual that indicates each chapter of this title under which such individual may proceed.

What does this mean? We will explain everything so you don't need to worry about confusing legal language and terms that make you want to run away. The law basically states that you have a right to declare bankruptcy. And because there are various types of bankruptcies, you have to pick the right type of filing for the kind of debt you have.

Each bankruptcy court is in charge of a geographic area; some states have just one district, larger states have more districts. There are 94 bankruptcy districts across the country. The bankruptcy courts generally have their own clerk's offices (where you go to file your petition).

> The procedural aspects of the bankruptcy process are governed by the Federal Rules of Bankruptcy Procedure (often called the Bankruptcy Rules) and local rules of bankruptcy. The Bankruptcy Rules contain a set of official forms for use in bankruptcy cases. The Bankruptcy Code and Bankruptcy Rules (and local rules) set forth the formal legal procedures for dealing with the debt problems of individuals and businesses.

Types of Bankruptcy Filings

Every year more than a million and a half people exercise their right to eliminate their debts and start over again. You, too, can exercise this right, eliminate your debts, and start rebuilding your financial affairs.

General information on the main Chapters of the Bankruptcy Code and definitions of bankruptcy terminology are available in the form of a Public Information Series, comprised of a series of fact sheets on these topics. Anyone may obtain the Public Information Series by writing to the Administrative Office of the United States Courts, Bankruptcy Judges Division, One Columbus Circle, N.E., Washington, D.C. 20544. The fact sheets have been combined in the publication *Bankruptcy Basics*, which is available at the federal judiciary's Internet web site, www.uscourts.gov.

Bankruptcy filings vary, whether you're an individual or business looking for relief from your debts in the form of debt elimination or restructuring the terms of repaying those debts. Here's a basic breakdown:

- Both individuals and businesses can file under Chapter 7 to eliminate their debts, which is also referred to as total liquidation.
- Individuals can restructure their debts by filing for relief under Chapter 13.
- Businesses can restructure their debts by filing for relief under Chapter 11.
- A family farmer can restructure his debts under Chapter 12.

In the United States in 2003, approximately 1,100,000 individuals were able to wipe out their debts under Chapter 7. Almost half a million were able to restructure their debts under Chapter 13. Approximately 100,000 businesses were able to eliminate their debts under Chapter 7 or restructure and reorganize their debts under Chapter 11. We will revisit these types of bankruptcy in more detail in chapter 3 of this book.

You might wonder why bankruptcy filings have to come under chapters. That's how the law works. United States Codes are laws. They are usually called titles and their subsections are broken down into chapters. Hence, we have the Bankruptcy Code labeled as Title 11 in the U.S. Codes, and under Title 11 are various chapters—or types—of bankruptcies. We know it can get confusing, but you'll get used to hearing these terms.

How Do I File without An Attorney?

Yes, bankruptcy is the legal process, but no, you do not need an attorney to complete the paperwork and file the forms with the court.

You have the right to represent yourself in the bankruptcy court. This is referred to as doing it *pro se*. A large number of people have filed their own bankruptcies and have done so successfully. That is because filing bankruptcy is simply a matter of completing the forms required by the bankruptcy courts. The official bankruptcy forms published by the federal judiciary are accepted in all bankruptcy courts. So you can go to the court and get a packet of all the official forms (you may have to pay a small fee). The easiest way to start is to go to www.wethepeopleforms.com and download (and print) all necessary forms. Instructions on the site will tell you which ones you need. Use this book to understand how to fill them out. If you do not have access to a computer or the Internet, you can visit your local public library, or a store such as Kinko's that offers Internet and printing services. You can also download these same forms at www.uscourts.gov/bankform/. Links from this main site to your local

> ## TIME OUT! *I Don't Understand What You Mean By . . .*
>
> **Insolvency.** The state of being unable to pay your debts because you owe more than you have.
>
> **Debt.** Something owed, an obligation to pay.
>
> **Debtor.** The person (such as you) who owes a debt.
>
> **Creditor.** The person to whom money is owed.
>
> **Exemptions.** The rules that allow you to keep some of your assets in your bankruptcy. Generally, exempt assets are what you can keep. Nonexempt assets are what you cannot keep. But there is some flexibility here, as we'll see.
>
> **Collateral.** Assets used as security (a pledge or promise) for the repayment of a loan. Many people use large assets like homes, cars, and home furniture as collateral for loans.
>
> **Equity.** The money value of your property, such as a home, that does not include the lender's portion of the value. Equity is the difference between the value of the asset and what you owe on the asset. Example: Your home is worth $250,000. When you bought it for $230,000, a bank loaned you the money in a mortgage. You've paid $40,000 against the principal of your loan (this excludes any interest on your loan), so your equity is roughly $60,000 ($40,000 plus the increase in the home's value of $20,000). Another example: Your car has a value of $4,000 but there is a $3,500 lien on it (you owe someone money because you've used your car as collateral for a loan) so your car now has an equity value of only $500. This $500 would be the amount subject to exemption.
>
> **Discharge.** To dismiss or release from obligation to pay, such as your debts. When a bankruptcy discharges your debts, you are no longer responsible for paying those debts—ever again. This word can also be used as a noun: A discharge is a release of obligation to pay. Hence, the court discharges your debts, and you receive a discharge.

court's web site will allow you to download any local forms you need. Alternatively, you can walk into a We The People office, fill out all the information on the worksheets we provide, and have us type the forms for you. You don't need an attorney to hold your hand and explain to you how to fill out the forms. If the forms intimidate you, think about setting more time aside to focus on the documents. You can do it, and we are here to ensure that you do it successfully.

People are intimidated by the thought of going to a court and appearing before a judge. Much of the bankruptcy process is administrative, however, and is conducted away from the courthouse. A debtor's involvement with the bankruptcy judge is usually very limited, if at all. If you're filing under Chapter 7, you will not appear in court and you will not see the bankruptcy judge unless an objection is raised in your case (unlikely), or you plan to reaffirm, or keep, a debt such as your car loan. Some judges require that debtors who file for bankruptcy

---

TIME OUT! *I Don't Understand What You Mean By . . .*

Assets. Your stuff. Specifically, any real property (your house), personal property (your car), or intellectual property (your patent rights to an invention) in which you own an interest (a legal share). Money owed to you and portions of property (such as half of a house you share with your wife) are also examples of assets. The words "property" and "asset" can be used interchangeably.

Automatic Stay Provision (or Order). An automatic and instant relief from your creditors' attempts to collect from you.

Income. How much you make from all sources, or the amount that appears on your pay stubs.

Expenses. What you spend, or the money that you need to pay for monthly expenses, such as food, rent, etc.

Trustee. The person appointed by the bankruptcy court to take possession of all your nonexempt assets, reduce them to cash, and make distributions to creditors (subject to your right to retain some exempt assets and the rights of secured creditors). Your trustee's job is to make sure that your documents are complete and to review your list of assets for items that are not protected by law. In no-asset cases, where you don't have assets worth selling for money to pay creditors, your trustee gets only a flat fee to manage your case. Your trustee is a fair and impartial participant in your bankruptcy. The U.S. Trustee is the bankruptcy arm of the Justice Department.

Liquidate. To sell your assets in an attempt to repay some of your debts. Your trustee will liquidate any nonexempt assets you have once you file. For the majority of Chapter 7 filers, there are no assets worth selling, so the trustee has nothing to liquidate.

---

without an attorney appear before them to confirm these reaffirmation agreements. (We will explain this process later.)

If you're filing under Chapter 13 you may only have to appear before the bankruptcy judge at your plan confirmation hearing. Usually, the only formal proceeding at which you must appear is the meeting of creditors, which is usually held at the offices of the United States trustee. Your trustee is the impartial representative in your bankruptcy case who deals with the distribution of your nonexempt assets.

Most Common Type of Bankruptcy Filing

Chapter 7 is the most common type of bankruptcy. It is commonly referred to as a washout or straight bankruptcy. With a Chapter 7, you are able to totally discharge almost all of your debts without having to repay them. You will also be allowed to keep most of your assets, possibly including your home. A husband and wife may file jointly in a bankruptcy and obtain a discharge of all their marital debts, as well as the debts they each incurred before the marriage. A Chapter 7 bankruptcy allows you to start fresh without having to pay back the majority of your debts.

A common factor of all bankruptcies is the automatic stay provision. This puts any act to collect assets or to recover a claim against you in an immediate hold position. The stay takes place once the petition is filed. It obviously allows you some breathing room from bill collectors. So the moment you file your bankruptcy petition is the moment you

> Under Chapter 7, an individual or business is discharged of any liability on most—if not all—of their *unsecured* debts and on unsecured portions of *secured* debts. A discharge means the debtor (you) no longer has legal obligation to repay the debt.

don't have to answer to all the people who hound you down for money. Your creditors can no longer call, write, harass, or threaten in any way. It also stops wage garnishment (the taking of your money out of your wages). Once you file your initial papers with the court, you can notify your creditors (especially the problem ones) of your bankruptcy, and they will have to stop taking any actions against you. If your wages are being garnished, you will want to notify your employer immediately so that stops happening. Your trustee will also mail your creditors an official notice of your bankruptcy filing. (Included in your paperwork is a list of all your creditors and their contact information.)

You may claim some of your assets as exempt under governing law. If you have nonexempt assets subject to seizure, the trustee will try to sell any valuable assets and use the proceeds to pay your creditors according to the priorities of the Bankruptcy Code. For details about the role of the trustee and how your assets—if you have any the trustee sees as worth selling—get seized and sold, go to chapter 6 of this book.

Three Types of Debt

While there are 34 categories of assets, there are only three types of debt.

1. **Unsecured Debt:** Debts that cannot be repossessed or foreclosed on, such as credit card debt, personal loans, and medical bills. An unsecured creditor is one who holds no security or collateral for its loan. In other words, your credit card company cannot reclaim the things you've purchased on the card to help pay for the money it is owed. Unsecured debts generally are characterized as those debts for which credit was extended based solely on the creditor's assessment of your future ability to pay.

2. **Secured Debt:** Debts where the assets securing the debt can be repossessed or foreclosed on, such as your home mortgage, car loan, rented furniture, etc. A secured creditor is one who holds an item of yours as security for the debt. The bank that loaned you the money to buy your house holds a mortgage or trust deed lien on your house as security for the loan; therefore, the mortgage company is a secured creditor.

3. **Priority Debt:** Debts granted special status by the bankruptcy law, such as debts to a government agency (like the Internal Revenue Service or state income tax board), child support payments, and student loans.

Remember these terms. They become important when you officially file, because each of these three types of debts is handled differently in a bankruptcy proceeding. We will describe these debts throughout this book.

The Process of Filing For Bankruptcy—At a Glance

Most debtors who file bankruptcy, and many of their creditors, know very little about the bankruptcy process. The following are the basic steps you take when completing a bankruptcy proceeding:

→ Decide that bankruptcy is right for you (see chapter 2 of this book).

→ Decide which type of bankruptcy is right for you (see chapter 3 of this book).

→ Gather and record all the information you need to fill out the actual forms (including your petition, schedules, and statement of financial affairs).

→ Use the worksheets explained in chapter 2 to help you organize your assets and understand your expenses.

→ Download the forms provided at www.wethepeopleforms.com. Print up several copies of the forms on regular, 8½ by 11 inch paper.

→ Find out if your local court requires any additional or special forms.

→ Follow the instructions in chapter 4 to fill out the official documents for the court.

→ Double-check and review your forms, making sure you've dated and signed everything. Make sure they are complete.

→ Make at least four copies of your documents in addition to the original for your own records.

→ Locate the court where you need to file your forms (see Appendix B).

→ Go to this court and file the forms with the clerk.

→ Pay the filing fee directly to the court with a money order payable to the U.S. Bankruptcy Court.

→ Look at the case number for your bankruptcy filing at the time of your filing. The clerk will note this at the top of your copy of the petition.

→ Get the name and phone number of your appointed trustee at the time of your filing.

→ Look at the tentative court's date, location, and time of your mandatory creditors' meeting. The court will send you an official notice of this meeting, usually about 35 days after you filed.

→ Enjoy the temporary relief that the automatic stay provides, stopping your creditors from attempting to collect from you. (Breathe your first sigh of relief!)

→ You must attend your meeting of your creditors with your trustee (not a judge). If you file under Chapter 13, you will have to attend a hearing before a judge to explain your plan.

→ Await the court's formal notice in three to four months that discharges all your debts except the debts that are not dischargeable. Many debtors receive their discharge about 90 days after they file.

→ Breathe another sigh of relief and begin to rebuild your credit—and a new life!

Before filling out those forms, we have provided a workbook-like exercise in chapter 2 of this book that gets you thinking about what assets you have. These pages will prepare you for

TIME OUT! *I Still Don't Understand What You Mean By . . .*

Petition. A formal written request. A bankruptcy petition is your request to the court to discharge your debts. You will complete all the forms that make up your petition to the bankruptcy court.

Schedules. Lists that you must provide as part of your bankruptcy filing, such as a list of your real estate property (Schedule A), a list of your personal property (Schedule B), a list of your exempt property (Schedule C), and so on.

Statement of Financial Affairs. Information about you, such as how much you earned this year to date, how much you earned last year and the year before, and who helped you prepare your petition. This statement is a series of questions you must answer in writing concerning sources of income, transfers of property, lawsuits by creditors, and so on. There is an official form you must use, and we discuss it in detail in chapter 4.

---

filling out and completing the official forms. The forms should be typed and neatly prepared. If you'd prefer someone else to do the actual creation of your official forms for you, you can contact a We The People office and our services can help you out.

We can also assist you with specific forms and requirements you must meet locally. You can always seek this information from your local bankruptcy court clerk, another bankruptcy petition preparer (nonattorney), or an attorney. The information and the people you need to help you are readily available. The bankruptcy court web sites have become sophisticated enough to meet most other needs you may have in addition to the information we provide in this book and on our web site at www.wethepeopleforms.com.

Filing Fees

You can expect the following fees when filing for bankruptcy:

- Chapter 7: $209
- Chapter 13: $194
- Chapter 11: $839

These fees are subject to change, so contact your local court to confirm these fees. Once you file your forms with the court and obtain a notice of your creditors' meeting, all collection efforts, including lawsuits, foreclosures, repossessions, wage garnishments (creditors taking money directly out of your income to pay for your debts), bill collector telephone calls, collection letters, and similar actions by your creditors are stopped automatically. The automatic stay is effective even when a creditor is not listed on your petition.

To stop any collection actions by your creditors, you simply provide them with your filing information: the name of the bankruptcy court, the Chapter under which you are filing, the filing date, and the case number. Your creditors must comply or the bankruptcy court can charge them with violating the automatic stay order.

As a general rule, excluding cases that are dismissed or converted (to other Chapters), individual debtors receive a discharge in more than 99 percent of Chapter 7 cases. In most cases, unless a complaint has been filed objecting to the discharge or the debtor has filed a written waiver, the discharge will be granted to a Chapter 7 debtor relatively early in the case, that is, 60 to 90 days after the date first set for the meeting of creditors.

How Long Will This Take Me?

It might take you a few days to sort through your personal information and gather the right information for filling out the official forms. Customers who visit our offices generally pick up questionnaires and spend about 20 to 30 minutes filling them out over the kitchen table. Take your time and be careful and thorough. If you're filling out the documents on your own, assuming this is the first time you've ever had to fill out such forms, you might need more time for the sake of being precise and detailed. It's important that you don't rush through this initial phase and make careless mistakes on your paperwork that will slow the process down later.

Once the court receives the documents, it is likely that a creditors' meeting will be scheduled in the next one to two months, after which you await the final notice from the court of your bankruptcy's completion. Be forewarned that once secured creditors receive notice of your bankruptcy, some will file a motion for relief from stay, which is their way of asking the court to lift the automatic stay so they can take back secured assets, such as your home or car. Courts usually grant this permission, but you can negotiate to some degree with your secured creditors and keep the asset in the end (we will explore your options later). Without extraordinary motions, hearings or proceedings, the Notice of Discharge is entered approximately 90 days after the date of filing. So the entire process (for a Chapter 7) takes about four to five months from the day you first file with the court. Chapter 13 cases typically take more time, because you need the court to approve of your plan, plus three to five years before your plan is completed (more on Chapter 13 later).

The Cast of Characters

As complex as a bankruptcy proceeding might appear to be, you can count the number of people involved in the process on your hands, unless your situation gets complicated with lawyers and creditors that emerge to challenge your filing. For most who are simply filing a personal bankruptcy under Chapter 7, the process is easy and the number of people with whom you deal is small. We already defined the following characters (see Figure 1.1 and Figure 1.2).

What You Can Gain

Peace of mind! The purpose of discharging you of certain debts in a bankruptcy is to give you a fresh start in life. Nobody is perfect. The Bankruptcy Code originated from the need to release people from incurable debts that prevent them from living and pursuing their goals. The Code also stems from the belief that there should be no stigma or shame involved in needing to seek relief in bankruptcy.

If you've been struggling financially for a long time, you might feel isolated, on an island with no raft to take you back to civilization (or drowning while trying to find your way back to the mainland's shore). Filing for bankruptcy can give you that raft, and then you can begin to paddle back to civilization on that raft. But understand that you're not alone in

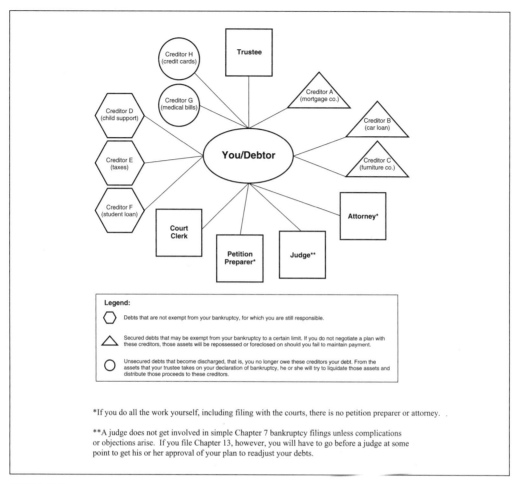

Figure 1.1

this journey. More than a million and a half people every year seek relief in bankruptcy. That's a lot of people.

People seek relief in bankruptcy for a variety of reasons. Here are some sample scenarios.

1. Joe finally got a job—after nearly a year of unemployment. During that time, his bills added up and he began using his credit cards to pay for rent, food, and basic living expenses. His new job didn't pay him enough to put a dent in his debt, and he worried about being able to keep up with the creditors once they started calling. He didn't want to put his family of five through the pain of crawling out of a deep hole that he couldn't see himself ever getting out of.

2. Mary started a small business a few years ago with a friend, who later left when the business started to go downhill. Within two years of her partner's departure, the business went belly-up and Mary had lost everything, including personal savings, personal loans from friends and family, and all that she had to keep herself above water. She sold her car and tried to pawn her jewelry before thinking about bankruptcy, but nothing was going to help wash away her $95,000 of unsecured debt.

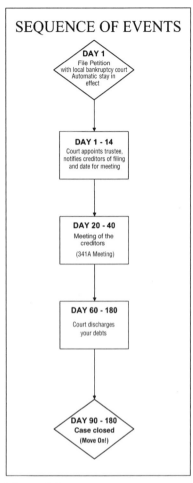

SEQUENCE OF EVENTS

DAY 1
File Petition
with local bankruptcy court
Automatic stay in
effect

DAY 1 - 14
Court appoints trustee,
notifies creditors of filing
and date for meeting

DAY 20 - 40
Meeting of the
creditors
(341A Meeting)

DAY 60 - 180
Court discharges
your debts

DAY 90 - 180
Case closed
(Move On!)

Figure 1.2

3. After a car accident, Ellen was out of work for nearly six months. The medical bills stacked high, and she didn't have adequate health insurance to help pay. When she went back to work, everything she made seemed to go to medical bills and taking care of her two daughters as a single mom. There was little left to pay regular bills.

These people sought relief in bankruptcy and it changed their lives for the better.

What You Can Lose

Bankruptcy should be considered a financial protection of last resort. When you're desperately in the red and cannot pay your bills to the point that your quality of life is severely diminished, the pros of filing for bankruptcy far outweigh the cons. But you should be aware of what you stand to lose during a bankruptcy.

First, you will lose assets that are not exempt from your bankruptcy. In some jurisdictions, this includes a house with a substantial amount of equity. However, a large majority of bankruptcies filed under Chapter 7 are no-asset filings. In other words, you don't lose any properties. This is because the trustee may only take your nonexempt properties. Because the majority of your properties are exempt (and in some jurisdictions you can protect your home and personal automobile) the trustee cannot take them. The types and quantity of exempt properties are different from state to state. Some states' exemptions rules make it easier to keep a home than other states. More on this later.

Second, you will lose secured assets that you cannot continue to make payments on. For example, even though a portion of your automobile could be considered an exempt item, you financed the car and it remains security for the bank that loaned you the money to buy it. Let's say you still owe $18,000 on the car before the title to it is yours. If you cannot continue making payments on what you owe, the finance company has a right to file a motion with the

A **reaffirmation agreement** is a written agreement between a debtor and a creditor in which the debtor promises to pay a debt that is dischargeable. Such agreements are commonly used where the debt is secured by a lien on personal property, which a debtor owns (for example, where the creditor has a lien on the debtor's car to secure payment of a car loan). So you can reaffirm property that can be taken away by either the trustee or a secured creditor if you promise to continue making the proper payments.

court for relief from the automatic stay so that it can repossess that car. Secured creditors usually win these types of motions. The same holds true if you're behind on mortgage payments.

Third, you will lose points on your credit rating. A bankruptcy stays on your credit report for 10 years. But as soon as your bankruptcy case is closed, you can begin the process of rebuilding your credit. Although it may not be wise to jump into using credit again, you'll find creditors willing to extend credit to you quickly. Creditors look for steady employment and a history (since the bankruptcy) of paying for purchases on credit. Many creditors totally disregard a bankruptcy after five years. In Chapter 8 we'll talk about life after bankruptcy and give you tips for rebuilding your credit and using money wisely so you never have to consider bankruptcy again.

Finally, and most importantly, you lose your dischargeable debts in bankruptcy. A Chapter 7 bankruptcy eliminates most of your debt by wiping out the following bills:

- Credit cards
- Medical bills
- Most personal judgments
- Personal loans
- Loans you have personally guaranteed or cosigned

With a bankruptcy filing, you lose all that stress and the burdens related to barely keeping your head above water. You lose the feeling of being out of control, cornered, thrown down a hole with no way out, or left out to sea with no life jacket.

And you lose your fear and trepidation of living and making the most out of your life.

Conclusion

Consider what the Supreme Court said about the purpose of bankruptcy in its 1934 ruling in *Local Loan v. Hunt:*

> [I]t gives to the honest but unfortunate debtor . . . a new opportunity in life and a clear field for future effort, unhampered by the pressure and discouragement of preexisting debt.

Giving debtors a financial fresh start from burdensome debts is the fundamental goal of the federal bankruptcy laws enacted by Congress. They are there for your protection. If you are an honest person unable to get out of serious debt and you've made every good faith effort to repay your debts, bankruptcy might be right for you. Bankruptcy represents the most devastating debt solution for the debtor's credit while providing the most complete elimination of the debt. A Chapter 7 personal bankruptcy can wipe out all of a person's debts, allow that person to keep all of his or her possessions, and give him or her a fresh start again. Exactly who can qualify to have his or her debts discharged in a no-asset case where he or she

No matter why you opt to file for bankruptcy, what kind of debt you carry or where it came from, all bankruptcy filings assume that you are an honest person who chooses to use a bankruptcy in good faith. In other words, you won't use bankruptcy to run away from civil or criminal lawsuits and debts you can pay, and once you've filed, you won't hide assets or shelter assets that should be used to repay your debts.

retains everything varies by state. In Chapter 13 bankruptcy cases debtors reorganize their finances by paying a portion of what they owe as settlement in full of their debts.

This chapter gave you an overview of bankruptcy and opened the door to exploring more about the topic and how you can proceed in a bankruptcy filing.

In the next chapter, we'll discuss some of the alternatives to bankruptcy that you should consider before filing for bankruptcy. Generally, any initial step should include negotiating an agreement with your creditors or those you owe in a liability case, but sometimes that's not possible and bankruptcy becomes the only way. We'll look at all the alternatives so that you can ultimately decide which road to take.

CHAPTER 2

Is Bankruptcy Right for Me?

Confusion.
  Guilt.
    Stress.
      Denial.
        Shock.
          Embarrassment.
            Panic.
              Humiliation.
                . . . Depression.

The hardest part of filing for bankruptcy is deciding whether or not to do so. You don't accept the contemplation of bankruptcy with a happy face and big smile. To the contrary, it frightens you to the core and changes how you think, how you feel, and how you live every day. You worry about what your family and friends think, wondering how long the stigma of declaring bankruptcy will last. You think about your situation when you wake up and when you try to go to sleep at night. The words "failure" and "loser" continue to harass you and drain your energy. Having all those emotions move through you at a time like this doesn't make deciding what to do any easier. If anything, all those emotions make it harder.

If you're asking yourself, *How did this happen to me?,* keep in mind that one of the reasons bankruptcies overall are on the rise is simple economics: Americans have been experiencing higher costs of living and falling median family incomes. Since 2000, housing costs have risen 17 percent; childcare, 18 percent; and health insurance, 40 percent. Meanwhile, the median family income has fallen 2.8 percent. While workers can expect modest pay increases of 3.3 percent in 2004 and 3.5 percent in 2005, those increases are barely ahead of inflation. So any sudden unbudgeted expenditure, such as an accident, divorce, business failure, or job loss, can make the slippery slope into debt even more slippery. Having enough savings to cushion any unexpected expenses in life can prevent the fall into bankruptcy, but truth is, most Americans are living paycheck to paycheck and don't have a trust fund or a whopping savings account balance to be the savior at the end of the day.

Also keep in mind that the world tells you every day to buy, buy, buy. Politicians like to urge people to spend money because it puts a spark in the economy. When our government leaders advise us to spend, telling us that it's our duty to help the economy and save jobs, how can we say no? Consumer spending is central to the American economy, and excessive spending has become central to the American lifestyle. Later, in Chapter 7, we'll provide tips to managing money and preventing another fall into bankruptcy.

In this chapter, we discuss in detail who qualifies for bankruptcy and provide some of the alternatives to filing that might be better for you. We cannot make this decision for you, but we can provide the information for assisting you in your thinking.

> Bankruptcy is something we help people with every day. But for some of those people, they choose not to proceed with a filing once they sit and think about their situation, as well as other options. Our services guide people who have already decided to file and simply need information and the forms typed for them. For legal advice, finding an understanding attorney who specializes in advising people on bankruptcy might be a good idea for those who cannot make that decision on their own.

Overcoming Your Fears

Now is the time to stop and take a deep breath. Understand that it's totally normal to feel overwhelmed and under the weather right now. But try to look beyond the negative aspects to this moment in your life and focus on what you can do to turn it around. Now is the time to think positively, stop blaming yourself, and take action in a way that will move you forward successfully and lay a new foundation for your future. Light shines at the end of every tunnel—if you walk with the determination and an openness to learn a new set of skills.

If you're like most who contemplate bankruptcy, you think that it's the only way out of your current troubles. And your desire to get your life back on track as soon as possible drives your thinking more than a realistic and rational look at your situation does. Take one thing at a time, and proceed one step at a time. You'll be able to get through your current situation more easily and feel more in control. Try not to see this as a crisis but as a challenge to overcome.

Qualifications for Bankruptcy

Qualifying for bankruptcy is less about meeting strict legal requirements than it is about making the decision to accept what bankruptcy laws can (and cannot) do for you. Why? You don't have to satisfy a dozen legal requirements before you can file for bankruptcy. Remember: Filing for bankruptcy is like claiming your right to start over within certain limits provided by the court. As an honest individual, you have a right to delete burdensome debt through the bankruptcy discharge, the sole purpose of which is to provide a fresh start. In return for this grant of a fresh start, you might have to relinquish some assets to the court and accept that you will have to rebuild your credit once the bankruptcy is complete.

In order to qualify for relief under the Bankruptcy Code, you must be an individual, a partnership, or a corporation (farmers also have access to relief, described later). We focus on Chapter 7 bankruptcy, however, which is how individuals with mostly consumer debt (and not many large assets to protect) get rid of their debt.

Relief is available under Chapter 7 irrespective of the amount of your debts or whether you are solvent (able to pay your debts) or insolvent (unable to pay your debts). We say this with a word of caution: If you can pay for your debts—or part of them—because you have significant free cash after expenses, the bankruptcy court can dismiss your case under reason of bad faith or force you to convert to a Chapter 13 filing where you pay back most of your debt. A person who carries largely consumer debts (example: credit card debt) but has enough income to put a portion toward debt every month can expect to face a trustee who is very skeptical of the bankruptcy petition. United States Trustees are taking aggressive positions in these circumstances; and the bankruptcy courts do not want to condone consumer credit abuse by allowing debtors to

> Chapter 7 is the Bankruptcy Code's liquidation Chapter. Lawyers sometimes refer to it as a straight bankruptcy. It is used primarily by individuals who wish to free themselves of debt simply and inexpensively, but may also be used by businesses that wish to liquidate and terminate their business.

erase their debts while they continue to earn plenty of income for everyday living, including living above their means. We don't see many customers who file in bad faith, but once in a while someone walks into our offices with less-than-good intentions for filing a Chapter 7 bankruptcy. If, when you compare your expenses to your income, your numbers do not reflect a need for bankruptcy, review your reasons for filing as well as those numbers.

You cannot file under Chapter 7 or any other Chapter, however, if during the preceding 180 days a prior bankruptcy petition was dismissed due to your willful failure to appear before the court or to comply with orders of the court, or due to you voluntarily dismissing the previous case after creditors sought relief from the bankruptcy court to recover property on which they hold liens. You also cannot file for bankruptcy (under Chapter 7) if you've already done so in the past six years.

You are a candidate for bankruptcy if the following statements are true:

- ☑ I am an individual, a partnership, or a corporation.
- ☑ I have not filed for bankruptcy within the last six years.
- ☑ I have not had a bankruptcy petition dismissed in the preceding 180 days.
- ☑ I cannot make ends meet and pay down my debts.

Moreover, you are a good candidate for bankruptcy if the following are also true:

- You have no money left after you pay your normal living expenses (rent, car payments, food, insurance, utilities, etc.).
- You have recently lost your job or had a decrease in your normal income due to medical or personal problems.
- You have gotten divorced or separated from your spouse and the debts are too much for you to handle.
- Your debts are mostly unsecured debts, like credit card bills, medical bills, loans you've made to others, or other kinds of debts that are not backed by a mortgage, pledge of collateral, or other lien.

I think I qualify for bankruptcy, but I still don't know if it's right for me. Read on. . . .

Getting to Know Your Financial Situation

Before rushing into filing for bankruptcy, a good thing to do is organize your financial paperwork so you have a clear idea of just where you stand with regard to debt. It's okay if you haven't handled your finances as carefully as you know you should or if you know you're sloppy when it comes to keeping track of your expenses and balancing your checkbook every month. Forget about what you haven't done in the past, and focus on what you can do today for your future. Believe it or not, studies have shown that alongside losing weight, losing debt is on everyone's minds come those New Year's Resolutions. But like losing weight and keeping it off, becoming debt-free requires a lifestyle change that starts with getting to know your finances. (And this doesn't require complex algebra and calculus! All you need is the courage to look and see.)

→ Do you know exactly how much you need to cover your fixed monthly living expenses, or how much you spend on a daily, weekly, or monthly basis?

→ Do you know how much money sits in your bank accounts (or, more specifically, your monthly deposits versus withdrawals) and how much you are paying in interest on credit cards?

→ Do you know how much you owe and how long it will take to pay off your debts given your current abilities to pay and the interest rates that are accumulating more debt?

The average American is in debt. Although the credit card industry says average household consumer debt comes to $9,000 (not including car and home loans), it is actually closer to $13,000 when the roughly 40 percent of households that pay their balances each month are taken out of the equation. That means the majority—60 percent—do not pay off their credit cards every month. And that translates to three out of five United States households with credit card debt. Many have debts in the tens of thousands. Did you think you were the only one?

Credit has never been more available—and more socially acceptable—than it is today. The widespread use of credit has made us all champion shoppers, and hesitant savers. Credit card companies love people who don't pay their bills in full every month because that's how the credit card companies make money—and lots of it. In 2002, the average household consumer debt translated into $1,700 a year in finance charges and fees.

Credit card companies are also very aggressive in their pursuit of customers, offering high credit terms and introductory rates that allow people to live well above their means until a day of reckoning comes. When was the last time a credit card company solicited you? Today? Yesterday? More than likely, you amass a decent number of credit card solicitations each year, many of them pre-approved—and even if you're already in debt with other cards. In this case, you get balance transfer offers, where one credit card company offers you a low introductory rate if you transfer your existing balance on a high-interest card over to another. But that credit card company is banking on your inability to pay off all that debt within its introductory rate period, thereby snagging you as a customer who, over time, will pay out more money to the credit card company's benefit.

According to Robert D. Manning, author of *Credit Card Nation: The Consequences of America's Addiction to Credit,* our credit card problems are rooted in the way credit cards have come to imply social status. They are "yuppie food stamps" akin to "social-class entitlement" rather than an earned privilege. Manning also points to the hidden costs of buying on credit that many don't take into consideration until they're drowning in fees, finance charges, and rising interest rates. The cost of borrowing (on credit) has tripled in real terms since the early 1980s. So once those zero percent introductory rates expire, people are paying exorbitantly high interest rates. New kinds of so-called hybrid financial institutions and loan products have further muddied the waters by offering good-looking deals from the outside, which are riddled with high long-term costs on the inside. For example, some rent-to-own places advertise irresistible offers, but when you do the math on those offers, you end up paying more than 200 percent a year on interest!

Despite your reluctance to face your financial problems and look at those bank and credit card statements in detail, now's the time to put on your thinking cap and get ready to take charge. When you file for bankruptcy, you'll need to complete various lists of what you have, such as assets and income, so there's no better time to take inventory of your stuff (including stuff you may not even need for filing for bankruptcy) before beginning the bankruptcy process. Why? Because some of what you uncover will affect your decision. For example, once you look at your credit card situation (assuming you have one), you might be able to go the credit counseling route instead of a bankruptcy filing, saving you some of the more serious ramifications of an actual filing. But until you do that personal financial assessment, you won't know which route is best for you.

> If payday-in-advance outlets have gotten your attention, beware! You are borrowing money at a premium. Some advance payday shops aren't so upfront about the price you actually pay for their loan, but you could be paying more than 900 percent interest and not even knowing it! That makes those 20 percent high-interest credit cards not look so bad in comparison.

Take an Inventory of Your Finances

Don't be afraid! Even if you dread math and looking at your financial statements, this is a necessary part of the process of taking charge of your financial life and moving forward. If you can get through this initial phase, you're well on your way to building a better situation for yourself that will reward you for years to come.

Find a good place to scatter your paperwork and organize your finances to study and evaluate. If you've never been neat and tidy with paperwork, do your best to organize your stuff here. Use manila folders or files with labels if you like: one for "Things I Own" and one for "Things I Owe." Or, alternatively, you can see how you want to organize your files once you finish taking inventory. If you have piles and piles of miscellaneous papers, such as receipts, bank and credit card statements, and copies of bills, put them in an empty shoebox or basket—you'll get to them later. You can use those receipts for figuring out an average for your monthly expenses.

Set yourself up at a cleared kitchen table or dining room table with a beverage and remove any distractions. Get some blank paper, such as a lined notepad, a calculator, and a good pen and highlighter. And get comfortable!

Use the pen to write down your estimates for the following four categories, and highlight the sums so you can glance back at them when you're done. We've included a worksheet in the back of this book (see Appendix A, Worksheet A) that you can tear out or download and use for filling in blanks. A sample completed worksheet is included here. (See Figure 2.1.)

The first goal is to figure out your total monthly expenses, including taxes and insurance. Tally up those living expenses, using averages for things like food and gas that fluctuate from month to month. Include the following:

CATEGORY 1: Monthly expenses

EXPENSE	MONTHLY PAYMENT
Rent	
Mortgage	$1,600
Electric	60
Gas	55
Phone	65
Water/sewer	45
Home maintenance	150
Cable TV/internet access	40
Phone/cell	45
Food	250
Clothing	150
Gasoline/transportation costs	150
Entertainment/newspapers	50
Incidentals–gifts, laundry	60
Medical and dental	60
Taxes not deducted from paycheck	
Miscellaneous	

Installment payments   Car
                     Furniture
        Other _____
	360
	_____
	_____

Children's tuition/education	
Payments to dependents outside the home	
Alimony	

Insurance premiums   Health
                  Home
                  Auto
	
	90
	105

Charitable contributions	40
TOTAL	$3,320

CATEGORY 2: Credit card balances

CREDIT CARD	BALANCE
Citibank	$4,000
Citibank	3,000
Household Bank	4,377
Providian	1,000
Sears	3,650
TOTAL	$16,027

CATEGORY 3: Other debts

DEBT	BALANCE
IRS	$32,000
Ford Motor Credit	21,150
Crown Mortgage	153,000
TOTAL	$206,150

Figure 2.1 Worksheet A: Taking Inventory of Your Finances

CATEGORY 4: Property/assets (what you own)

ASSET	QUICK SALE VALUE*
Homes**	$160,000
Cash	$240
Checking, savings, CD's	$425 (checking)
Security deposits held by utilities or landlord	
Household goods/furniture/electronics/appliances	$500
Books/pictures/art objects	$100
Clothing	$200
Furs/Jewelry	$300
Sports/hobby equipment/firearms/gadgets	$150
Cash value in insurance policies	
Annuities	
Interest in pension or profit sharing plans	
Stocks and interests in incorporated business	
Interest in partnerships/joint ventures	
Bonds	
Accounts receivable	
Alimony or family support to which you are entitled	
Tax refunds	
Equitable or future interests or life estates	
Interest in estate of descendent or life ins plan	
Other liquidated debts owed to you (claims, funds due you, benefits)	
Patents, copyrights	
Licenses and franchises	
Car(s) ***	$16,000
Boats/motors & accessories	
Aircraft and accessories	
Office equipment & supplies	
Machinery/fixtures	
Inventory (business)	
Animals, crop, farm supplies etc. (for farmers)	
TOTAL	$177,915

* A quick sale value is what you think your assets would sell for if sold quickly.
  Consider how much your assets would sell for in a pawnshop or a yard sale.

** If you have a mortgage on your home, list any home equity loans and liens you have here.

Total liens and mortgages = $153,000
Total ownership equity
(Home value less total liens/mortgages) = $ 7,000)

*** Use the current value of your car today if you tried to sell it quickly.

MONTHLY INCOME

Gross monthly	$3,150
Deductions	
Payroll taxes/Social Security	220
Insurance	60

YEARLY INCOME

This year to date	$28,350
Last year	37,800
Year before last	37,800

Category 1: Fixed Monthly Overhead

- Rent/mortgage payment
- Utilities
- Water/sewer
- Home maintenance
- Cable/television/high-speed Internet access
- Phone/cell
- Food
- Clothing
- Car payments
- Gasoline/transportation costs
- Entertainment, recreation, newspapers, magazines
- Miscellaneous expenses like trash disposal
- Incidentals (such as gifts, house cleaning service, laundry, and dry cleaning)
- Children's tuition and related education or extracurricular activity costs
- Payments to support dependents not living in the home
- Insurance premiums (health, home, auto, life, other)

Look at this roundabout number and compare it to your current take-home pay. How much is left over? Do you put any of this leftover money into savings, retirement plans, or investments? If so, how much?

If you're running a small business or are declaring a bankruptcy for a failed business, be sure to include your business's operational and other expenses. We've included another worksheet you can use (see Appendix A, Worksheet B) for business debtors. The information you provide on Worksheet B will become attached to Schedule J of your official forms.

Category 2: Credit Card Balances

Next, get your most recent credit card statements out and note each one's balance and interest rate:

Credit card 1: _____ (balance) _____

Credit card 2: _____ (balance) _____

Credit card 3: _____ (balance) _____

Credit card **debt TOTAL**: $_____

How much money do you allocate each month for paying down this debt? Do you know how long it will take you to pay off your credit card debt—plus interest—at the current rate you're making payments? If you can only afford to pay the minimum required amount every month, it will take you *decades* to pay off a card with a high balance and a high interest rate. Example: You owe $6,000 on a credit card and can only afford to pay the minimum payment of $150 a month. Given the interest rate is 12 percent, it will take you 331 months to pay off the debt, and by then you've paid $8,615.25 in interest—more than what you initially owed in principal. That's 27½ years of making payments! This is an ugly path to take.

Category 3: Other Debts

List all other debts you pay out each month here, such as student loans, child support/alimony, rental fees, medical and dental bills, judgments against you, counseling or consulting, union or professional group dues, charitable contributions, taxes not taken out of your paycheck, etc. It's okay to make an estimate here.

Other debts total: $_____

Have any of your debts resulted in repossessions, foreclosures, or returns? Has any of your property been garnished, seized, or attached under any legal or equitable process in the past year? Have creditors threatened or instigated lawsuits against you in their attempts to receive payment?

Category 4: Property/Assets

Here's where you consider what you own, whether you own it outright, share an interest in it, or have financed it through a bank or lender. List all your property, and for little things like household goods and furniture, guesstimate the total value instead of itemizing every item. Sample pieces of property include the following items:

- House(s)
- Cash
- Checking, savings, CDs, other bank accounts
- Security deposits held by utilities or landlord
- Household goods/furniture/electronics/appliances
- Books, pictures, art objects, records, CDs, collectibles
- Clothing
- Furs and jewelry
- Sports, photographic and hobby equipment; firearms/gadgets
- Cash value in insurance policies
- Annuities
- Interest in pension or profit sharing plans
- Bonds
- Accounts receivable
- Alimony or family support to which you are entitled
- Tax refunds
- Equitable or future interests in life estates
- Interest in estate of descendent or life insurance plan or trust
- Other liquidated debts owed to you (claims, funds due you, benefits)
- Patents, copyrights, and other intellectual property
- Licenses and franchises
- Car(s), including trucks, trailers, and accessories
- Boats, motors, and accessories

- Aircraft and accessories
- Office equipment and supplies
- Machinery, fixtures
- Inventory (business)
- Stocks and interests in incorporated/unincorporated business
- Interest in partnerships/joint ventures
- Animals, crops, farm supplies, etc. (for farmers)

How many of these above items can be sold to pay for your debts? Some of these assets may be exempted from seizure in a bankruptcy, but exemptions vary by state. Thus, whether your house, car, clothing, jewelry, and other types of property can be exempted will depend on your state's laws. (Go to www.wethepeopleforms.com for detailed lists of exemptions.)

If you were able to exempt the most important things on this list from seizure, such as your home, car, and retirement savings (assuming you can continue to make monthly payments to those secured creditors), will wiping out your debts give you the fresh start you need? Do the numbers you arrived at in Categories 1 through 3 frighten you to the point that losing some of the items listed in Category 4 wouldn't be so bad? Remember: You have a right to retain certain exempt property, subject to the rights of secured creditors. If you have little or no nonexempt property, you can file a Chapter 7 and it's called a no-asset case. If your above assets (your property in Category 4) are not significant, but your debts are very significant, then you are among the many who would use a Chapter 7 bankruptcy to make effective changes to your financial life.

Because there is usually little or no nonexempt property in most Chapter 7 cases, there may not be an actual liquidation of the debtor's assets. These cases are called no-asset cases. A creditor holding an unsecured claim will get a distribution from the bankruptcy estate only if the case is an asset case and the creditor files a proof of claim with the bankruptcy court. In most Chapter 7 cases, the debtor receives a discharge that releases the debtor from personal liability for certain dischargeable debts. The debtor normally receives a discharge 90 to 120 days after the petition is filed.

If you're considering filing a joint petition with your spouse, you'll have to gather detailed data for both you and your spouse.

Nonetheless, given the kind of debt you carry (your liabilities) and the type of property you have (assets), Chapter 7 might not be the Chapter for you when filing for bankruptcy. Other types of bankruptcy, such as Chapter 13 (where you can adjust your payment terms to work your way out of debt without liquidating your assets), are better routes to take for certain people. We'll explore these other types of bankruptcies in the next chapter of the book.

Consider Your Age and Your Lifetime Goals

If you're young and declare bankruptcy, you have lots of time on your side to recover and rebuild your credit. Although a bankruptcy on your record may prevent you from getting a loan for a business venture until your thirties or forties, that's within plenty of time to reach your goals and do what you want to do. If, however, you are over 50 and want a loan for a new venture, having the bankruptcy on your credit record for 10 years is an especially long time and may prevent you from ever getting into that new venture since you may not be able to get credit until too late in life. Older people generally have more assets to protect, so a liquidation of their property in a Chapter 7 bankruptcy might not be as beneficial as a debt adjustment in Chapter 13.

Understand that a bankruptcy will stay on your credit record for 10 years, while unfavorable information in your credit file will stay there for only seven years. A bad credit report will make getting credit in the future more difficult. For example, a credit record with unfavorable information may make it more difficult for you to get a mortgage for your house, to rent an apartment, or to obtain a car loan. In addition, bankruptcy does not necessarily erase (or discharge) all of your debts, which means that you will remain liable for most taxes, alimony, child support, and student loans, even after going through the bankruptcy process.

Taking these concerns into consideration alongside your age and what you want to accomplish in the next 10 years should have an effect on your decision to file.

Alternatives to Bankruptcy

You can take several avenues before filing for bankruptcy. These alternatives are particularly useful for debtors who carry mostly consumer debts, meaning unsecured debt that is not backed or underwritten by an asset like a house or car.

1. Contact your creditors.
2. Contact a credit counseling service.
3. Consider a debt management firm.
4. Sell assets to pay off debt.
5. Resort to a debt consolidation loan.

1. Contact Your Creditors

Talk with your creditors. Many creditors will want to work with you rather than forcing you into bankruptcy. Although a bankruptcy proceeding can be initiated by your creditors, they really would rather work through your problems with you before reaching that point. If you file for bankruptcy, many of your debts will be discharged and your creditors will get little or nothing as a result. Creditors want to help you repay your debt. By explaining to them the reason that you have fallen behind in payments (such as divorce, losing a job, or an illness), many creditors are willing to work with you to satisfy your obligation.

Some creditors are willing to settle their claim for a smaller cash payment that they get right away. For example, if you owe $5,000 on a credit card, you might be able to reach a debt settlement whereby you pay the credit card company a lump sum of $3,500 in cash instead of the full $5,000. Negotiating these kinds of settlements, however, might require the help of a debt management firm (described below).

Other creditors are willing to stretch out payments so long as you are making a good faith effort to meet, rather than to avoid, your financial obligations. So long as you stay in touch with your creditors and tell them when you need more time, they likely will be willing to work within your means. It's in their best interest to help you repay your debt *before* you file for bankruptcy.

If you look at your debts and realize that you cannot pay them off within three years on the present terms, contacting a consumer credit counselor can help you make a budget and negotiate a repayment plan. Creditors generally cease collection actions against those participating in such plans.

2. Contact a Credit Counseling Service

If you're unable to get your finances back on track yourself through talking with your creditors, a debt counselor might be helpful. The more than 1,000 accredited nonprofit agencies of the National Foundation for Credit Counseling help 1.5 million households annually. Certified counselors at agencies like these help clients to make budgets, cut spending, and negotiate with creditors to lower payments. They can reduce your interest payments, sometimes eliminating interest entirely. Reputable agencies tailor payment plans to the circumstances of each client, sometimes offering services for free.

Some programs allow debtors to use a period of interest reduction to pay down their debt. Repayment of the principal balance of the debt through credit counseling generally requires full dollar-on-a-dollar payment without reduction or discount. Often these firms maintain nonprofit status, but they are not government sanctioned or public service companies. These organizations work with you and your creditors to develop debt repayment plans. Such plans require you to deposit money each month with the counseling service. The service then pays your creditors.

Because millions of Americans are in debt, many of whom would benefit from counseling, debt services have sprung up everywhere—including abusive ones that will make your situation worse. You've seen television, radio, Internet, and billboard ads on the highway that target debtors with seemingly unrealistic promises. "No credit? Bad credit? No problem! We'll get you out of debt and erase those negative marks on your credit report today!" Some of these advertisements read like a fad diet that promises you all the rewards with little or no work involved. They are trouble. Double trouble.

Be careful, because many of these debt counselors are not reputable. Senate investigators have found that consumers who struggle with credit card debt increasingly are being victimized by poor service, hidden charges, and high fees charged by credit counseling agencies that leave debtors in even deeper debt. When you're drowning in debt, you're vulnerable to abuse, so it's important to stay tuned in to what actions you are taking and why. As we said at the beginning of this chapter, contemplating bankruptcy is a transaction that stirs a lot of unwanted emotions, which can in turn affect the way you respond and act. Credit counseling and debt management firms know the psychology involved in bankruptcy considerations, and they can easily play into your fears and use those fears to *their* advantage instead of *your* advantage.

Consumer complaints are on the rise as new companies come into the counseling business and abuses multiply. Watch out for up-front fees that never lead to any debt solutions or even

> **WARNING:** Beware of scams! Any advertisement that makes wild promises to get you out of debt quickly may be a method for obtaining a large, up-front fee or a disguised way of stealing your identity. In addition, it is illegal to represent that negative information, such as bankruptcy, can be removed from your credit report. Promises to "help you get out of debt easily" are a red flag. Be especially wary of these offers. Be wary of your junk mail and electronic spam mail, too. If you pay attention to the spam mail that clogs e-mail boxes, offers to get rid of your debt outnumber the pornographic solicitations. Don't be fooled by these powerful messages that bombard you daily. (If you are feeling vulnerable, this is a good reason to block as much spam as you can!)

Tips to Finding Reputable Credit Counselors

- Get references.

- Avoid giving your personal information until you are confident that the counselor works for a legitimate entity.

- Beware of unsolicited e-mails or regular mailings that make irresistible claims to take care of all of your debt problems quickly and easily.

- Watch out for deceptive and misleading practices (example: nondisclosure of fees).

- Beware of high fees or required voluntary contributions that, with high monthly service charges, may add to your debt and defeat your efforts to pay your bills.

education about debt solutions. Some so-called nonprofit agencies are really for-profit agencies that aggressively sell you plans that are not tailored to your specific needs and that take precious money away from you.

The following red flags were published in a 2003 report by the Consumer Federation of America, a nonprofit association of consumer groups, and the National Consumer Law

The Red Flags: Agencies to Avoid

High fees. If your set-up fees and monthly fees seem expensive, they probably are. Generally, if the set-up fee for a debt management plan is more than $50 and monthly fees exceed $25, look for a better deal. If the agency is vague or reluctant to talk about specific fees, go elsewhere.

Voluntary fees. Don't be bullied into paying these fees. If the full fee is too much, don't pay more than you can afford.

The hard sell. If a representative talks from a script and pushes debt savings or the possibility of getting a consolidation loan, hang up.

Employees working on commission. Most credit counseling agencies are nonprofit organizations that are supposed to consider your best interests when offering you information. Employees that receive commissions for placing consumers in debt management plans are more likely to be focusing on their own wallets than yours.

They flunk the "Twenty Minute Test." Any agency that offers you a debt management plan in less than 20 minutes hasn't spent enough time looking at your finances. An effective counseling session, whether on the phone or in person, takes a significant amount of time (30 to 90 minutes).

One size fits all. A good agency should talk to you about whether a debt management plan is right for you rather than assume that it is. If the agency doesn't offer any educational options, such as classes or budget counseling, consider one that does.

Aggressive ads. There are quality agencies out there as aggressive as the dubious ones. Don't respond reflexively to television and Internet advertising or telemarketing. Get referrals from friends and family. Find out which agencies have been subject to investigations and complaints. You local Better Business Bureau might be helpful here.

> To contact the National Foundation for Credit Counseling 24-hour hotline, call 1-800-388-2227 or access it on the Internet at www.nfcc.org.
>
> To contact the Consumer Credit Counseling Service in your area, call 1-800-388-2227 or access its web site at www.cccservices.com.
>
> To find a lawyer to help you weigh the pros and cons of bankruptcy, check with your local or state bar association and ask for the names of lawyers who specialize in bankruptcy practice. To find the name of a lawyer referral service in your area, access its web site at http://www.abanet.org/legalservices/lris/directory.html.

Center, a nonprofit organization specializing in consumer issues on behalf of low-income consumers. This is a version of that publication.

The Federal Trade Commission also keeps an enormous volume of resources on its web site (www.ftc.gov) that can provide you with valuable information about credit, credit repair, and your rights as a consumer.

3. Consider a Debt Management Firm

These are the firms that can help you negotiate new payment terms with your creditors. Firms that perform this type of work may identify themselves as debt management, debt reduction, debt relief, debt workout, debt settlement, or a host of other names implying they help with debt, even sometimes including debt consolidation. However, think of debt consolidation as a reorganization of your debt through an approved loan to pay off your debts in full, which will be discussed below.

Debt settlement firms operate by contacting your creditors and negotiating settlements on each of your debts. Most of these firms set their goal at reducing your debt down to 30 to 50 cents on the dollar through their efforts. Your payments may stretch out over a term of years. You can use a debt settlement firm regardless of your home ownership status or your credit.

While you can try to work out your debt repayments by yourself, most people don't know how to negotiate a debt settlement or what a proper debt settlement would be. A debt management professional working in this field will know most individual creditors, including what their standard acceptance offer will be (because their job is to work with these creditors on a daily basis). A creditor might take your offer more seriously if it's done through a debt management professional. Plus, when someone else is negotiating for you, the letters and calls from the collectors end up going to the debt management professional you have hired to work for you, thus making the entire debt settlement process less stressful. However, these kinds of firms, which are not nonprofit entities and do make money by charging fees that you pay through your debt plan, are also subject to corrupt characters. You must choose a debt management firm wisely.

Most debt reduction firms work with basic credit card debt (unsecured commercial creditors), but some may also work

> Most credit card debt elimination plans last three years or less, but in some cases, credit card debt management plans may last up to four years or longer. Costs are generally 8 to 15 percent of your total outstanding debt. Firms can calculate your fees based on the money they save you, taking 25 to 33 percent of those savings.

with medical bills, auto deficiencies, and other similar unsecured debt. If you're in need of help with secured debts, such as your mortgage or car loan, you'll need to find a firm that specializes in these kinds of secured debts.

Finally, be sure to ask any debt reduction firm that's working with you what it does when one of your creditors refuses to negotiate.

4. Sell Assets to Pay Off Debts

A Chapter 7 bankruptcy will seize your nonexempt assets in an attempt to sell them and apply those proceeds to your debt. If you are trying to avoid filing for bankruptcy, and you have assets that you think you can sell to pay down a good portion of your debt, it doesn't hurt to try this approach. Any balance due can be negotiated with your creditors—outside of a bankruptcy filing.

> Choose a program that deals with all your debt. Some debt counselors exclude your obligations for nondischargeable child support, unpaid taxes, or the crushing car loan. In effect, they ignore the debts that are most important, while channeling your money to creditors whose claims can be discharged in bankruptcy. Knowing the kind of debt you have—and kind of firm that can help you and your debt—is key.

Selling assets these days is easy and painless with Internet auction houses like eBay and the like. Just be sure that you sell assets that you already own outright. In other words, don't place an ad for a car you have leased or furniture you have rented! Also note that the Bankruptcy Code allows a court to look into any transactions that occurred within the last 90 days before a filing. This discourages any debtor from paying friends and family with scarce resources and then filing for bankruptcy to stiff other creditors. There's nothing wrong, however, with honestly trying to repay your debts through selling off of things you think will help pay for your debts before considering bankruptcy. If you are, in fact, contemplating bankruptcy seriously—and think you will end up having to file—do not begin to sell your assets and pay off creditors whom you prefer, such as your parents or a close friend. These kinds of transfers will be considered preferential transfers. And some transfers made before filing for bankruptcy can be seen as fraudulent, though rarely does this happen, because they stiff other creditors to whom you owe money.

5. Resort to a Debt Consolidation Loan

Debt consolidation loans allow you to consolidate many of your debts into one loan with one payment each month. Note that this is a loan—so this method of climbing out of debt forces you to take on another loan that you have to repay. Generally, interest charged on these loans falls far below the interest charged on most credit card debt, thus allowing easier repayment of the debt. But they are often secured by your home or some other asset that you can use as collateral. You must be able to make those monthly payments, or you risk going into deeper debt and losing your home.

> *Do I cash out my retirement savings?* Consider long and hard before resorting to liquidating IRAs or 401K plans to pay creditors: These assets are generally protected from collection actions by creditors. They are hard to replenish once spent; but most importantly, using retirement savings to pay creditors may create new debt in the form of income taxes and penalties for early withdrawal. Your good intentions to repay creditors may just end up substituting Uncle Sam as a tax creditor in place of your existing creditors.

By consolidating your debts, you only have to deal with one creditor. However, weighing the risks of losing the asset you put up as collateral for the loan is important. With

> **Remember: Choose any credit counselor, debt management, or consolidation firm wisely. There are people who will take your money and make your life more miserable, and there are people who can truly help you repay or restructure your debts.**

record-low interest rates, debt consolidation firms have been happy to market their programs and plans aggressively. Home equity loans in particular are abundant. You've seen these ads on television as well: "Cash out the equity in your home to pay off high-interest debts," or "Get cash today to use toward those mounting credit card bills with a second mortgage." Some firms even offer people loans equal to 125 percent of the value of their home. This all sounds spectacular, but these loans come with costs that are high to bear. If it sounds too good to be true, it probably is.

Questions to ask your lender:

- What are the exact terms, interest rate, and fees related to this loan?
- Will the loan pay off over the life of the loan, or will I owe a balloon (think "lump sum") payment at the end?

Your Rights as a Debtor

Outside of our discussion of bankruptcy, we want to alert you to your rights as a debtor, regardless of your contemplation of bankruptcy. The fact that you owe people money does not mean you have no rights as a debtor or that you lose rights as a consumer. You are responsible for your debts, but when you fall behind in paying your creditors or an error is made on your account, debt collectors soon become a problem in your life. (If you are already contemplating bankruptcy, then you probably know what we mean.)

Some debt collectors are not related to the person or company to whom you owe money but are hired solely to collect your debt. A debt collector is any person, other than the creditor, who regularly collects debts owed to others. This includes lawyers who collect debts on a regular basis. This includes collections companies and individuals who make a living by pursuing debtors ferociously. Debt collectors rarely share any kind of pre-existing relationship with you, which makes it easy for them to be firm, unmoved by your situation, and downright unpleasant. They are hired to do a job and get it done no matter what. They will do anything within the law to get money from you. (Sometimes, they break the law.) However, you have the right to be treated fairly by debt collectors. You do not need to tolerate unfair or even illegal debt collections tactics.

The Fair Debt Collection Practices Act

The Fair Debt Collection Practices Act (FDCPA) is a law that applies to personal, family, and household debts. This includes money owed for the purchase of a car, for medical care, or for charge accounts. The FDCPA prohibits debt collectors from engaging in unfair, deceptive, or abusive practices while collecting these debts. Your rights under the Fair Debt Collection Practices Act are as follows:

- Debt collectors may contact you only between 8 AM and 9 PM
- Debt collectors may not contact you at work if they know your employer disapproves.
- Debt collectors may not harass, oppress, or abuse you.

- Debt collectors may not lie when collecting debts, such as falsely implying that you have committed a crime.
- Debt collectors must identify themselves to you on the phone.
- Debt collectors must stop contacting you if you ask them to in writing.

As you course your way through dealing with your debts, keep the preceding rights in mind. We know how hard it can be to deal with uncaring debt collectors when you are trying your best to figure out your financial life. If any debt collector disobeys any of your rights listed above, remind them of your rights and inform them that if they ignore your rights, you may press charges.

Death and Taxes Are Two Certainties in Life

Benjamin Franklin said it best: ". . . in this world nothing can be said to be certain, except death and taxes."

If your debt is mainly tax-related, you can find a solution to your problems by dealing directly with the Internal Revenue Service (IRS). Some taxes are not dischargeable in a bankruptcy, so you are responsible for these taxes no matter what. You can't file for bankruptcy in an attempt to run from Uncle Sam. But you can negotiate a tax plan whereby you pay your taxes at a steep discount in a lump sum (called an Offer in Compromise by the IRS) or pay your full tax debt over the course of a longer period.

Because tax issues can become complex and you don't know how to negotiate such deals with the IRS (maybe the thought of even calling the IRS makes you quiver), it's best to find someone who deals with these kinds of plans. To maximize your chance of having an Offer in Compromise approved by the IRS, having a professional to assist you is beneficial. Typically those who put together these plans are attorneys or accountants who once worked as agents for the IRS or specialized in debt or taxes.

Chapter 13 Instead of Debt Management

In the next chapter we'll visit the types of bankruptcy that fit your needs. Another alternative to filing for a Chapter 7 bankruptcy is to file a Chapter 13. Chapter 13 bankruptcy is a repayment plan in which you propose the percentage that you can repay creditors, and on confirmation, the court makes it binding on creditors.

WARNING: The IRS treats debts that are forgiven or reduced, outside of bankruptcy, as taxable income! That means that if your creditor agrees to settle a debt for 50 percent of what you actually owe, without actually filing for bankruptcy, the other 50 percent will be reported to the IRS as income. So you'll have to pay taxes on that 50 percent as though your creditor wrote you a check for that amount! What this means: If you negotiate major deals on your debt with your creditors without declaring bankruptcy, you will have to pay tax on that relief, so be ready.

Consumers with debts they sincerely want to pay back within reasonable terms and who don't want the hassle of negotiating with their creditors or hiring an agency to help out, can seek relief through a Chapter 13 bankruptcy proceeding that is backed by the safety of the court system. A debtor pays a court filing fee ($194) and is ensured that the plan is enforced by a federal judge. The ongoing cost is the commission of the trustee, calculated at a percentage of the payments you make to the plan, usually between 4 and 10 percent.

At the end of the plan, the dischargeable debt is no longer enforceable. Better still, there are no tax consequences to the cancellation of debt in bankruptcy, as there are in debt management programs.

Chapter 13 requires creditors

- to stop collection action when the case is filed; and

- to accept payments as provided in the Chapter 13 plan.

No creditor can refuse to go along with a confirmed plan. We'll explore more about this type of bankruptcy in the next chapter.

What You Should Know about Credit Reports

In this information-based economy, Fair, Isaac and Company (FICO) scores are essential personal information. Has a lender or an acquaintance at a dinner party during talk about home-buying asked, "What's your FICO score?"

Fair, Isaac and Company develops the mathematical formula used to obtain snapshots of your credit risk at a given point in time. These scores are the most widely used and recognized credit ratings. FICO scores are calculated by the three major credit reporting agencies (Experian, TransUnion, and Equifax), and your score determines how easily you can obtain credit or apply for a loan. Factors that determine your FICO score include the following:

- Payment history

- Amount owed

- Length of credit history

- New credit

- Types of credit in use

FICO scores are the SAT scores for adults. As SAT scores facilitate the passage into college and beyond, FICO scores facilitate the passage into adulthood with the purchase of large assets (think houses) and good lines of credit (think credit cards and loans). FICO scores range from a low 500 to a high of 850.

Have your credit report in front of you when you sit down to look at your finances and think about bankruptcy. Make a separate file for it.

It's a good idea to check your credit report at least once a year for errors. Now you can obtain one free credit report per year from each of the three national credit bureaus. The first site to offer this resource is www.annualcreditreport.com, but eligibility for free reports is being phased in over 10 months. Those who live in the East Coast may have to pay a small fee until they are fully eligible for their free report in September 2005. You are also entitled to a free copy of your credit report

> **WARNING:** Beware of identity thieves that target debtors! You worry so much over your debts that you never think to look at your credit report carefully. Identity thieves love people who are already in serious debt; thieves assume you won't be keeping track of your finances or monitoring your credit to notice any problems. Before you consider a bankruptcy, be sure that all of your debt is indeed your debt—and no one else's!

if you are unemployed, on welfare, or were recently denied credit, or if your report is inaccurate because of fraud. The three major credit bureaus (listed later in this chapter) do not contain identical information, so it's worth your while to order all three. Obtaining your FICO score (in addition to the comprehensive information contained in your report) may require a small fee.

You can learn how to read a report by contacting the credit bureaus or by simply doing a search online for advice. In addition to your debts and payment history, credit reporting agencies also provide general data (name, social security number, marital status, addresses—past and present), your employer's name and address, inquiries of your credit file, and public record information such as bankruptcies and liens. Credit reporting agencies do not, however, maintain files regarding your race, religion, medical history, or criminal record.

Review your report carefully to make sure no unauthorized charges were made on your existing accounts and that no fraudulent accounts or loans were established in your name.

Should there be errors on your report, you should contact the credit bureaus and start the process of correcting the information. Having erroneous negative information about you on your file should be cleared up as soon as possible, because such information can have lasting damage on your report and will complicate your attempts to repay your debts or proceed in a bankruptcy. You can find information about reporting errors on the Federal Trade Commission's web site (www.ftc.gov) or by contacting the credit bureaus.

We The People can provide credit reports through an independent service, which is especially licensed to provide reports to attorneys, paralegals, and legal document services like us. The company's reports come from Experian and TransUnion and are especially tailored for use with bankruptcy filings. These reports contain the necessary information you need for filing, such as a summary of accounts, current trades, collection accounts, public records such as tax liens and judgments, a detailed creditor list showing all accounts and their status, as well as the proper mailing addresses and phone numbers for all listed creditors. The key to accessing your credit report is making sure you use a service that is reliable and will provide accurate and comprehensive information about you.

The Big Three Credit Bureaus

Below, you'll find the information you need to access all three major credit bureaus in the event you prefer to contact them directly or if you need to correct a mistake on your record.

Equifax (www.equifax.com)
- To dispute information in your report, write to Equifax Service Center, ATTN: Dispute Department, P.O. Box 740256, Atlanta, GA 30374.
- To order a credit report, call 1-800-685-1111 or write to Equifax Service Center, ATTN: Disclosure Department P.O. Box 740241, Atlanta, GA 30374.

- To remove your name from pre-approved offers of credit and marketing lists, call 1-888-567-8688 or write to: Equifax Options, P.O. Box 740123, Atlanta, GA 30374-0123.

Experian *(www.experian.com)*

- To order a credit report, call 1-888-397-3742 or write to Experian, P.O. Box 9066, Allen, TX 75013.

- To dispute information in your report, call 1-800-493-1058 or write to Experian, P.O. Box 9556, Allen, TX 75013.

- To remove your name from pre-approved offers of credit cards, call 1-888-567-8688. To remove your name from marketing lists, call 1-800-407-1088.

TransUnion *(www.tuc.com)*

- To order a credit report, call 1-800-916-8800 or write to TransUnion LLC, Consumer Disclosure Center, P.O. Box 1000, Chester, PA 19022.

- To dispute information in your report, call 1-800-916-8800.

- To have your name removed from pre-approved offers of credit and marketing lists, call 1-888-567-8688 or write to TransUnion LLC's Name Removal Option, P.O. Box 97328, Jackson, MS 39288-7328.

A final note about credit reports: Just as you would choose a debt counseling agency or debt management firm with caution, should you seek the help of a credit repair or credit-monitoring service company, do your homework before you hire. And remember: No one can remove a legitimate mark on your credit report for any amount of money. Anyone that claims he or she can magically erase your bad credit is lying—and probably making money in a scam, too.

Conclusion

One way to organize your search for information about bankruptcy is to look at the kinds of debts you owe and how those kinds of debts are treated in the various Chapters of bankruptcy. Where is your debt?

- ☑ Credit cards
- ☑ Taxes
- ☑ Student loans
- ☑ Secured debts
- ☑ Support
- ☑ Lawsuits
- ☑ Home loans

While Chapter 7 is the most common type of bankruptcy, there are several alternatives to Chapter 7 relief. We've explained out-of-court alternatives to bankruptcy in this chapter, but other types of bankruptcy can also provide relief. For example, debtors who are engaged in business, including corporations, partnerships, and sole proprietorships, may prefer to remain in business and avoid liquidation. Such debtors should consider filing a petition under Chapter 11 of the Bankruptcy Code. Under this Chapter, the debtor may seek an adjustment of debts, either by reducing the debt or by extending the time for repayment, or the debtor may seek a more comprehensive reorganization. Sole proprietorships may also be eligible for relief under Chapter 13 of the Bankruptcy Code.

In addition, individual debtors who have regular income may seek an adjustment of debts under Chapter 13 of the Bankruptcy Code. Indeed, the court may dismiss a Chapter 7 case filed by an individual whose debts are primarily consumer rather than business debts if the court finds that the granting of relief would be a substantial abuse of the provisions of Chapter 7. A number of courts have concluded that a Chapter 7 case may be dismissed for substantial abuse when the debtor has the ability to propose and carry out a workable and meaningful Chapter 13 plan.

As we stated at the beginning of this chapter, we cannot tell you whether you should file for bankruptcy. It's a decision you have to make on your own. You have to look at your numbers and decide what's best for you and your future. There's no equation you can do that will give you a yes or no answer. Some experts and attorneys will suggest sample scenarios and say that if you fall into one of those scenarios, then it's good to file. But again, there are no hard lines when it comes to making the decision to file. Only you know what's best for you. And now that you have more information—the knowledge to empower you—you can make a sound decision.

Let's move on and get to the specifics of these types of bankruptcies in the next chapter. The information will add to your knowledge.

CHAPTER 3

Types of Bankruptcy

Understanding the different types of bankruptcy is equally important to understanding your financial situation. Depending on your unique situation, such as your ability to generate an income, the magnitude of your assets, and the kind of debt you carry, you can determine which type of bankruptcy best fits your needs.

Each type of bankruptcy entails different kinds of relief, with different processes to follow, different time frames to expect, and different forms to fill out. We focus on Chapter 7 bankruptcy in this book, but in this chapter we'll expand our discussion to include the other kinds of bankruptcy so you can learn the scope of bankruptcy and increase your knowledge on the topic. Remember: Knowledge is power.

The debts discharged vary under each Chapter of the Bankruptcy Code. Section 523(a) of the Code specifically disallows various categories of debts from the discharge granted to individual debtors. Therefore, you must still repay those debts after bankruptcy. Congress has determined that these types of debts are not dischargeable for public policy reasons (based either on the nature of the debt or the fact that the debts were incurred because of improper behavior of the debtor, such as the debtor's drunken driving).

The five types of bankruptcy are as follows:

- Chapter 7: Liquidation (discharge most of your debts)
- Chapter 13: Individual Debt Adjustment (pay back your debts through a payment plan)
- Chapter 11: Reorganization (for certain types of businesses)
- Chapter 12: Family Farmer
- Chapter 9: Municipality

A filing under Chapters 11, 12, or 13 involves the so-called rehabilitation of the debtor to use his or her future earnings to pay off creditors. In these cases, a trustee may or may not be appointed to supervise the assets of the debtor—depending on how much money the debtor owes and how angry the creditors are about not being paid. Although a Chapter 7 is the most common way for people to free themselves of debt simply and inexpensively, there are good reasons to consider other kinds of bankruptcy, specifically Chapter 13, which we'll explain.

In most cases, companies file under Chapter 11; that's how big companies like Kmart and Tower Records stay in business while reorganizing and working their way out of debt. United Airlines filed for Chapter 11 in the aftermath of 9/11. Some companies don't survive a restructuring, however. Montgomery Ward said goodbye at the end of 2000 after the 128-year-old retailer failed to come out of Chapter 11 and eventually liquidated (sold everything and closed up shop).

Individuals typically file under Chapter 7 or 13. Chapter 9 bankruptcies are the least common: They apply to government entities that go broke (think schools, cities, and water districts). We will concern ourselves with the other four, more common types of bankruptcy (with minimal talk about the family farmer). And we begin with Chapter 7, the straight bankruptcy.

Chapter 7's Liquidation

A Chapter 7 bankruptcy is called a liquidation of debt because it wipes out all debts, except certain exclusions, and exposes debtors to a loss of property.

Remember: When you see the word "liquidate," think of "to pay off," "to get rid of," or even "to kill." When you liquidate your debt, you get rid of it! This is accomplished by selling your assets and giving any proceeds to your creditors. Sidenote: The word "liquid" is often used to describe money, and in particular, cash. Why? Cold, hard cash is the most liquid form of money—you can use it anywhere. It's the most versatile form of money, or legal tender. You can also think of it this way: Your Rolex watch isn't as liquid as the cash that sits in your wallet, because you can't use your Rolex to pay for groceries at the supermarket. If you were to convert your Rolex to cash by selling it in a pawnshop, however, you would be liquidating it. And then you could go buy groceries.

Sometimes a Chapter 7 bankruptcy is called a straight bankruptcy because it's simple—cut and dry. In a best case scenario, a Chapter 7 usually takes about four to six months to complete, costs about $209 in filing and administrative fees, and commonly requires only one trip to the courthouse. More often than not, you never have to go in front of a judge. Instead, you deal with people who sit across a table in a regular meeting room. No fancy outfits or courtroom dynamics.

The goals of a Chapter 7 bankruptcy include

- wiping out (most of) a debtor's debts, particularly the unsecured ones;
- allowing people a fresh start who cannot pay their debts from their income; and
- converting what assets can be seized into cash to help pay creditors back (in other words, liquidating!).

In a Chapter 7 case, the court usually grants the discharge promptly on expiration of the time fixed for filing a complaint objecting to discharge and the time fixed for filing a motion (a legal action) to dismiss the case for substantial abuse (60 days following the first date set for the creditors' meeting). Typically, this occurs about four months after the date the debtor files the petition with the clerk of the bankruptcy court.

Under this Chapter, the individual debtor is permitted to exempt or keep certain property. The remaining property is liquidated or sold by a court-appointed trustee and the money from the sale is handed over to the creditors. At the end of the case, the individual debtor receives a discharge that cancels his or her obligation to pay debts listed in the bankruptcy petition. Some debts may not be discharged. A discharge may be denied if the debtor received a discharge in a previous

Chapter 7 case within the past six years. Because each debtor may receive a Chapter 7 discharge only once every seven years, it is important that the decision to file a petition not be made lightly.

Also, if a previous Chapter 7 (or Chapter 13) case was dismissed within the past 180 days because you (1) violated a court order or (2) requested the dismissal once a creditor asked for the automatic stay to be lifted, you cannot file for Chapter 7 bankruptcy.

The court may dismiss a Chapter 7 case filed by an individual whose debts are primarily consumer, rather than business debts, if the court finds that the debtor is substantially abusing

> Chapter 7 is for those individuals with little or no income beyond that which is necessary for food, shelter or other necessities. A Chapter 7 relieves you permanently of any obligation to pay your dischargeable debts that arose before you filed your bankruptcy petition. That means you become no longer liable for those burdensome debts.

the provisions of the Chapter 7. This may include having substantial income in excess of your debts. Among the documents you will include in your bankruptcy petition is one that lists all of your current expenses, so if your current financial obligations do not exceed your income in a manner that justifies declaring bankruptcy, be ready to encounter resistance to your filing. To this end, note that it is extremely unwise to use a bankruptcy filing as a way of avoiding those credit card bills after you have recklessly abused them with no intention of ever paying for your purchases. If you have abused your privileges as a credit card holder, the court will challenge your bankruptcy filing. Moreover, if you know that you intend to file for bankruptcy and proceed to rack up enormous credit card bills, thinking that these debts will be discharged automatically, you're likely to encounter some problems in your filing.

A Red Flag

If you've recently run up a tab for large debts that are not necessary for day-to-day living, such as vacation, a hobby, or entertainment, filing for bankruptcy won't help you. Most luxury debts incurred just before filing are not dischargeable if the creditor objects. And getting further into debt shortly before filing makes the court very suspicious about your entire bankruptcy case. Honest people who have to resort to bankruptcy aren't likely to be taking vacations and incurring new debt from the purchase of luxury items before filing.

Last-minute debts presumed to be nondischargeable include the following:

- Debts of $1,150 or more to any one creditor for luxury goods or services made within 60 days before filing
- Debts for cash advances in excess of $1,150 obtained within 60 days of filing for bankruptcy

Note: Filing for bankruptcy may become more difficult in the future if Congress enacts new laws that change the rules of bankruptcy. Because credit card companies lose millions of dollars when their credit card holders file for bankruptcy and get those charges erased, they have lobbied aggressively for new rules that make it harder for the bankruptcy court to discharge unsecured, consumer debts. When this book went to press, Congress had not changed the rules, but we suggest you keep abreast of potential new rules by asking a We The People office or by referring to information provided on our exclusive web site. Visit www.wethepeopleforms.com, and enter your password: WTPBK.

To discharge luxury debts, you'll have to prove that extraordinary circumstances required you to make the charges and that you really weren't trying to pull a fast one on your creditors. This is not an easy case to prove. Judges often assume that people who incur last minute charges for luxuries are on their final buying binge before going under and losing their power to buy for a long time in the future.

Objections to Your Discharge

If you file a Chapter 7, you don't have an absolute right to a discharge. A creditor can file an objection to your discharge, and so can your trustee or the U.S. Trustee. Creditors receive a notice shortly after your case is filed that details important information, including the deadline for objecting to your discharge. If one of your creditors decides to object, the creditor must file a complaint in the bankruptcy court before the deadline indicated in the notice. Filing of a complaint starts a lawsuit referred to in bankruptcy as an adversary proceeding. If the issue of the debtor's right to a discharge goes to trial, the objecting party has the burden of proving all the facts essential to the objection. (More on credit card fraud and objections to your discharges later in this chapter.)

A Chapter 7 discharge may be denied for any of the reasons described in section 727(a) or 707(b) of the Bankruptcy Code:

- You transferred or concealed property with intent to hinder, delay, or defraud creditors.
- You destroyed or concealed books or financial records.
- Your committed a perjury or other fraudulent acts.
- You failed to account for or satisfactorily explain any loss of assets.

Or, as we've already mentioned:

- You violated a court order.
- You had an earlier discharge in a Chapter 7 or 11 case that commenced within six years before the date the petition was filed.
- Your petition was not filed in good faith.

The forms in a Chapter 7 filing, which we'll review in the next chapter, are straightforward once you acquaint yourself to them. A filing begins with a two-page petition, which you fill out in addition to several other forms that all get filed in your local bankruptcy court. In simple terms, the forms ask for details on the following information about you:

- Your property
- Your current income, its frequency and sources
- Your current monthly living expenses (food, clothing, shelter, utilities, taxes, transportation, medicine, etc.)
- Your debts and the nature of your creditors' claims
- Assets you think the bankruptcy law allows you to keep
- Assets you owned and money you spent during the previous two years
- Assets you sold or gave away during the previous two years.

How hard can that be? If someone were to ask you about these bulleted items in a conversation, you'd be able to talk without much struggle. So the challenge in filing a Chapter 7 is sitting down to put all that information in written form. Your information gets written down in the form of a detailed list, which the court likes to call a schedule. And then you sign and deliver (or mail) these papers.

The moment you file, that automatic stay we talked about in previous chapters takes effect. This means that the creditors can no longer hound you like sharks following a bleeding animal. They cannot initiate any lawsuits against you, call you incessantly and demand payments, or harass you in any way. Neither can creditors legally garnish (grab) your wages, drain your bank accounts, go after your car or prized possessions, cut off your hot water and electricity, or call your wealthy grandmother. You don't even have to notify them of your bankruptcy filing, as the clerk of the court will take care of that promptly upon your first filing of your petition. If any creditors call you after you file (because the court needs a few days and sometimes a week or two to get your notice sent out about your bankruptcy), you simply give them your case number and the date of your filing. Inform them that they are required by law to stop contacting you.

Letting the Bankruptcy Court Handle Your Case

Filing for a Chapter 7 sets in motion a sequence of events that eventually lead to the total discharge of (most of) your debts. And until your bankruptcy case ends, your financial problems are in the hands of the bankruptcy court. The court assumes legal control of the assets you own (except your exempt assets, which are yours to keep) and the debts you owe as of the date you file. Nothing can be sold or paid without the court's consent. You have control, however, with a few exceptions, of assets and income you acquire after you file for bankruptcy.

The court-appointed trustee is an important player in a Chapter 7. Later in this book, we'll go into detail about the trustee and give you tips for dealing with him or her.

The primary role of your trustee is to liquidate (sell) your nonexempt assets in a manner that gets the most money to your unsecured creditors. (And the more assets the trustee recovers for creditors, the more the trustee is paid.) To accomplish this, the trustee attempts to sell your nonexempt assets, such as assets that you own free and clear of liens and your assets that have market value above the amount of any security interest or lien and any exemption that you hold in the property. Example: You own, as a second vehicle, a Harley-Davidson motorcycle that is worth about $20,000, and you've paid it off. Your trustee surely will take your motorcycle and sell it. Another example: You've collected museum-quality Navajo rugs and artifacts that are worth a lot more than what you can exempt. Your trustee will take these items and sell them.

The trustee also pursues claims for damages or money owed to you. Finally, the trustee can use so-called avoiding powers to take back any preferential transfers you made within 90 days of your bankruptcy filing. If, for example, you paid off a creditor in contemplation of bankruptcy, this act of transferring money or assets to one creditor (over others you owe) is essentially defrauding your other creditors. Your trustee can recover any such transfers and include them in your overall bankruptcy petition as a listed creditor so all creditors get treated fairly and

The commencement of a bankruptcy case creates an estate. (And you thought you were poor!) Your estate technically becomes the temporary legal owner of all of your assets. It consists of all legal or equitable interests you have in assets at the beginning of your case, including assets owned or held by another person if you have an interest in the asset. Generally speaking, your creditors are paid from nonexempt assets of the estate.

> As a debtor, don't worry about how your trustee sells any assets he or she manages to take, or how your trustee pays back creditors. Your main concerns are your exempt assets and any debts that cannot be discharged by your bankruptcy, such as alimony and child support. You want to keep as many assets as you can by using your exemptions, and you want as much of your debts to be discharged as possible.

equally. In some situations, a trustee can recover large transfers made within two years of your bankruptcy filing.

There are 18 categories of debt excepted from discharge under Chapters 7, 11, and 12. A more limited list of exceptions applies to cases under Chapter 13.

About Exempt Property

One of the schedules that you will file is a schedule of exempt property. Federal bankruptcy law provides that an individual debtor can protect some property from the claims of creditors either because it is exempt under federal bankruptcy law or because it is exempt under the laws of the debtor's home state. Many states have taken advantage of a provision in the bankruptcy law that permits each state to adopt its own exemption law in place of the federal exemptions. In other jurisdictions, the individual debtor has the option of choosing between a federal package of exemptions or exemptions available under state law. Thus, whether certain property is exempt and may be kept by you is often a question of your state's law. We have provided every state's list of exempt property on our web site at www. wethepeopleforms.com. Simply enter **WTPBK** as your password to access everything you need.

At your creditors' meeting, which will occur about 20 to 40 days after your petition is filed, your trustee will go through the papers you file and ask you questions. You must attend this meeting, which is also known as a 341(A) meeting for its reference in the Bankruptcy Code. Don't worry too much about this meeting: Your actual time before the trustee is not likely to last more than five minutes (but waiting for your turn might take an hour or so!). Creditors may attend, too, but rarely do. (Chapter 6 of this book is dedicated entirely to describing and preparing you for this meeting. You will also learn about trustees, how they sell your property—if they do—and how you need to act when you meet your trustee face to face. If you're curious enough to skip ahead to this chapter in the book, go ahead!)

> Don't let any ruthless creditor who shows up at your creditors' meeting intimidate you. The court is in charge of the bankruptcy proceeding and will serve as a moderator to any disputes should someone arrive on the scene to challenge your bankruptcy. And, while a huge multimillion-dollar company like Macy's or Home Depot (probably) won't send any representatives to your meeting, be ready to have those companies cancel your store card as soon as they get word of your filing. It's okay. In most cases, you can get another card once the bankruptcy is over or prepay for one.

Because these store cards are more or less credit cards, which are discharged routinely in bankruptcy, courts do not like hearing this argument and challenge these companies' practice. If you meet opposition from Sears or any other store for which you hold a card, stick to your guns and don't feel pressured to reaffirm a debt to a retail store, as the court will likely side with you and allow the card's balance to be discharged. As we'll explain later, you can never be forced to reaffirm a debt. The worst that can happen is you lose the asset.

What's Dischargeable and Not Dischargeable in a Chapter 7?

If most of your debt cannot be discharged by a Chapter 7 bankruptcy, then filing will do you no good.

The most common types of nondischargeable debts are as follows:

- Certain types of tax claims (1040 taxes that have not been assessed for more than three years)

We've said that creditors don't usually show up at creditors' meetings. But if you carry debt on a retail store card, you may face a representative from that company in your meeting. In the past, Sears has aggressively tried to prove to bankruptcy courts that their store cards are secured by the items purchased on the cards. A rep from Sears may try to get you to reaffirm (keep) your debt, redeem your debt by paying current market value for the goods you've purchased on the card (example: paying $350 for the refrigerator you originally bought on the card for $800), or give back the items you bought with the card. Other electronics and home appliance companies such as Circuit City and Best Buy may also make this argument, pointing to fine-point language in the terms to your credit card agreement.

- Debts not included on the lists and schedules that you must file with the court
- Debts for spousal or child support or alimony
- Debts for willful and malicious injuries to a person or property
- Debts to governmental units for fines and penalties
- Debts for most government-funded or guaranteed educational loans or benefit overpayments (unless you can prove undue hardship, explained later)
- Debts for personal injury caused by your operation of a motor vehicle while intoxicated
- Debts for certain condominium or cooperative housing fees

In addition, the following debts may be declared nondischargeable by a bankruptcy judge if a creditor challenges your request to discharge them. These debts may be discharged in Chapter 13, however, because you can include them in your plan, and at the end of your case, the balance is wiped out.

- Debts you incurred on the basis of fraud, such as lying on a credit application
- Credit purchases of $1,150 or more for luxury goods or services made within 60 days of filing
- Loans or cash advances of $1,150 or more taken within 60 days of filing
- Debts from willful or malicious injury to another person or another person's property
- Debts from embezzlement, larceny, or breach of trust
- Debts you owe under a divorce decree or settlement unless after bankruptcy you would still not be able to afford to pay them or the benefit you'd receive by the discharge outweighs any detriment to your ex-spouse (who would have to pay them if you discharge them in bankruptcy)

Other debts can be discharged in a Chapter 7 bankruptcy. These typically include credit card bills, medical bills, most personal judgments, personal loans, and loans you have personally guaranteed and cosigned for.

For Assets You Own Free and Clear. If you decide you want to keep assets that your trustee has a right to take and liquidate (sell), you can request that you retain that property if it's listed as one of your exemptions allowed by the bankruptcy court. For example: If your state law provides an exemption for a car up to a $2,500 value, and your car is worth $2,500 or less, you can claim the exemption and keep the car. If the car is worth more than $2,500 and you want to keep it, then you may have to pay the trustee the value of the vehicle that is

As a practical matter, unless there is substantial excess value, your trustee will not bother pursuing an exempt property. Keep in mind that the exemption only applies to your equity in the exempt property. So, if your car is worth $2,500 and you owe $2,500 to the bank that lent you the money to buy it, you don't have any equity and the exemption will not help you. You can still keep the car, but you will have to agree to reaffirm your contract with the bank and continue to make your payments.

over the $2,500, unless there is another exemption that can be used to protect the balance.

For Assets You Do Not Own Free and Clear. If you want to keep property that a secured creditor has a right to take back in the event of your bankruptcy, you can negotiate new terms for paying the debt with the creditor and reaffirm that property (retain that debt and continue to make payments on it). Remember: A reaffirmation is an agreement between you and a creditor that you'll pay all or a portion of the money owed, even though you've filed for bankruptcy. In return, the creditor pledges not to repossess or take back the property.

For example: Let's say you owe $3,400 to ABC Bank on your car loan. But your car is only worth $2,000. You can try to negotiate with ABC Bank to continue paying for the car (using a reaffirmation agreement, which we'll explain later), but only paying for its current value—$2,000. If ABC Bank refuses to negotiate with you, it will have to think twice about repossessing the car. Why? Because if ABC Bank repossesses the car, it will only be able to get $2,000 for it. And, if it costs ABC Bank $500 just to repossess the car, store it, and try to sell it, ABC Bank ends up losing $500 when it could have agreed to let you pay only $2,000 to keep it. ABC Bank will let you reaffirm your debt.

What Is a Nonexempt Asset?

A nonexempt asset is any asset you own that is not listed under the exemption laws of your state or under the federal exemptions where applicable. For example, let's say that your state law exempts only one car, but you have two cars. If you own both cars free and clear of any liens, you can protect only one with your state exemption and the other will be a nonexempt asset.

Can I Keep Any Nonexempt Assets?

Yes, you can always buy the nonexempt asset back from the trustee. If the property has very little value, you could file a motion with the court (that is, ask the court formally) to have the trustee abandon (that is, not pursue) the property. The trustee usually will not object or oppose to your request if the asset has little or no value and the asset will become a burden to the estate. However, you will have to file a motion and attend a hearing in the bankruptcy court before you can get the property abandoned. The court may also deny your motion.

NOTE: Because the various bankruptcy courts disagree about whether a debtor whose debt is not in default may retain the property and pay under the original contract terms without reaffirming the debt, you should consider getting some legal counsel to ensure that your rights are protected and that any reaffirmation is in your best interest. If you choose to reaffirm debt, the reaffirmation should be done before the granting of a discharge. A written agreement to reaffirm a debt must be filed with the court and, if you are not represented by an attorney, a judge must approve the agreement. More on reaffirmation agreements in chapter 5 of this book.

Chapter 13's Debt Adjustment

A Chapter 13 bankruptcy is a court-supervised reorganization of your debts. It reduces your monthly payments over a specified period of time. In other words, you don't let go of your debts in a discharge like you do in Chapter 7. Instead of surrendering your debts, you retain them and attempt to repay them under a plan you create and that the court must approve.

The main goal of a Chapter 13 filing is to reduce the payments to your creditors as low as the court will allow and at the same time secure protection from your creditors. You must first list all your assets (assigning each its proper value) along with your total outstanding debts. It's important to take the maximum exemptions, because it will determine the minimum amount of money you will be allowed to pay into your plan to satisfy your unsecured creditors.

Having a realistic plan is key to your ability to come out of a Chapter 13 bankruptcy successful. Scrutinize your budget and statement of income to ensure that the payment schedule you adopt can be realistically met within your budget. It does not help if the plan payment schedule is too high.

Once you establish what you earn and your realistic budget of expenses, you can compute what you can comfortably afford.

The Chapter 13 Plan

All debts in a Chapter 13 bankruptcy are divided into three major categories:

- Priority
- Secured
- Unsecured claims

Priority claims have to be paid in full over the term of the plan. Taxes are typical priority claims (that is, property taxes, income taxes, and so on). For example, if you owe $3,000 in taxes, you can pay them over a 36-month period. It is not advisable to go beyond 36 months on a *pro se* (representing yourself) bankruptcy, unless you can prove substantial hardship to the court.

The next category is the secured debts. Secured debts relate to a specific asset such as a car, furniture, or home. This category is further divided into money owed on a home and money owed on everything else (that is, car, furniture, and so on).

Unsecured claims consist of credit card bills, doctor and hospital bills, and so on.

Chapter 13 is the debt repayment chapter for individuals (including those who operate businesses as sole proprietorships) who have regular income and whose secured debts do not exceed $871,550 and whose unsecured debts do not exceed $290,525. (Note that these debt limitations change from time to time.) Chapter 13 is not available to corporations or partnerships. Chapter 13 generally permits individuals to keep their property by repaying creditors out of their future income. Each Chapter 13 debtor proposes a repayment plan that must be approved by the court. The debtor pays the amounts set forth in the plan to the Chapter 13 trustee, who distributes the funds for a small fee. The Chapter 13 debtor receives a discharge of most debts after the debtor completes the payments required under the plan.

How Your Home Mortgage Is Paid in Chapter 13

You cannot modify the rights of the creditor who has a lien on your home. You must make the same payments each month that you originally contracted to pay. However, if you are several months behind on your mortgage payments and the lender is about to foreclose on your property, the filing will prevent the lender from taking your home. You will be given the opportunity to pay the past due amounts, plus interest, over the term of the plan.

In regards to an automobile, let's assume your original obligation was $10,000 with monthly payments of $350. Assuming the value of your automobile today is only $6,000, it is that value that you will be paying over the term of the plan. This actually results in you paying the secured creditor a lower overall amount than you originally contracted.

You May Not Have to Pay 100 Percent of Your Debt in Chapter 13

Unsecured debts are dealt with last. The rule is that the unsecured creditor must receive, over the life of the plan, as much as they would have received if you had filed Chapter 7. For example, if you have $1,000 in nonexempt property, you will be required to pay $27.77 a month to your unsecured creditors over a 36-month term. That amount represents the minimum; if you can pay more (after living expenses, priority claims, and secured claims), the court will want you to do so.

If you cannot pay at least 70 percent of your unsecured debt through a Chapter 13, your case gets treated as a Chapter 7 in the sense that you cannot file a Chapter 7 within the next six years.

Making Payments on Your Plan

Approximately 30 days after you file your plan with the court, you will be expected to start making payments. You will make your payments directly to your appointed trustee. This requires living on a fixed budget for a prolonged period. This also requires you to not make any new credit obligations without consulting your trustee, as such credit obligations may affect the execution of your plan.

Some districts allow you to mail in your payments, while other districts require the payment to be deducted directly from your paycheck. If the latter is required in your area, make sure you notify your employer first.

After your plan is filed, your bill collectors should cease all collection activity. If you notify your creditors on the day you file of your intent to adjust your debt, your call can stop all foreclosures, repossessions, and legal actions from occurring.

Your employer is not allowed by law to discriminate against you because you have filed a Chapter 7 or Chapter 13 bankruptcy. A governmental unit or private employer may not discriminate against a person solely because the person was a debtor, was insolvent before or during the case, or has not paid a debt that was discharged in the case. This means that your employer cannot terminate your employment because you have filed for bankruptcy and/or have failed to repay a discharged debt.

Meeting with the Trustee

This meeting is also known as the first meeting of the creditors because your creditors may attend to determine how their claims are being treated under your plan. The trustee may have already begun to review your plan. The purpose of the review is to determine whether your budget will allow reasonable amounts for each category. The trustee will not recommend an adjustment in your plan if you have not budgeted enough money for your personal needs.

After presiding over the creditors' meeting, the trustee will either recommend or oppose confirmation of your plan. The trustee may oppose it if he believes the plan is either impractical, submitted in bad faith, cannot be complied with, or does not represent your best efforts. Cooperating with the trustee is to your advantage, as he or she carries substantial influence with the judge. Trustees vary a great deal in the degree to which they will assist. Some districts offer debtor schools that teach skills in financial matters; other districts have the trustees available to discuss individual financial questions you might have. Check with your bankruptcy trustee's office to find out what assistance is available to you.

How Trustees Are Paid

The general guideline is 10 percent of what you pay toward your debt is directed toward administrative costs and salary of the trustee.

Again, we'll go into great detail of this meeting and the role of your trustee in chapter 6.

How Claims Are Treated

Priority claims must be paid in full. If you owe federal income taxes, which are the most common priority claim, the tax owed can be paid out in monthly installments over the term of the plan. While you are under the protection of your Chapter 13 bankruptcy, the IRS cannot put their collection process in motion.

There are several ways to handle secured claims. First, the collateral (the item secured by your creditor) may be returned to the creditor. If the creditor sells the asset and does not recover the total obligation owed by you, the remaining balance is still owed and then becomes an unsecured debt.

An automobile is a common secured item. Chapter 13 allows you to pay the bluebook or current market value of the automobile only. Your monthly payments will therefore be greatly reduced. Paying just the current market value of the car can be used in the same manner for furniture, boats, or any other personal property—except your home.

Your home mortgage cannot be modified; however, defaults in your mortgage payments can be cured through your Chapter 13 plan. You can pay off your late payments while you continue to make your current payments.

Non-possessory secured liens are when you have borrowed money from a finance company and have put up your household goods (that you own outright) as collateral. In this kind of secured claim, the law gives you a break. The bankruptcy can void (eliminate) the lien and then you can treat it as an unsecured debt. Remember: Unsecured claims are debts for which there are no physical assets, such as a washing machine or a car, to back up (secure) the debt.

Example: You borrow $5,000 and put up your oak bedroom set and living room furniture as security for the loan. In your bankruptcy, you list these items as exempt, and if their value is less than your exemption limit, you can keep the assets and the court will eliminate the lien. Or, if you cannot entirely exempt your bedroom and living room sets using your exemptions, the court will reduce the amount of your lien by the difference between the exemption limit and either the asset's value or the amount of the debt, whichever is less.

So, on a $5,000 lien:

Value of asset	= $3,500
Minus exemption amount	= $3,000

Amount of lien remaining:	$500 (this is what you'd owe now)

Chapter 13: Adjustment of Debts for Individuals

Ten chronological steps usually make up a Chapter 13 adjustment of debt program:

1. Just as in Chapter 7 bankruptcy, you will **fill out forms** that reveal your assets and debts. Again, completeness and accuracy are important.

2. You should **understand** the different types of debts that can be treated in a Chapter 13 bankruptcy.

3. The **plan of reorganization** will be prepared at this time. You will attempt to lower your overall payments to creditors and, at the same time, ensure that you will keep those assets you want to maintain. Be sure you understand the plan that is being proposed on your behalf and your related obligations.

4. You will **file the petition** to stop all creditors' activity against you. After you file the necessary papers with the court, notice will be given to your creditors.

5. Thirty days after the filing of your petition and proposed plan of reorganization, you must **begin paying** the trustee according to your plan. Most trustees in the United States insist that payments be deducted automatically from your paycheck; some trustees, however, may allow you to pay directly.

6. Before your creditors' meeting, you will **negotiate with creditors** to avoid objections to your plan of reorganization.

7. At the **creditors' meeting** (approximately 40–60 days after the filing of your petition), you will attempt to complete any negotiations with creditors. Creditors might attend the meeting to find out how they are going to be treated in your plan. The trustee will conduct the meeting and ask questions to determine if your plan is feasible. The trustee will either recommend confirmation of your plan or suggest changes that must be made before recommending the plan to the judge. Your secured creditors will decide whether to file a motion with the court to obtain their collateral or to file an objection to your plan. Either they will determine they are not being treated fairly or they will accept the payment plan you are offering.

8. After the creditors' meeting, there will be a **confirmation hearing** before the judge. Some districts conduct the hearing on the same day; others three to four weeks later. If there are no objections, the judge will confirm the plan. If there is an objection, the judge will hear it and then decide whether or not to confirm your plan. If the plan is not confirmed, the court will usually give you time to change your plan and propose it at a later date.

9. After the plan is confirmed, you will **continue to pay the trustee** for a specific period of time—usually three years. During that time, if you have problems making your payments, you can modify your plan to change the way you are paying or you can convert your case to a Chapter 7 liquidation bankruptcy.

10. When you have completed your plan, the **court** will give you a **discharge.** Any unsecured debts that have not been paid in full will be wiped out.

The court can make a substantial reduction in your payments. Unsecured creditors do not receive interest; therefore the interest you are presently paying is eliminated. As long as all unsecured creditors are treated equally and you pay at least 70 percent of what you owe them, your plan should be successful. No preference can be given to one credit card company— even if you'd like to give preference to one because you want to keep that card.

Objections to Your Plan

Before your plan is confirmed to the court, your creditors can object to its confirmation. If you have followed the guidelines we discussed, particularly as they relate to unsecured creditors, there should be no problems. Even though in most cases there are no objections, you should be aware that the possibility exists.

It's important to make sure that you are current with your payments to the trustee by the time of your confirmation of the plan. Do not start off in a default position as your case could be denied and dismissed.

Discharges of Debts in a Chapter 13

A broader discharge of debts is available to a debtor in a Chapter 13 case than in a Chapter 7 case. As a general rule, if you file for Chapter 13, you are discharged from all debts provided for by the plan except certain long-term obligations (such as a home mortgage), debts for alimony or child support, debts for most government-funded or guaranteed educational loans or benefit overpayments, debts arising from death or personal injury caused by driving while intoxicated or under the influence of drugs, and debts for restitution or a criminal fine included in a sentence on your conviction of a crime. Although a Chapter 13 debtor generally receives a discharge only after completing all payments required by the court-approved (confirmed) repayment plan, there are some limited circumstances under which you may request the court to grant a hardship discharge even though you have failed to complete plan payments. Such a discharge is available only to a debtor whose failure to complete plan payments is due to circumstances beyond his or her control.

The scope of a Chapter 13 hardship discharge is similar to that in a Chapter 7 case with regard to the types of debts that are excepted from the discharge. A hardship discharge also is available in Chapter 12 if the failure to complete plan payments is due to "circumstances for which the debtor should not justly be held accountable."

How bad was this woman's debt? When the 52-year-old woman filed for bankruptcy, she claimed she couldn't afford the $917 monthly payments on $85,000 in school debt because she had reached a plateau in her career as a drafting technician, in which she earned $40,000 annually. The woman also argued she had no reasonable prospects for earning more in the area where she lived. Her monthly income of $2,299.33 just covered her monthly expenses of $2,295.05. And when she retires in 13 years, her income will drop to $1,000 a month.

Although her discharge was initially denied by the bankruptcy court, on appeal she won— and her $85,000 was discharged.

Student loans are not typically discharged in a bankruptcy, but they can be a source of serious debt for people—far more serious than credit card debt. Proving a hardship discharge for a student loan might become easier in the future. In 2004, a California court ruled that a woman did not have to prove exceptional circumstances in order to show that continuing to make payments created an undue hardship. According to that court, even a person well above the poverty level can have debt relief in bankruptcy as long as the individual's financial straits prevent repaying the loan in the future.

Chapter 7 or Chapter 13?

There are a number of reasons why filing a Chapter 13 is preferable to a Chapter 7, even though the vast majority of people who file for bankruptcy do so under Chapter 7. Some of those reasons for picking Chapter 13, however, include the following:

- You have valuable nonexempt property (example: a lot of equity in your home).
- You have debts that cannot be discharged in Chapter 7 (example: taxes).
- You're behind on your mortgage or car loan. In a Chapter 7, you might have to give up the asset or pay for it in full during your bankruptcy case. In Chapter 13, you can repay the arrears through your plan and keep the asset by making the payments required under the contract.
- You have codebtors on personal (nonbusiness) loans. In a Chapter 7, the creditors will go after your codebtors for payment, which can mean your business partners and/or close friends. In Chapter 13, the creditors may not seek payment from your codebtors for the duration of your case. Keep in mind this is true for consumer, not business, debts. And your plan must pay off 100 percent of your debt or your creditors may go after your codebtor.
- If you've filed for a Chapter 7 or 13 in the previous six years, you cannot file for a Chapter 7 bankruptcy (unless you've paid off at least 70 percent of your unsecured debts in a Chapter 13 bankruptcy); however, you can file for Chapter 13 bankruptcy at any time.

Also, if you feel a moral obligation to pay your debts, filing a Chapter 7 will not give you that satisfaction. You can use your bankruptcy as a period to excel in money management skills and practice those skills through a Chapter 13, which basically grants you the right to work through your debt problems in an organized, active, and planned manner. Moreover, there's a chance that creditors will extend better credit lines to you once you've recovered from a Chapter 13 bankruptcy than had you filed for Chapter 7.

Two influential factors in one's choosing a Chapter 7 or Chapter 13 bankruptcy are

- income power (how much the person makes and stands to make in the future to pay off debts); and
- asset power (how much the person has in assets).

1040 taxes due on filed returns that have been assessed are dischargeable after three years from the date of assessment. Example: You owe the IRS back taxes for 10 years. Any taxes that were assessed three years or later before your bankruptcy filing can be discharged, but you will owe the taxes due from the past three years.

People with large assets and/or a decent, steady income (with perhaps the ability to increase that income in the future) have more reasons to consider a Chapter 13 over a Chapter 7. It is also a good option for those barred from Chapter 7 because of a pre-existing filing within six years. (If, however, you obtained a Chapter 13 discharge in good faith after paying at least 70 percent of your unsecured debts, the six-year bar does not apply. The six-year period runs from the date you filed for the earlier bankruptcy, not the date you received your discharge.)

For those with few or little assets but an enormous amount of unsecured debt, Chapter 7 is usually the answer.

Think about How Chapter 7 Can Affect Others

When people take on loans with others for a business venture or piece of property, they often do so with friends, family members, or relatives. Those loans are joint obligations to pay and once you file for a Chapter 7 bankruptcy, you, in effect, make your partners in that obligation wholly responsible for the debt. Let's say your father cosigned a loan for you as a favor, and you never intended for him to pay any part of that loan. It was always your responsibility and you simply needed his cosignature to get the loan approved in the first place. If you file for bankruptcy, you immediately make your father responsible for the loan. And now he has to pay for it and deal with the lenders that go after him when he fails to make the payments that were supposed to be yours. He's on the hook

> If your monthly income exceeds your monthly expenses, giving you disposable income that can be used to pay your debts, you're at risk of having your Chapter 7 case dismissed unless you agree to convert it to a Chapter 13 bankruptcy. Also, there is no hard and fast rule about how much you'd have to be able to repay in a Chapter 13 case before the judge will toss out your Chapter 7 case.

that you created, and it has the potential to do financial harm to him both now and in the future. If you don't want to subject someone to this kind of liability, paying off your debt over time with a Chapter 13 is better than discharging it in a Chapter 7.

Based on your income and ability to pay some or all of your debts, a bankruptcy judge could decide that you better qualify for Chapter 13 and thus deny or dismiss your Chapter 7. Usually, a trustee will raise this issue before a judge, who then decides that to grant you a discharge would be a substantial abuse of the bankruptcy laws.

There is an exception, however, for people whose debts are primarily business-related. If your debts are business-related, you are less at risk of being denied a Chapter 7. If they are consumer-related (example: you owe $55,000 spread over four credit cards) and your income is substantial, you're likely to meet a Chapter 13.

Don't File for Bankruptcy If . . .

1. You Want to Prevent Seizure of Property and Wages

Let's assume that you don't file for bankruptcy and a creditor files a lawsuit against you in an attempt to get payment. And, let's say that creditor wins and tries to collect that judgment from your property and income. A lot of your property, however, including food, clothing, personal effects, and furnishings, is probably protected by law (exempt) from being taken to pay the judgment. And, quite likely, your nonexempt property is not worth enough to tempt a creditor to go after it, as the costs of seizure and sale can be quite high.

If the creditor goes after your income, the law still protects you, as only 25 percent of your net wages can be taken to satisfy a court judgment (up to 50 percent for child support and alimony). And often, you can keep more than 75 percent of your wages if you can demonstrate that you need the extra amount to support yourself and your family. Income from a pension or other retirement benefit is usually treated like wages. Creditors cannot touch public benefits such as welfare, unemployment insurance, disability insurance, or Social Security.

Bottom line: You may not need to file for bankruptcy to keep creditors from seizing all your property and wages.

FRED'S STORY

> **I am still shocked** at how fast my life fell apart. Three years ago my wife and I had everything . . . and then lost everything in a very short period. We felt wealthy with good jobs and the dual income to buy a beautiful house, filling it with exactly the kind of furniture and home décor we wanted. We even had a wine cellar and two BMWs. And we had plenty of money for traveling, fine dining, and planning how we'd start a family and buy a second home for vacationing in the mountains. Life was perfect.
>
> Within two weeks, our lives were turned around. It started when my wife was bedridden with a difficult pregnancy. A week after she gave birth to twins, I broke my collarbone in a backyard accident that involved a ladder. Two days later, my company announced cutbacks and I was laid off. My broken collarbone made it difficult to find another job quickly. My wife had the two infants at home and wasn't planning on going back to work anytime soon. Within a couple of months, we were behind in our bills. We had missed mortgage payments and car payments, and I was using the credit cards to pay for medical bills, food, diapers, formula, and gas to get around for job interviews and to run errands for my wife.
>
> We filed for Chapter 7 bankruptcy when the babies were six months old. By then, BMW was threatening to take our cars, the mortgage lender was sending notices threatening foreclosure, and our credit card bills exceeded $100,000. We had gone from making six figures to owing six figures! I just didn't understand it.
>
> Initially, my wife didn't want to file for bankruptcy, but when I explained to her how severe our debts were, she agreed. The day after we filed the papers for bankruptcy, two amazing things happened: The creditors stopped calling, and I got a great job offer that would pay me more than what I was making before. I took the job and began to see the light at the end of the tunnel. But when we went into my creditors' meeting a month later, my trustee advised us to convert our filing to a Chapter 13. He said that we had too much equity in our home and that my new job had the potential to bring us out of debt with careful planning over the next 36 months. We had to sell a few things and downsize our cars to one, less expensive car, but we were okay with that.
>
> I walked out of that creditors' meeting two years ago, and life is almost back to normal. My wife and I worked hard at climbing out of debt with the plan we made through Chapter 13. We didn't have to lose our home, and we managed to keep the vast majority of our assets; we worked out a plan whereby we paid cents on the dollar of our debts instead of the whole enchilada. Going through a Chapter 13 bankruptcy taught me a lot. Once we took inventory of our assets in relation to our debts, we realized where we had gone wrong: We had never saved. So when we needed extra money to pay for accidents, incidentals, or to help cushion serious changes in life (like my job loss and my wife's pregnancy), we didn't have it. Our money had already been spent. And the downward spiral began.
>
> I don't think we'll ever be in that position again. We save now more than we spend. We don't buy as many luxury items and fancy gadgets as we used to, but we live knowing that we're prepared for the unexpected. That gives us enormous peace of mind.

2. You Want to Stop the Creditors from Harassing You

Don't file for bankruptcy if your only concern is related to the harassing creditors that call and call and threaten you with legal action if you don't pay today. Bankruptcy can always be an option, but if you're able to pay off your debts outside a bankruptcy filing, and you just need to find a way to keep the creditors at bay, review your state's web site and look for an explanation of both federal and state debt collection laws. Laws exist to protect you from abusive and harassing debt collector conduct.

3. You Defrauded Your Creditors

We've already talked about the dangers of abusing the bankruptcy laws, but it bears repeating: Bankruptcy is designed for honest people who simply get into too much debt, to their dismay, and who never planned on being in so much debt, either. A bankruptcy court will not help someone who has been unfair with creditors or who has abused their privileges to credit.

Courts and trustees see certain activities as red flags. If any of the following red flags pertain to you within the past year, you should consult with an attorney before proceeding in a bankruptcy by yourself:

- You've unloaded assets to your friends or relatives to hide them from creditors or from the bankruptcy court.
- You've incurred more debt for nonnecessities when you were clearly broke.
- You concealed assets or money from your spouse during a divorce proceeding.
- You lied about your income or debts on a credit application.

As more people file for bankruptcy and more people seek relief of debts caused by consumer abuse of credit, it's no surprise that credit card issuers have become more aggressive with their objections to a discharge of debt. A court that must determine whether a person has committed a fraud with regard to his or her debts will look at the following factors:

- How long was the period between incurring serious debt and filing for bankruptcy?
- Did the person consult with an attorney before incurring more debt?
- Are there recent charges that amount to more than $1,150? Luxury items? Multiple charges on the same day?
- Are there many charges less than $50 (to avoid pre-clearance of the charge by the credit card issuer) once the person reached his or her credit limit?
- Were there charges after the card issuer ordered the person to return the card or sent several past due notices?
- Are there indications on the credit card that the person acted out of character, such as taking multiple trips to exotic locations without a history of much travel?
- Are there excessive charges after the person obviously became unable to pay for bills?

Although there's no formula for weeding out the fraudulent bankruptcy filers, it doesn't take much effort to look at a potential bankruptcy candidate's debts and determine his or her level of honesty and integrity. You should consider your profile before facing your trustee and the questions you're likely to encounter when defending your case. Later on, we'll give you some tips for dealing with your trustee and handling any challenge that you might encounter along the way.

The bankruptcy court will dismiss your bankruptcy case and possibly jail you if you defraud the court. If you lie, hide, cheat, or swindle the court, you will face more problems than your current debt crisis. In fact, your fraud can possibly haunt you for the rest of your life. Remember: You must sign your bankruptcy papers under penalty of perjury, swearing that everything in them is true. If you deliberately fail to disclose assets, omit material information about your financial affairs, or use a false Social Security number (to hide your identity as a prior filer), and the court discovers your action, your case will be dismissed and you may be prosecuted for fraud.

Chapter 11's Reorganization

While individuals are not precluded from using Chapter 11, this type of bankruptcy is more typically used to reorganize a business, which may be a corporation, sole proprietorship, or partnership. When you hear about a company filing for bankruptcy in the news, you probably hear "Company X filed for Chapter 11 today . . ." and you know that the company won't be closing its doors tomorrow. Chapter 11 is how big companies such as the airlines, giant retailers, and telecommunications corporations restructure their debt and use the protections allowed in Chapter 11 to stay in business. A good way to think of Chapter 11 is to equate it with super large debts—debts in the millions. And individuals don't usually have debts in the millions unless they are tied to a company.

They can take years to resolve, and people or businesses that file for Chapter 11 generally don't proceed through the process alone. If you have any questions about this type of bankruptcy, consult an attorney.

Relief for Family Farmers

Chapter 12 of the Bankruptcy Code provides debt relief to financially-strapped family farmers with regular annual income. The process is much the same as that under Chapter 13, under which the debtor files a plan to repay debts over a period of time. The farmer continues to operate the farm while making regular payments.

Chapter 12 is tailored to meet the economic realities of family farming; with the introduction of Chapter 12, Congress has eliminated many of the barriers that family farmers had faced when seeking to reorganize successfully under either Chapter 11 or 13 of the Bankruptcy Code.

Farmers eligible to file under Chapter 12 include

1. individuals or individual and spouse; and

2. a corporation or partnership.

Each must meet certain criteria as of the date the petition is filed in order to qualify for relief under Chapter 12. Chapter 12 is more streamlined, less complicated, and less expensive than Chapter 11, which is better suited to the large corporate reorganization. In addition, few family farmers find Chapter 13 to be advantageous, because it was designed for wage earners who have smaller debts than those facing family farmers. In

Chapter 11 is more expensive and complex than a Chapter 13, but not everybody qualifies for Chapter 13 bankruptcy. Consumers with secured debts less than $871,550 and unsecured debts less than $269,250 can file for Chapter 13. Consumers with debts in excess of the Chapter 13 debt limits and businesses can file for Chapter 11.

Chapter 12, Congress sought to combine the features of the Bankruptcy Code, which can provide a framework for successful family farm reorganizations. Because Congress has revisited Chapter 12 and closed the availability of this Chapter in the past, check with your local court if you are a family farmer looking to voluntarily file for bankruptcy under this Chapter.

> Chapter 12 of the Bankruptcy Code was enacted by Congress in 1986, specifically to meet the needs of financially distressed family farmers. The primary purpose of this legislation was to give family farmers facing bankruptcy a chance to reorganize their debts and keep their farms.

Conclusion

Choosing the right kind of bankruptcy will have a direct effect on your ability to recover from your debt and move forward in your life. Of the five different types of bankruptcy, Chapter 7 is how the majority of individuals get a relief from their debts quickly and inexpensively. People with sizeable assets and interest in property typically try to pay back their debt through a debt adjustment in Chapter 13.

Our government has designed bankruptcy law to aid and protect debtors. It provides for the development of a plan that allows a debtor who is unable to pay his creditors to resolve debts through the division of assets among the creditors. This court-supervised division allows the interests of all creditors to be treated with some measure of equality. Certain bankruptcy proceedings allow a debtor to stay in business using revenue that continues to be generated to resolve debts. An additional purpose of bankruptcy law is to allow certain debtors to free themselves (to be discharged) of the financial obligations they have accumulated, after their assets are distributed, even if their debts have not been paid in full.

Stories in the news have chronicled people who manage to avoid bankruptcy despite the odds against them. Take O.J. Simpson for example, who was ordered to pay the families of his ex-wife and her friend $33.5 million in the wrongful death civil lawsuit. He didn't have enough cash to pay for the judgment against him, but he had other valuable assets that were vulnerable to seizure in the judgment. What did he do? Instead of filing for bankruptcy and letting bankruptcy law protect him, he used other laws that helped him shelter what assets and little cash he had, and he avoided bankruptcy. This meant moving to Florida, where Florida laws prevent a person from selling a home that is owned outright; converting most of his remaining assets into untouchable pension and retirement funds; moving money into his children's estate; and cashing out on assets that were subject to seizure. O.J. did lose his Los Angeles home and watched his Heisman Trophy go for $255,000 at auction (something the court did seize), but he luckily had sources of income that no judge could order him to surrender. So he could keep on living regardless of the money he had to convert to other, untouchable forms.

O.J. Simpson's situation was very unique, and even the craftiest person with the smartest attorneys working for him or her cannot always avoid a bankruptcy. Avoiding a bankruptcy can be more harmful than bankruptcy itself, and the bankruptcy laws are stronger than any other laws you can use to protect you. That's a key word to keep in mind: protect. Bankruptcy law exists to protect people.

Most people aren't like O.J. You don't have millions to shuffle around and tuck into untouchable accounts or a Ferrari and a Warhol serigraph to sell. You don't have a bulletproof pension from the NFL. You simply want to release your debts and recover from bankruptcy as an honest, goal-oriented individual. Welcome to Chapter 7 bankruptcy in the next chapter.

CHAPTER 4

Completing and Filing Your Paperwork

Here is where the real work begins. This chapter contains the step-by-step instructions for filling out the official forms. Included throughout this chapter are sample forms already completed.

If this part overwhelms you, you can always visit one of our stores and have us type your petition for you. If you come across a word that you don't understand or that lacks definition here, refer to chapter 9 where we give you a glossary of common bankruptcy terms. Similarly, you can consult any bankruptcy petition preparer (nonattorney) or a bankruptcy attorney. If you have someone helping you complete your forms, use this chapter to understand your paperwork and how your information gets incorporated into the official documents. You should become familiar with these forms regardless of whom you hire to help you complete them. This will ultimately prepare you for meeting your trustee and keeping your bankruptcy process moving smoothly.

Things You Need Before You Get Started

Comfortable work area

Completed Worksheet A from chapter 2

A clean set of printed, official forms

A calculator

Pens—two different colors, preferably

Typewriter

A courageous smile

All official forms are available to download online at www.wethepeopleforms.com. Access to all of the state exemption tables is also on this site. We mentioned earlier that you can also find the official forms for bankruptcy on the U.S. court's main web site (www.uscourts.gov). Click on "U.S. Bankruptcy Courts," and then click on "U.S. Bankruptcy Court web sites," which is a link in the lower left-hand corner. Continue to click your way through the sites until you land in your jurisdiction. Navigating the bankruptcy courts' web

Alternatively, you can write a letter to your local bankruptcy court asking for information. (See Figure 4.1.) Enclose a self-addressed stamped envelope. Be formal. If you do not hear back from your court, call of visit the court in person. You can also log on to the bankruptcy court's main web site at www.uscourts.gov and double-click your way to your local court's web site. People who live in small communities may find their local bankruptcy court very responsive; however, if you live in a large city, or if your court has to deal with several regions, it may be more difficult to get the court to respond to you by mail. Most web sites are quite thorough and will give you all the information you need, including the local forms for you to download. This is the easiest and quickest way to get the information.

sites is pretty easy, but you'll find it very difficult to locate exemptions tables. Local courts' web sites contain lots of information except for the rules you need to know about the property you can keep. This is why we've created a user-friendly web site that allows you to download all the forms you need, as well as print out your specific set of exemptions that pertains to you. To access downloadable forms, go to www.wethepeopleforms.com and enter **WTPBK** as your password. We suggest you print out one complete set, make several copies of each of them, and have them neatly available in a nearby folder. If you decide to have a We The People office fill out the official forms for you, you can use this workbook in preparation to visiting one of our stores and proceeding.

Note that we give you all the official bankruptcy forms that every bankruptcy court uses. Your local bankruptcy court, however, might require additional forms that you'll need to obtain and file. If your papers don't meet local requirements, the clerk may reject them. You can get local forms from your local court or at your local We The People store. We have most local forms required and know exactly what most local courts request upon a bankruptcy filing. As part of our job, we keep up with local rules that govern the court's procedures in districts where we have We The People stores. For example, if you are a debtor filing for bankruptcy in New York City, one of our Manhattan stores can provide the local forms and tell you exactly what you can expect when you proceed through your bankruptcy in that district.

In your letter, be sure to include the following:

- Address the court clerk of your local bankruptcy court.
- Request copies of local forms for the type of bankruptcy you're filing and for making changes to your paperwork.
- Ask about how many copies or sets of papers you need to make before filing.
- Ask in what order your forms should be submitted.
- Ask if there are special instructions related to the mailing matrix (the list of creditors and their contact information).
- Confirm the filing fee and the best way to submit it (certified bank check, cash, or money order).
- Ask about the presentation of your paperwork, such as stapling, hole-punching, using paper-clips or bluebacks.
- Ask about any other information and instructions that you should know and that are not typical of the normal federal guidelines.

Marilyn McSample
1218 Glendon Avenue
Los Angeles, CA 90024
(123) 555-4567

5 August 20XX

United States Bankruptcy Court
Edward R. Roybal
Federal Building and Courthouse
255 East Temple Street
Los Angeles, CA 90012

ATTN: Court Clerk

To the Court Clerk:

As a possible Chapter 7 bankruptcy filer, please send me the following
information in the enclosed self-addressed stamped envelope:

- Copies of your local forms for an individual filing a Chapter 7 bankruptcy,
  plus any forms for making amendments or changes
- How many copies or sets your court requires
- How I should order my forms
- How I should deliver the paperwork (hole-punch? stapled?)

I understand that the filing fee is $209. If this fee has changed, please let me
know. Finally, any instructions you can provide for completing the mailing matrix
is appreciated.

Thanks.

Sincerely,

M. McSample

> ☺ **Encouragement Alert!** This part isn't as hard as you think if you take it step by step. If, at any time, you feel overwhelmed or too tired to continue, take a break and come back to it later. Go for a walk (or a run if you're so inclined). Call a friend. Watch a movie. Read a book. Working on the forms is not like running a marathon, but it can seem that way in the very beginning. Keep yourself energized and look toward the goal. You *will* get there!

Gearing up for Filling out the Forms

Before you tackle the official forms, have the worksheet you filled out in chapter 2 nearby. Having a list of your assets and debts will make the process easier. If you did as we suggested and you organized your financial paperwork into neat folders and files, keep those available for reference during this process. You may need to refer to specific bank statements, credit card statements, lender information, insurance and judgment information, and specifically, your "Things I Own" and "Things I Owe" folders that we told you how to set up in chapter 2. The more organized you are before getting to your forms, the better equipped you'll feel for filling them out successfully.

Tips to Completing Your Forms

The following are guidelines to use when completing your paperwork.

Type Your Forms. Courts prefer that your papers be typed, not handwritten. If you do not have access to a typewriter and do not want a legal document company to type the forms for you, ask your local court if a handwritten bankruptcy filing is acceptable, or if it has other options available to you (such as electronic filing).

Get to Know Your Local Court. You'll find that we say "ask your local court" or something similar throughout this book. Every bankruptcy court has its own way of doing things, and there is no way to know what your court's preferences are unless you ask. Preferences can also change. Don't be afraid to call or write to your local court (always with a self-addressed stamped enveloped for a reply) if you need information. As the courts move toward creating digital instead of paper records of cases, you may find that your court does not require you to submit more than one original copy of your petition. Some courts are more technologically advanced than others and will scan your original into a computer to create multiple electronic copies. If this is the case at your local court, then when we talk about making multiple copies of your documents, you can disregard that instruction and follow your own court's directions. The point is to know what your local court requires, follow its rules and guidelines, and be ready to make changes to your petition in order to meet those requirements.

Libraries, universities, community centers, and junior colleges in your area may be able to provide a typewriter for you. Ask your friends if they have any or know where you can find one. At We The People, part of our services includes typing the official forms for customers.

Answer Every Question to the Best of Your Ability and Knowledge. Don't leave any questions unanswered. Most of the forms have a box to check if your answer is none. But if you come across a question that does not apply to you and there are no boxes to indicate that, simply put "N/A" for not applicable.

If you leave any sections blank, the trustee might think you didn't complete your form. If a question that does not apply to you has a number of blanks, put "N/A" in the first blank if it's obvious that this applies to the other blanks as well. To be most clear, use "N/A" in every place.

Disclose Everything, Even When You're Unsure of Where to Put It on the Forms. If you have trouble categorizing a debt or asset on a form, do the best you can and make a note next to your entry that you're uncertain. Your trustee can sort through those uncertainties and place them in the appropriate place if necessary. Don't leave anything out just because you didn't know where to put it.

Be Honest and Brutally Careful. Approach this task with your mind in overdrive. You'd rather supply too much information than not enough—even when that means repeating information multiple times in your paperwork. The less room you leave in your forms for your trustee to doubt, question, suspect, or investigate your paperwork, the better. Anything you fail to disclose, including debts, opens the door to your entire case being dismissed—or worse, dischargeable debts not being discharged. Listing all of your assets can be tiring, but it's part of the process and you cannot get careless or lazy about doing it. You increase the chance of having your case challenged or dismissed if you don't take your paperwork seriously. Also, if you fail to complete your paperwork carefully, you run the risk of losing assets that you could have kept.

Use Continuation Pages. If you run out of room on a particular form that doesn't give you enough space to complete your answers, create your own continuation page by using another page of the exact same style. In other words, go back to your untouched original copies of your forms, and make duplicate copies of any forms for which you need to create more pages. Example: If you run out of room on Schedule F when you list your creditors holding unsecured nonpriority claims, make a photocopy of a blank Schedule F and use that as your continuation sheet. Be sure to type in your name at the top as it appears on all of your official documents, and make a note that this sheet is a continuation page (example: Sheet no. 2 of 2 sheets attached to Schedule of Creditors Holding Unsecured Nonpriority Claims).

To File Jointly or Not

First, you must be married to file jointly. Second, if you are married, you cannot avoid losing nonexempt assets in a bankruptcy by filing alone and transferring assets into your spouse's name. Married couples naturally acquire assets together, so if one person files for bankruptcy in a 10-year marriage, your trustee is going to ask questions about your spouse's separately owned property, confirming that the spouse's assets are, in fact, owned separately. If they are not, the trustee will wonder why you filed alone, and doubt your honesty.

In some states, notably the community property states, all assets acquired during the marriage are considered community property (owned jointly by both spouses). So if you file alone—without your spouse—and you live in a community property state, your trustee will try to take both your share of community property and your spouse's. Consider filing separately in a marriage only if your spouse acquired substantial assets before the marriage and you haven't been married that long. Otherwise, you're likely to run into problems when you defend your separate filing before your trustee.

> Community property states include: Alaska (with an agreement), Arizona, California, Idaho, Louisiana, Nevada, New Mexico, Puerto Rico, Texas, Washington, and Wisconsin. If you live in one of these states, are married, and file separately (that is, your spouse is not part of your bankruptcy), your trustee can go after your spouse's portion of the assets you share. With some minor exceptions, all of the assets you own as community property with your spouse will become part of your bankruptcy estate whether you have filed jointly or not. Two more things to note: (1) Creditors cannot later go after community property acquired after the case is filed from the nonfiling spouse; and (2) The nonfiling spouse may receive a discharge of community debts without filing under Chapter 7. (Because the nonfiling spouse's assets shared with the filing spouse get pulled into the bankruptcy, any discharged debts shared by both spouses become entirely discharged.)

If you file jointly, all of your marital assets will be considered part of your bankruptcy estate. Exceptions to this rule include assets that one spouse exclusively received, such as an inheritance or gifts meant for one spouse only. When filing jointly, be sure to gather detailed data for both you and your spouse.

Bottom line: If you are married and are thinking about filing alone, you must consider how your state deals with property acquired during your marriage. It's possible that not all of your marital property will be part of your bankruptcy estate, but which assets are part of your bankruptcy is a question that every state answers differently. For more information on the laws that govern your state with regard to assets in your bankruptcy estate, contact a local law library or an attorney.

Federal versus State Exemptions—What You Can Keep

One of the forms you will complete is a schedule of exempt property—assets that can be excluded from your bankruptcy and that you can keep. Federal bankruptcy laws establish exemptions for some types of assets. However, many states have taken advantage of a provision in the law that permits each state to adopt its own exemption law in place of the federal exemptions. Thus, whether certain assets, such as a house, car, clothing, jewelry, etcetera, is exempt—and therefore may be kept out of bankruptcy—can be question of state law. Refer to the exemptions tables for your state at www.wethepeopleforms.com.

The exemptions you can use in your bankruptcy will depend on the state where you file. Debtors in Arkansas, Connecticut, the District of Columbia, Hawaii, Massachusetts, Michigan, Minnesota, New Jersey, New Mexico, Pennsylvania, Rhode Island, Texas, Vermont, Washington, and Wisconsin can choose between their state's exemptions or the federal exemptions. Bankruptcy filers in these states must choose which system of exemptions they want to use—they cannot mix up the systems to create their own set of exemptions.

If you live in the following states, you can choose between a set of federal exemptions or your own state's exemptions: Arkansas, Connecticut, the District of Columbia, Hawaii, Massachusetts, Michigan, Minnesota, New Jersey, New Mexico, Pennsylvania, Rhode Island, Texas, Vermont, Washington, and Wisconsin. When you review the exemption tables in the back of the book, compare between the federal exemptions and your own state above. The federal exemptions were revised in late 2004.

A set of other exemptions called the federal nonbankruptcy exemptions are available for bankruptcy filers who use their state exemptions or, in the case of Californians, System 1. The federal nonbankruptcy exemptions apply to the rights of federal employees; it's best to think of them as supplemental federal bankruptcy exemptions. You can use any exemptions listed in the federal nonbankruptcy exemptions in addition to your state's exemptions—but if you choose the federal exemptions, you cannot also use these supplemental exemptions. Most people, however, don't qualify to use these exemptions because they generally deal with government benefits for federal employees such as civil service employees, railworkers, veterans, longshoremen, and harbor workers. If you are an employee of the government, don't forget to glance at these exemptions in case you can and do qualify to use any of them. We have included the federal nonbankruptcy exemptions on the web site as well.

You have three choices in picking exemptions, depending on the laws of your state:

- Use state exemptions only.
- Use federal exemptions only.
- Use state exemptions and federal nonbankruptcy (or supplemental) exemptions. If you live in California, you must choose between your state's System 1 and System 2. System 1 is best for homeowners.

California has adopted two systems from which Californians can choose (System 1 and System 2). If you live in California or any of the states not listed above, you cannot use the federal exemptions and must comply with your state's exemption system. You will want to choose exemptions (and, if it pertains to you, an exemption system) that protect your most important assets.

Starting Your Bankruptcy Case

In order to start a bankruptcy case, you must file the following Official Bankruptcy Forms:

Form 1—Voluntary Petition (2 pages)

(Yes, we know 2 through 5 are missing! Don't worry about it.)

Form 6—Schedules A through J, Summary, and Declaration

Form 7—Statement of Financial Affairs

Form 8—Statement of Intention

In addition, you must also file any local forms required by your court.

For example, in California, a Creditor Matrix (a list of people you owe money to, with complete addresses) and a Verification of Creditor Matrix form must be included. If you are filing under Chapter 13, you must also file your Chapter 13 Plan. With respect to Forms 1, 6, 7, and 8, you must file the original and three copies. However, only one matrix is required. You may pay the filing fee by cash, money order, or certified bank check. The Clerk's Office does not accept personal checks. Courts in different districts vary in how they like bankruptcy papers completed and submitted, so please be sure to inquire about how many copies you need to provide—in addition to the originals—and find out how your court wants to receive its money. The above information is for California filers only. Your court may be different.

If you need to start your case quickly, you may file only the Voluntary Petition (the original plus three copies) and your Creditor Matrix with the accompanying Verification (in California). You have an additional 15 days to file the rest of your bankruptcy papers, commonly known as Schedules. This is a so-called emergency, or skeleton, filing, which people use when they must stop creditors from filing lawsuits against them. Filing the initial paperwork activates the automatic stay, which also stops the creditors from their attempts to collect. If you need to do an emergency filing, we suggest you contact your local court to inquire specifically about what's required at your local level to execute your bankruptcy. Some courts require a special cover sheet or form in addition to the basic petition. If you fail to submit the remainder of your paperwork within 15 days of your emergency filing date—no matter your state—you risk having your bankruptcy case dismissed. All bankruptcy courts require that the complete set of paperwork be submitted within 15 days of the first date of filing.

You don't need to worry about forms 2, 4, and 5 if you're filing for Chapter 7. If you need to pay the filing fee in installments, you may do so by filling out Form 3: Application to Pay the Filing Fee in Installments and Order. Your local court might provide a local form for this application as well. However, if you've paid an attorney or bankruptcy petition preparer (such as We The People) to help you with your forms, that payment must be refunded and not paid

---

The Official Forms that Comprise Your Bankruptcy Petition

Form 1: Voluntary Petition

Form 6: (Schedules)

    Schedule A—Real Property

    Schedule B—Personal Property

    Schedule C—Property Claimed as Exempt

    Schedule D—Creditors Holding Secured Claims

    Schedule E—Creditors Holding Unsecured Priority Claims

    Schedule F—Creditors Holding Unsecured Nonpriority Claims

    Schedule G—Executory Contracts and Unexpired Leases

    Schedule H—Codebtors

    Schedule I—Current Income

    Schedule J—Current Expenditures

    Summary Schedules A through J

    Declaration Concerning Debtor's Schedules

Form 7: Statement of Financial Affairs

Form 8: Chapter 7 Individual Debtor's Statement of Intention

Form 21: Full Social Security Number Disclosure

Mailing Matrix

Any required local forms

N/A–N/A–N/A–N/A–N/A–N/A–N/A

Does N/A mean you're not available to answer the question? No! N/A means not applicable. Get used to typing this abbreviation: You will use it a lot when you fill out your forms. There are lots of forms to fill out, but not every single form applies to you. However, you cannot exclude any of the forms in your paperwork. For example, if Schedule D and E do not pertain to you and you have nothing to report in these forms, you must still complete them by indicating "none" or "N/A" where appropriate on the forms and include them in your filing. If you leave important sections blank, your trustee will question you and ask you to amend your paperwork so everything is complete and thorough (thus lengthening the time it takes to receive your discharge). Forgetting to type "N/A" down a column of questions that do not apply to your situation may result in complications that will frustrate, annoy, and exhaust you further. Be clear, be concise, and be stubbornly thorough. Pretend you're in kindergarten and all you want to do is impress your teacher by showing off how well you can follow rules and exceed expectations!

---

again until the filing fee has been paid in full. In other words, you cannot pay someone to type your forms and then apply for the installment option. You must pay the total of the filing fee and do so within three installments.

In the following sections, we will use a fictitious filing to demonstrate a completed set of documents. Use the sample as a guide for filling out your own forms.

Form 1: The Voluntary Petition

The voluntary petition is a two-page document. Before you begin, find the name of the bankruptcy court in your state and, specifically, your area if there is more than one district in your state. In our sample, Jack B. Smith lives in Brooklyn, New York, so he would use the Eastern District of New York's courts. Refer to Appendix B for a list of bankruptcy court addresses.

First Page

Court Name. In the first blank space (top left corner), fill in the name of your judicial district, such as "Eastern District of New York." If your state only has one district, type "XXXXXX" in the first blank. If your district is further divided into divisions, type the division after the state, such as "Central District of California Northern Division."

Name of Debtor. Fill in your name: last name, first name, middle. Use the name you normally use in official documents, which should correlate to your driver's license, passport, identity cards, or other formal documents. If you and your spouse are filing jointly, you will enter your spouse's name in the same way in the blank labeled "Name of Joint Debtor" to the right of your name. If you are filing alone, type "N/A" in the joint debtor box. (Remember: don't leave anything blank! You will type "N/A" or "none" a lot in these forms!)

All Other Names. Fill in this box only if you've used other names to identify yourself in the previous six years, such as a married name, maiden name, unusual nickname, or trade name.

(Official Form 1) (12/03)

FORM B1	United States Bankruptcy Court Southern District of New York	Voluntary Petition

Name of Debtor (if individual, enter Last, First, Middle): **Smith, John**	Name of Joint Debtor (Spouse) (Last, First, Middle):
All Other Names used by the Debtor in the last 6 years (include married, maiden, and trade names):	All Other Names used by the Joint Debtor in the last 6 years (include married, maiden, and trade names):
Last four digits of Soc. Sec. No. / Complete EIN or other Tax I.D. No. (if more than one, state all): **xxx-xx-9878**	Last four digits of Soc. Sec. No. / Complete EIN or other Tax I.D. No. (if more than one, state all):
Street Address of Debtor (No. & Street, City, State & Zip Code): **2500 Maganolia Street New York, NY 10034**	Street Address of Joint Debtor (No. & Street, City, State & Zip Code):
County of Residence or of the Principal Place of Business: **New York**	County of Residence or of the Principal Place of Business:
Mailing Address of Debtor (if different from street address):	Mailing Address of Joint Debtor (if different from street address):
Location of Principal Assets of Business Debtor (if different from street address above):	

Information Regarding the Debtor (Check the Applicable Boxes)

Venue (Check any applicable box)

■ Debtor has been domiciled or has had a residence, principal place of business, or principal assets in this District for 180 days immediately preceding the date of this petition or for a longer part of such 180 days than in any other District.

☐ There is a bankruptcy case concerning debtor's affiliate, general partner, or partnership pending in this District.

Type of Debtor (Check all boxes that apply)		**Chapter or Section of Bankruptcy Code Under Which** **the Petition is Filed** (Check one box)
■ Individual(s)	☐ Railroad	■ Chapter 7 ☐ Chapter 11 ☐ Chapter 13
☐ Corporation	☐ Stockbroker	☐ Chapter 9 ☐ Chapter 12
☐ Partnership	☐ Commodity Broker	☐ Sec. 304 - Case ancillary to foreign proceeding
☐ Other_____	☐ Clearing Bank	

Nature of Debts (Check one box)		**Filing Fee** (Check one box)
■ Consumer/Non-Business	☐ Business	■ Full Filing Fee attached

Chapter 11 Small Business (Check all boxes that apply)

☐ Debtor is a small business as defined in 11 U.S.C. § 101

☐ Debtor is and elects to be considered a small business under 11 U.S.C. § 1121(e) (Optional)

☐ Filing Fee to be paid in installments (Applicable to individuals only.) Must attach signed application for the court's consideration certifying that the debtor is unable to pay fee except in installments. Rule 1006(b). See Official Form No. 3.

Statistical/Administrative Information (Estimates only)

☐ Debtor estimates that funds will be available for distribution to unsecured creditors.

■ Debtor estimates that, after any exempt property is excluded and administrative expenses paid, there will be no funds available for distribution to unsecured creditors.

THIS SPACE IS FOR COURT USE ONLY

Estimated Number of Creditors	1-15	16-49	50-99	100-199	200-999	1000-over
	■	☐	☐	☐	☐	☐

Estimated Assets							
$0 to $50,000	$50,001 to $100,000	$100,001 to $500,000	$500,001 to $1 million	$1,000,001 to $10 million	$10,000,001 to $50 million	$50,000,001 to $100 million	More than $100 million
☐	☐	■	☐	☐	☐	☐	☐

Estimated Debts							
$0 to $50,000	$50,001 to $100,000	$100,001 to $500,000	$500,001 to $1 million	$1,000,001 to $10 million	$10,000,001 to $50 million	$50,000,001 to $100 million	More than $100 million
☐	☐	■	☐	☐	☐	☐	☐

You don't need to list abbreviations of your name unless they are very different from your official name and a creditor might not recognize you. If you've been a sole proprietor of a business and operated it under a specific name, list it here preceded by "dba" for "doing business as." Examples: "Jonathan Brown" or "dba JDB Digital." Fill in any variation for your spouse if filing jointly. If neither of you have variations to include in your paperwork, type "N/A."

Social Security/Tax ID Number. Enter "xxx-xx" for the first five digits and then enter the last four digits of your Social Security number. If you also have a taxpayer's ID number, enter that entire number. Do the same for your spouse in the right-hand box (or enter "N/A" if filing alone).

Street Address of Debtor. Enter your home street address. Do not list a P.O. box if you pick up your mail at the post office.

Street Address of Joint Debtor. Enter your spouse's current address, even if it's the same as yours. If filing alone, type "N/A."

County of Residence. Enter your county. Enter your spouse's county as well, or type "N/A" if filing alone.

Mailing Address of Debtor. If your mailing address is the same as your street address, type "N/A" and do the same for your spouse if that applies. If, however, you use a different mailing address, such as a P.O. box, type that address here.

Location of Principle Assets of Business Debtor. The bankruptcy court may consider you a business debtor if you or your spouse (if filing jointly) have operated a business as a sole proprietor and were self-employed within the last two years. The court will request additional information on Form 7. If this situation applies to you and you own business assets as a result (examples: inventory, computers, machinery, office supplies), list their primary location here. If your business assets are located at your home or mailing address, enter that address here. Refer to the next chapter for more information on business bankruptcies.

Venue. Fill in or check the top box. This confirms that you're filing in the judicial district where you've lived for most of the previous 180 days.

Type of Debtor. Fill in or check the first box, "Individual(s)." Fill in or check this box even if you've operated a sole proprietorship or have been self-employed within the last two years.

Nature of Debts. Fill in or check "Consumer—Non-Business" if you haven't operated a business in the last two years or if you own most of your business's assets. If your business owns most of your debts, then you would fill in or check the "Business" box. If you are confused about which assets box to check (because you have operated a business as a sole proprietor but don't know how much of your assets are considered personally owned), consult an attorney.

Chapter 11 Small Business. Leave these boxes blank or type "N/A" in the boxes.

Chapter or Section of Bankruptcy Code Under Which the Petition is Filed. Fill in or check "Chapter 7."

Filing Fee. Fill in or check the first box if you can pay the entire filing fee upfront. If you fill in or check the second box, you will have to complete the application for paying the fee in installments, which is Form 3.

Statistical/Administrative Information. The next four boxes reveal general information about your assets and debts. You may have to come back to this part of the petition later, once you've worked through listing your assets and debts more thoroughly. If you're making an emergency filing, you will have to make a good guess as to your answers and use the worksheet you completed in chapter 2 as a guide. Remember: These are estimates (of your number of creditors, value of assets, and value of debts). This is how you indicate whether your bankruptcy is a no-asset case or if you will have nonexempt assets that can be sold for distributing proceeds to creditors.

Second Page

Name of Debtor(s). Enter your name as you did on the first page. Add your spouse's name if filing jointly.

Prior Bankruptcy Case Filed Within Last 6 Years. If this is your first Chapter 7 bankruptcy filing, type "None" or "N/A" in this box. You cannot file a bankruptcy if you already have within the previous six years. Also, if you filed a Chapter 7 and it was dismissed for a reason within the past 180 days, you may have to wait (consult an attorney if in doubt). If you (or your spouse, if filing jointly) have declared bankruptcy in the past but outside the six-year bar, enter the information related to your previous bankruptcy, such as its location, case number, and date filed.

Pending Bankruptcy Case Filed by any Spouse, Partner, or Affiliate of this Debtor. Type "None" or "N/A" in this box unless your spouse has a bankruptcy case pending anywhere in the country. This section is not for individuals filing Chapter 7.

Signatures. Sign your name above Signature of Debtor. If filing jointly, your spouse will sign above Signature of Joint Debtor. Your signature(s) confirm your understanding of the various chapters of bankruptcy available to you and your choice to proceed under Chapter 7. You also declare under penalty of perjury that the information you provide in your petition is true and correct. Add your phone number/fax if you are filing without an attorney. If you are filing alone, type "N/A" in the joint debtor's signature line.

Signature of Attorney. Type "None" or "N/A" on the line asking for Signature of Attorney for Debtor. Type "Debtor not represented by attorney" on the second line that asks for Printed Name of Attorney for Debtor.

(Official Form 1) (12/03)

Voluntary Petition
(This page must be completed and filed in every case)

Name of Debtor(s):	FORM B1, Page 2
Smith, John	

Prior Bankruptcy Case Filed Within Last 6 Years (If more than one, attach additional sheet)

Location Where Filed: **- None -**	Case Number:	Date Filed:

Pending Bankruptcy Case Filed by any Spouse, Partner, or Affiliate of this Debtor (If more than one, attach additional sheet)

Name of Debtor: **- None -**	Case Number:	Date Filed:
District:	Relationship:	Judge:

Signatures

Signature(s) of Debtor(s) (Individual/Joint)

I declare under penalty of perjury that the information provided in this petition is true and correct.
[If petitioner is an individual whose debts are primarily consumer debts and has chosen to file under chapter 7] I am aware that I may proceed under chapter 7, 11, 12, or 13 of title 11, United States Code, understand the relief available under each such chapter, and choose to proceed under chapter 7.
I request relief in accordance with the chapter of title 11, United States Code, specified in this petition.

X _____
Signature of Debtor **John Smith**

X _____
Signature of Joint Debtor
(212) 555-7399
Telephone Number (If not represented by attorney)

_____
Date

Signature of Attorney

X _____
Signature of Attorney for Debtor(s)
Debtor not represented by attorney
Printed Name of Attorney for Debtor(s)

_____
Firm Name

_____
Address

_____
Telephone Number

_____
Date

Signature of Debtor (Corporation/Partnership)

I declare under penalty of perjury that the information provided in this petition is true and correct, and that I have been authorized to file this petition on behalf of the debtor.
The debtor requests relief in accordance with the chapter of title 11, United States Code, specified in this petition.

X _____
Signature of Authorized Individual

_____
Printed Name of Authorized Individual

_____
Title of Authorized Individual

_____
Date

Exhibit A

(To be completed if debtor is required to file periodic reports (e.g., forms 10K and 10Q) with the Securities and Exchange Commission pursuant to Section 13 or 15(d) of the Securities Exchange Act of 1934 and is requesting relief under chapter 11)

☐ Exhibit A is attached and made a part of this petition.

Exhibit B

(To be completed if debtor is an individual whose debts are primarily consumer debts)

I, the attorney for the petitioner named in the foregoing petition, declare that I have informed the petitioner that [he or she] may proceed under chapter 7, 11, 12, or 13 of title 11, United States Code, and have explained the relief available under each such chapter.

X _____
Signature of Attorney for Debtor(s)   Date

Exhibit C

Does the debtor own or have possession of any property that poses a threat of imminent and identifiable harm to public health or safety?

☐ Yes, and Exhibit C is attached and made a part of this petition.
■ No

Signature of Non-Attorney Petition Preparer

I certify that I am a bankruptcy petition preparer as defined in 11 U.S.C. § 110, that I prepared this document for compensation, and that I have provided the debtor with a copy of this document.

Jennifer West-We The People
Printed Name of Bankruptcy Petition Preparer

123-45-6789
Social Security Number (Required by 11 U.S.C.ß 110(c).)

239 W. 72nd St.
New York, NY 10023
Address
(212) 555-7700
Names and Social Security numbers of all other individuals who prepared or assisted in preparing this document:

If more than one person prepared this document, attach additional sheets conforming to the appropriate official form for each person.

X _____
Signature of Bankruptcy Petition Preparer

_____
Date

A bankruptcy petition preparer's failure to comply with the provisions of title 11 and the Federal Rules of Bankruptcy Procedure may result in fines or imprisonment or both. 11 U.S.C. § 110; 18 U.S.C. § 156.

Signature of Debtor (Corporation or Partnership). Type "N/A" on the first line.

Exhibit A. Leave this section alone. It likely does not apply to you.

Exhibit B. Type "N/A" on the signature line, as this section also does not apply to you.

Exhibit C. If you have any property that "poses a threat of imminent and identifiable harm to public health or safety," fill in or check the Yes box. You will have to attach Exhibit C to your petition. Examples include toxic chemicals used in a cosmetics small business, explosives as part of a collection, or a house polluted with toxic substances (and we don't mean the Comet under your kitchen sink). Otherwise, fill in or check the No box.

Signature of Non-Attorney Petition Preparer. If you hire someone to type your forms, such as We The People, your bankruptcy petition preparer will have to complete this part. If you complete your paperwork yourself, type "N/A" on the first line.

Form 6: Schedules

Wa 'cha got?

Wa 'cha owe?

Wa 'cha make?

Wa 'cha spend?

A series of schedules (lists) make up Form 6 of your bankruptcy papers. Your schedules describe your financial situation in detail, so this may take you time to complete and ensure everything is accurate on every page. Don't forget anything! Any omission you make—either intentionally or not—can jeopardize your entire bankruptcy case. You will find that you have to repeat information over and over again across the various schedules. Once you get going, understanding and filling in the schedules becomes easier, and by the time you get to the later ones, you'll be able to use previous schedules to help fill in blanks. Two important things to remember to do on all forms:

- Type in your name at the top of every form where In re is indicated.
- If you use any continuation sheets, label them carefully and be sure they are numbered and incorporated into your paperwork correctly.

Schedule A. Real Property

In re. Type your name and the name of your spouse, if filing jointly. You will do this on every page of your bankruptcy papers, including schedules for which you have no listings. If you don't own any real property and this schedule does not apply to you, you still need to fill it out. Type in your name(s); under the Description and Location of Property, type "None" or "N/A"; and type "0" in the Sub-Total and Total boxes on the bottom right-hand corner of the page.

Case No. Leave this blank unless you filed an emergency petition and you know your case number. If you know your case number, include this number on every page of your paperwork—including your continuation sheets.

In re   **John Smith**   ,   Case No. _____

Debtor

SCHEDULE A. REAL PROPERTY

Except as directed below, list all real property in which the debtor has any legal, equitable, or future interest, including all property owned as a cotenant, community property, or in which the debtor has a life estate. Include any property in which the debtor holds rights and powers exercisable for the debtor's own benefit. If the debtor is married, state whether husband, wife, or both own the property by placing an "H," "W," "J," or "C" in the column labeled "Husband, Wife, Joint, or Community." If the debtor holds no interest in real property, write "None" under "Description and Location of Property."

Do not include interests in executory contracts and unexpired leases on this schedule. List them in Schedule G - Executory Contracts and Unexpired Leases.

If an entity claims to have a lien or hold a secured interest in any property, state the amount of the secured claim. (See Schedule D.) If no entity claims to hold a secured interest in the property, write "None" in the column labeled "Amount of Secured Claim."

If the debtor is an individual or if a joint petition is filed, state the amount of any exemption claimed in the property only in Schedule C - Property Claimed as Exempt.

Description and Location of Property	Nature of Debtor's Interest in Property	Husband, Wife, Joint, or Community	Current Market Value of Debtor's Interest in Property, without Deducting any Secured Claim or Exemption	Amount of Secured Claim
Home **2500 Magnolia Street** **Queens, NY 10137**	**Real Estate**	-	160,000.00	153,000.00

Sub-Total >	160,000.00	(Total of this page)
Total >	160,000.00	

__0__ continuation sheets attached to the Schedule of Real Property

(Report also on Summary of Schedules)

What Constitutes Real Property?

Your property (without the prefix "real") is everything you own. It's better to think of property as assets, because property usually makes people think of land and homes. In your bankruptcy papers, property refers to all that you own, including your personal belongings (such as clothing, jewelry, bug collection, family hand-me-downs, etc.), bank accounts, stocks, insurance, cars, and retirement funds. Only when you put the word "real" in front of property do you refer specifically to land.

If you own a home, you have real estate, or real property. In addition to your house being real property, you must include all types of property that you own fully or partially, even if you don't live in or use the piece of property. Include vacation homes, condominiums, duplexes, townhomes, business properties, rental properties, undeveloped land, boat slips (if you own it), and any buildings permanently attached to land. If you live in a community property state and your spouse owns real property, include it here. If you know you are entitled to receive property at a future date out of a trust, list that property as well. If you lease or rent property, don't include it here. You will use Schedule G to list any and all timeshares, rentals, and leases.

Description and Location of Property. List each property, denoting each type of property (examples: single family home, vacation home, undeveloped land), and include their addresses.

Nature of Debtor's Interest in Property. Define your interest in the real property. You can simply type "real estate" for your home or other such property that you own.

Fee simple: Even if you still owe money on the property in terms of a mortgage, for example, you have the right to sell, make alterations, and leave it to children. Your mortgage company does not own the real estate unless it has already completed foreclosure proceedings. Alternatively, you can type "fee simple" for any property you own outright or through a loan, such as a mortgage. The following types of interest may pertain to you:

Future interest: Any rights you have to own property in the future as a result of a trust, will, or deed is a future interest. If you know you will inherit 50 acres of undeveloped land when your parents die, include that land here and type "future interest" in this part.

Lienholder: If you hold a mortgage, deed of trust, judgment lien, or other kind of lien on any real estate, you have an interest in that real property and are a lienholder.

Easement holder: If you have a right to use someone else's property in the form of an easement, list this piece of property and type "easement holder."

Life estate: If you have a right to possess and use property only during your lifetime—and you cannot sell or leave it to someone when you die—you have a life estate interest in that property. Life estates are typically established by trusts and wills, allowing sole owners of real estate to pass along that property to named individuals. For example, if your husband dies and leaves you the home in a life estate, you can live in the home for the rest of your life but when you die, it goes to whomever he named in the trust or will he set up, such as your children. You cannot sell it during your life.

Contingent interest: If you are entitled to interest in a property pending a condition you must meet, as outlined in a trust or will, you hold contingent interest. Example: Your mother leaves her art studio to you in a will so long as you use the studio to teach art classes. If you use it otherwise, the studio goes to your brother (who is a yogi). Both you and your brother hold contingent interest in the studio.

Power of appointment: If you are legally responsible for selling a specified piece of property that's not yours, you have the power of appointment. These powers are typically given by a will, trust, or transfer of real property. Power of appointment can apply to more than just the selling of property, and that property is not part of your bankruptcy estate.

Beneficial ownership under a real estate contract: If you're in the midst of negotiating a real estate purchase but have yet to complete the deal, you have beneficial ownership. If you've signed a binding real estate contract but await the property to clear escrow, you have beneficial ownership. (If you're going through a bankruptcy, you probably are not signing real estate deals and looking to buy more property.)

If these terms confuse you and you don't know how to list your property, contact an attorney. You can also refer to chapter 9 for more definitions to terms.

Husband, Wife, Joint, or Community. Type "N/A" if you are not married. If you are, enter the letter to indicate who owns what: the husband (H), the wife (W), jointly by the husband and wife (J), or jointly by the husband and wife as community property (C).

Current Market Value of Debtor's Interest in Property Without Deducting Any Secured Claim or Exemption. Enter the current fair market value of your interest in your real estate. You can obtain values from real estate agents or appraisers. Online search engines can also help you determine the value of real estate by giving you values of similar properties selling in your neighborhood. Do not deduct any liens or mortgages on your property or figure in any exemptions. Simply figure out the value of the assets and enter them here. If you list any assets that are jointly owed by someone else—and that person is not filing for bankruptcy—only include your portion of the asset. Example: If you and your sister own a home 50/50, list 50 percent of the home's current market value. If it's too difficult to put a value on your interest in an asset, do your best to give an estimate.

Amount of Secured Claim. This is where you list your mortgages and other debts secured by the asset. If you have no debts to the real estate, type "None" in this column. Be sure to enter all secured debts to the property—including mortgages, deeds of trust, home equity loans, and liens. The last statement you received from your lender should include the balance,

---

What's the Difference Between J and C?

Joint property and community property sound similar. Here's the general rule to follow when you complete your forms: If you live in a community property state (Arizona, California, Idaho, Louisiana, Nevada, New Mexico, Puerto Rico, Texas, Washington, and Wisconsin), consider all of your assets as community property unless a particular item is owned by only one of you, in which case you indicate husband (H) or wife (W). If you live in a non-community property state, sometimes referred to as a common law state (all the other states not listed above), consider all of your assets as owned jointly by you and your spouse unless a particular item is owned by one of you, in which case you indicate husband (H) or wife (W).

In re   **John Smith**   ,   Case No. _____

Debtor

SCHEDULE B. PERSONAL PROPERTY

Except as directed below, list all personal property of the debtor of whatever kind. If the debtor has no property in one or more of the categories, place an "x" in the appropriate position in the column labeled "None." If additional space is needed in any category, attach a separate sheet properly identified with the case name, case number, and the number of the category. If the debtor is married, state whether husband, wife, or both own the property by placing an "H," "W," "J," or "C" in the column labeled "Husband, Wife, Joint, or Community." If the debtor is an individual or a joint petition is filed, state the amount of any exemptions claimed only in Schedule C - Property Claimed as Exempt.

Do not list interests in executory contracts and unexpired leases on this schedule. List them in Schedule G - Executory Contracts and Unexpired Leases.

If the property is being held for the debtor by someone else, state that person's name and address under "Description and Location of Property."

Type of Property	N O N E	Description and Location of Property	Husband, Wife, Joint, or Community	Current Market Value of Debtor's Interest in Property, without Deducting any Secured Claim or Exemption
1. Cash on hand		**Cash on hand**	-	240.00
2. Checking, savings or other financial accounts, certificates of deposit, or shares in banks, savings and loan, thrift, building and loan, and homestead associations, or credit unions, brokerage houses, or cooperatives.		**Checking account** **Bank of America** **7258 Broadway** **New York, NY 10001** **Acct. 0585 0856 0859 7898**	-	425.00
3. Security deposits with public utilities, telephone companies, landlords, and others.	X			
4. Household goods and furnishings, including audio, video, and computer equipment.		**Household goods and furnishings**	-	500.00
5. Books, pictures and other art objects, antiques, stamp, coin, record, tape, compact disc, and other collections or collectibles.		**Books, pictures and other art objects; collectibles, CDs**	-	100.00
6. Wearing apparel.		**Wearing apparel**	-	200.00
7. Furs and jewelry.		**Jewelry**	-	300.00
8. Firearms and sports, photographic, and other hobby equipment.		**Firearms and sports, photographic and other hobby equipment**	-	150.00
9. Interests in insurance policies. Name insurance company of each policy and itemize surrender or refund value of each.	X			
			Sub-Total > (Total of this page)	1,915.00

  2   continuation sheets attached to the Schedule of Personal Property

In re   **John Smith**   ,   Case No. _____

                                                Debtor

SCHEDULE B. PERSONAL PROPERTY
(Continuation Sheet)

Type of Property	N O N E	Description and Location of Property	Husband, Wife, Joint, or Community	Current Market Value of Debtor's Interest in Property, without Deducting any Secured Claim or Exemption
10. Annuities. Itemize and name each issuer.	X			
11. Interests in IRA, ERISA, Keogh, or other pension or profit sharing plans. Itemize.	X			
12. Stock and interests in incorporated and unincorporated businesses. Itemize.	X			
13. Interests in partnerships or joint ventures. Itemize.	X			
14. Government and corporate bonds and other negotiable and nonnegotiable instruments.	X			
15. Accounts receivable.	X			
16. Alimony, maintenance, support, and property settlements to which the debtor is or may be entitled. Give particulars.	X			
17. Other liquidated debts owing debtor including tax refunds. Give particulars.	X			
18. Equitable or future interests, life estates, and rights or powers exercisable for the benefit of the debtor other than those listed in Schedule of Real Property.	X			
19. Contingent and noncontingent interests in estate of a decedent, death benefit plan, life insurance policy, or trust.	X			

Sub-Total >   0.00
(Total of this page)

Sheet __1__ of __2__ continuation sheets attached
to the Schedule of Personal Property

In re **John Smith**   ,   Case No. _____

                                    Debtor

SCHEDULE B. PERSONAL PROPERTY
(Continuation Sheet)

Type of Property	N O N E	Description and Location of Property	Husband, Wife, Joint, or Community	Current Market Value of Debtor's Interest in Property, without Deducting any Secured Claim or Exemption
20. Other contingent and unliquidated claims of every nature, including tax refunds, counterclaims of the debtor, and rights to setoff claims. Give estimated value of each.	X			
21. Patents, copyrights, and other intellectual property. Give particulars.	X			
22. Licenses, franchises, and other general intangibles. Give particulars.	X			
23. Automobiles, trucks, trailers, and other vehicles and accessories.		**2004 Ford Explorer**	-	**16,000.00**
24. Boats, motors, and accessories.	X			
25. Aircraft and accessories.	X			
26. Office equipment, furnishings, and supplies.	X			
27. Machinery, fixtures, equipment, and supplies used in business.	X			
28. Inventory.	X			
29. Animals.	X			
30. Crops - growing or harvested. Give particulars.	X			
31. Farming equipment and implements.	X			
32. Farm supplies, chemicals, and feed.	X			
33. Other personal property of any kind not already listed.	X			

Sub-Total > (Total of this page)	**16,000.00**
Total >	**17,915.00**

Sheet __2__ of __2__ continuation sheets attached
to the Schedule of Personal Property

(Report also on Summary of Schedules)

or you can call your lender and ask about your current balances. For liens made against your property, contact your county's land records office or order a title search through a title insurance company or real estate attorney. If you exhaust your efforts and cannot afford to pay someone to locate your liens and balances, type "unknown" in this column.

Total. Add up the dollar amounts you listed in the fourth column (under "Current Market Value") and enter the total at the bottom of the page.

Schedule B. Personal Property (Assets)

Like we mentioned above, personal property refers to everything you own, but specifically, to property that does not include land or homes. So think of personal property as everything else besides your home or any land/buildings you own. This schedule takes many pages to complete and requires your attention to detail.

In Re and **Case No.** Enter same information here as you did on Schedule A.

Type of Property. The form automatically lists the categories of personal assets you may or may not have. Go down the column, and for any numbered item(s) that you don't have, mark an "X" in the second column to indicate that you have none of these things. Use the worksheet you filled out in chapter 2 to guide you through this schedule. You should have already inventoried your personal assets in Category 4 of Worksheet A.

Description and Location of Property. For items that you do have, and which are valued more than $50, list them with details about their location. Example: If you have a checking and savings account with a bank, you would list that in number 2 as Checking account, #123-4567-89, ABC Bank, 5555 Main Street, Brooklyn and Savings account, #987-6543-21, ABC Bank, 5555 Main Street, Brooklyn. In number 4, don't itemize small assets like kitchen utensils and blenders and cookie sheets. Write "kitchenware." Similarly, combine your bed, tables, chairs, and couches into "household goods and furnishings." If most of your property is located in your home, you can write at the top of the column, "All personal property is located at my/our residence unless otherwise noted."

Husband, Wife, Joint, or Community. If you're not married, write "N/A" at the top of this column. If you are married, indicate whether the items listed are owned by you, your spouse, jointly, or as community property.

Current Market Value of Debtor's Interest in Property, Without Deducting Any Secured Claim or Exemption. Give fair estimates to the value of your personal assets. For items with obvious cash value, such as checking, savings, insurance, pensions, bonds, and so on, enter those actual values. For items difficult to valuate, do your best, consult with an appraiser, or use the Internet for arriving at fair amounts (example: www.Edmunds.com gives reliable car values). You want your estimates to be a low as possible but reasonable and within reality. Think quick sale value, or the amount one would get by having to sell the item quickly (at a pawnshop or in a yard sale) and without the luxury of waiting for the highest bidder. Do not give a range: If you think the property is worth $500–$600, provide the average, $550. Also, do not provide multiple figures for various items. For example, say you have the following

Tips to Completing Schedule B's Types of Property

Cash on hand: This means money in your wallet, at home, and so on.

Checking/savings/CDs: You will need to include complete names of all financial institutions, their addresses, the type of account (checking, savings, CDs, and so on), and the dollar amount in each account. Account numbers are optional. Unless required by your local court, keep them out. (Most courts do not require full account numbers anymore.)

Security deposits: List all security deposits that you have given. For example, security deposits given to a landlord, utility company, and the like.

Household goods: List items of value. Example: three rooms of furnishings, including TV, radio, VCR, and washer. List the quick sale value, which is the pawnshop value or yard sale value. List one total for everything in the final column (example: $800).

Books, pictures, etc.: Itemize items of value. Example: 50 books of personal first edition library, 50 unopened CDs, personal photos—total value, $250. Focus less on common items with no retail value and more on valuable collectors' items, such as art and coin collections.

Wearing apparel: This refers to used clothing or designer dresses.

Furs and jewelry: Itemize assets of value, but not costume jewelry, etc. Example: wedding ring, $100; watch, $50; and miscellaneous costume jewelry—total value, $175.

Firearms and sports, etc.: Itemize property of value. Example: Toshiba 325iDigital Camera, $300.

Cash value in insurance policies: List insurance company with address and cash value (surrender value) of policy. Term insurance has no cash value but should be listed anyway. Call your insurance company for this information. Example: CAN Life, 703 N. Bedford, Arlington, VA 22201, cash value $3,000.

Annuities: List annuity company with address and value of annuity. Call your annuity company for this information. Example: Classic Annuity, 123 Market Street, Boston, MA 02134, value $8,000.

Interests in pensions or profit sharing plans, including 401(k)s and Keoughs, etc.: List pension company with address and value of pension. Call your pension company for this information. Example: Motorola ERISA Plan, 226 Broadway, NY, NY 10017, value $22,000.

Stock: List company name and address and value of stock. For example, Xerox Company stock, 123 Copy Street, Chicago, IL 60623, value $1,200. List stock in closely-held companies, too; your value is capitalization value, such as $500.

Partnership: List percent ownership, name, address, and value of your ownership interest.

Bonds: List all bonds that you own with name, address, and value. Example: Series E Government Bond, Treasury Office, Washington DC 10001—value $50.

Accounts receivable: This is money that is owed to you in your business. List the name and address of the person who owes you money and the amount. Example: Alicia Smith, 435 Pinegrove Court, Chicago, IL 60614—$800 for printing services.

Alimony/family support: List money that is being paid to you as maintenance/alimony/support. List name and address of the person paying the money, and include the amount. Example: ex-spouse Jerry Kimmer, 327 Arnold Way, Chicago, IL 60623—$225 per month.

Liquidated debts owed to you: List all money owed to you, including name and address of the person who owes you money, and include the amount owed. Tax refunds owed to you must be listed. Example: Internal Revenue Service, Kansas City, MO 64999—2001 tax refund of $875.

Equitable or future interests: List all interests in property or items of value that you might be entitled to receive at a future date. For example, a settlement from a lawsuit, sale of real property, etc.

Interests in estates, life insurance, etc.: List all inheritances, life insurance, and financial benefits that you are currently entitled to receive as a result of someone's death. Example: Estate of Marge Smith, Case No 01-P233-D257; Estate attorney is Robert Klein, 100 N. LaSalle Street, Chicago, IL 60601—$20,000.

Other contingent and unliquidated claims: List any unresolved or uncertain claims for money or property that you have against person or entity. Example: personal injury lawsuit, Joe Debtor vs. Faulty Driver, 99 L 3456; attorney Pat Doey, 200 W. Randolph Street, Chicago, IL 60602, tel. 312-555-5681—value unknown.

Patents, copyrights, etc.: List all patents, trademarks, copyrights, etc., owned by you.

Licenses, franchise, etc.: List all licenses, franchises, and permits that you own.

Autos, trucks, etc.: List year, make, and model number, and quick sale value. Look for quick sale values by reading classifieds (in your local newspaper), an auto trader publication, Kelley Blue Books, or by checking online at sites like www.Edmunds.com, www.Ebay.com, or www.kbb.com (this is Kelley Blue Book's site).

Boats, motors, and accessories: List year, make, and model number, and quick sale value. Example: 1984 10 ft Bass aluminum boat with motor and trailer—value, $875.

Aircraft and accessories: List year, make, and model number, and quick sale value.

Office equipment and supplies: List details of the office equipment and quick sale value. Example: Computer—Dell 8600 laptop—value, $800.

Machinery, fixtures, equipment, and supplies used in business: List any of these items that are used in your business. Do not duplicate items listed previously.

Inventory: List all inventory and assets that you have in your business.

Animals: Farm animals with value, if any. Numbers 30 thru 32 don't normally apply to Chapter 7 filers so mark an "X" under None.

Other personal property: List all other property that you own that has not already been listed.

household goods: television, $150; VCR, $30; microwave oven, $50. Provide only the total value, in this case $230, and not the individual amounts.

The lower your estimates, the greater likelihood you'll get to keep your assets through your bankruptcy. However, if you grossly underestimate your assets, your trustee will notice and make your bankruptcy process more difficult. In this column, do not adjust your numbers to reflect exemptions or secured interest such as liens and loans.

Total. Add up the total amounts on every page, indicating subtotals on the bottom of every page, and enter the grand total on the last page of this schedule.

In re **John Smith**   ,   Case No. _____
                                                    Debtor

SCHEDULE C. PROPERTY CLAIMED AS EXEMPT

Debtor elects the exemptions to which debtor is entitled under:
[Check one box]

☐ 11 U.S.C. §522(b)(1):   Exemptions provided in 11 U.S.C. §522(d). Note: These exemptions are available only in certain states.

■ 11 U.S.C. §522(b)(2):   Exemptions available under applicable nonbankruptcy federal laws, state or local law where the debtor's domicile has
                          been located for the 180 days immediately preceding the filing of the petition, or for a longer portion of the 180-day
                          period than in any other place, and the debtor's interest as a tenant by the entirety or joint tenant to the extent the interest
                          is exempt from process under applicable nonbankruptcy law.

Description of Property	Specify Law Providing Each Exemption	Value of Claimed Exemption	Current Market Value of Property Without Deducting Exemption
Real Property **Home** **2500 Magnolia Street** **Queens, NY 10137**	NYCPLR § 5206(a)	7,000.00	160,000.00
Cash on Hand **Cash on hand**	Debtor & Creditor Law § 283(2)	240.00	240.00
Checking, Savings, or Other Financial Accounts, Certificates of Deposit **Checking account** **Bank of America** **7258 Broadway** **New York, NY 10001** **Acct. 0585 0856 0859 7898**	NYCPLR § 5205(d)(2)	425.00	425.00
Household Goods and Furnishings **Household goods and furnishings**	NYCPLR § 5205(a)(5)	500.00	500.00
Books, Pictures and Other Art Objects; Collectibles **Books, pictures and other art objects;** **collectibles, CDs**	NYCPLR § 5205(a)(2)	100.00	100.00
Wearing Apparel **Wearing apparel**	NYCPLR § 5205(a)(5)	200.00	200.00
Furs and Jewelry **Jewelry**	NYCPLR § 5205(a)(6)	300.00	300.00
Firearms and Sports, Photographic and Other Hobby Equipment **Firearms and sports, photographic and other** **hobby equipment**	NYCPLR § 5205(a)	150.00	150.00

___0___ continuation sheets attached to Schedule of Property Claimed as Exempt

Be Generous with Exempting Yourself

If you are unsure whether a certain exemption covers a particular asset, go ahead and claim that exemption. Your trustee will review your documents and raise any serious objections he or she has with the way you use your exemptions to shelter your assets. A trustee will try to honor your exemptions before challenging you. It is to your benefit to claim as many exemptions as you legally can. If you fail to be thorough and complete with using your exemptions, your trustee won't point them out and tell you how to use them. In other words, if you fail to use your exemptions wisely, you risk losing assets that you could have kept.

Schedule C. Property Claimed as Exempt

Dealing with exemptions is the trickiest part of your bankruptcy filing. Schedule C is where you indicate which of your assets are exempt from your bankruptcy (meaning they cannot be sold or taken away from you to pay creditors). For the vast majority of Chapter 7 debtors, all of the debtor's personal assets are exempt. To complete this schedule carefully, be sure to have Schedules A and B handy, as well as the list of the exemptions you elect to use—and are allowed to use—in your state. We suggest that you print out your exemptions from the web site.

In Re and **Case No.** Enter the same information here as you did on previous forms.

Debtor Elects the Exemptions to which Debtor Is Entitled Under. Once you decide which set of exemptions best protects your assets, indicate that here by filling in or marking an "X" in the box that pertains to those exemptions. So if you're allowed to use and are using the federal exemptions, mark the top box; if you're using your state exemptions, check the bottom box.

Description of Property. List the assets for which exemptions apply. Use your previously completed schedules to help you list those assets here. You may find it helpful to underline the category of exemptions allowed (as listed in your exemption table), and beneath that category, list your specific item. Example:

<u>Automobiles, Trucks, Trailers, and Other Vehicles</u>
2001 Dodge Ram Quad Cab
<u>Checking, Savings, or Other Financial Accounts, Certificates of Deposit</u>
Checking account #123-4567-89, ABC Bank, 5555 Main Street, Brooklyn
Savings account #987-6543-21, ABC Bank, 5555 Main Street, Brooklyn

Specify Law Providing Each Exemption. The citations you need to use are listed in the exemptions tables in Appendix A. Each state's exemptions list relevant statues to specific exemptions. We know these look confusing (and meaningless), but use them. Examples from various states: C.C.P. § 704.040; Conn. Gen. Stat. § 52-352b(a); LSA-R.S. § 13:3881(A)(4)(f); and N.J. Stat. Ann. § 2A:17-19.

Value of Claimed Exemptions. Enter the full value you are allowed to claim—but do not exceed the actual value of the item you're claiming. In other words, don't claim $1,000 in jewelry if you only valued your jewelry at $500. Most states allow married couples (filing

If you have options when it comes to picking an exemptions table, don't haphazardly pick one. Read them. Study them. Look at how each itemized exemption can apply to you and your assets. After letting your allowable exemptions sink into your mind, circle the ones that apply to you. You will need to list exemptions in order to keep the property. If exemptions are listed and no creditor has a security interest in the items, then you should be entitled to keep them. Also, if you list them you will be entitled to keep the property as long as the value (quick sale or pawn shop value) of the items is not greater than the dollar figure listed in the Exempt Amount column in the exemption lists. If exemptions are not listed, then you will not be entitled to keep the items of property.

jointly) to double some of their exemptions. Unless the exemption table for your state indicates that you cannot double your exemptions, go ahead and double the amounts allowed. You may want to contact your court or an attorney for more information about your specific state's doubling rules.

Current Market Value of Property without Deducting Exemptions. List the fair market values of each item you are claiming as exempt. Refer to Schedules A and B for items you've already valued, but be sure to place values on items you've listed separately here. Example:

Household Goods and Furnishings

Living room set	$500
Bedroom set	$200
Washer/dryer	$175

Making Sense of Exemptions and Learning How to Use Them

To reiterate, the assets you can keep despite your bankruptcy are your exempt property. Anything your trustee can take and use to pay creditors is nonexempt property. If you pick one set of exemptions and later decide that another would be better for you (and you live in a state that allows you to pick another set), you can amend Schedule C and change your exemptions.

If you apply an exemption to an asset that does not cover the asset completely, your trustee may take that asset and sell it. Example: You have a Honda Civic worth $1,000. Your car exemption allows you to exempt $1,900. This means that since $1,000 is less than $1,900, the car is completely covered by the exemption. Say the car is instead worth $2,500. The value of the claimed exemption is still only $1,900. This means that the car value in the amount of $600 is not covered by the exemption. Since the car is only partially covered by the exemption, there is a possibility that your trustee will sell it. You would receive $1,900, and the remainder would go toward paying your creditors. For a car that has a lien (you still owe money toward the car loan), the exemption typically only needs to cover the equity. Equity is the amount the car is worth to you. More specifically, if the car is worth $15,000 and you owe $14,000 to your creditor, the car has equity in the amount of $1,000. This is also less than the $1,900 exemption and so should be covered, if you claim the exemption and you choose to reaffirm it.

No Two State Exemptions Tables Are Alike. Exemptions vary state by state, and for the same reasons that traffic laws and licensing vary state by state. You'll notice that similar items are named differently in the exemption laws, and an exemption for one item may exist for one state but not necessarily for another. Generally, you can find an exemption category in which to place an item you want to exempt, but you may still be limited by an overall personal exemption. For example: Texas's exemptions have a category for "Sports and athletic equipment including bikes," but this category is limited to the overall personal property limit. If you live in Maine and want to exempt a bicycle, you can try using the wildcard exemption (see below) or include the bike in your household goods. Notice how Maine has a category for "Aid to needy persons" while Georgia has three categories for "Old age assistance," "Aid to the blind," and "Assistance to disabled." State exemptions reflect state customs, values, and histories that go back to the beginnings of this country (and even before it became an official country!).

If you live in New Mexico, but think Arizona's state exemptions are better, you cannot move to that state and then declare bankruptcy (another red flag for trustees). If you do move, you'll have to live in that state for at least 91 days to establish your residency in that jurisdiction. Unless you have the option of using the federal exemptions, or you live in California and can opt one of two systems, you'll have to accept your state's exemptions and work within those limits.

You'll find that exemptions typically cover part of the value of your assets, and not necessarily the entire thing. For example: Arizona's exemptions allow you to keep $5,000 of equity in a motor vehicle. Let's say you owe only $2,000 on a $18,000 car. Your trustee might force you to sell the car to help pay other creditors. Selling the car pays off the lender, pays your exemption (you get $5,000), and the trustee has $11,000 to use to pay other creditors.

You may live in a state where exemptions allow you to keep certain property regardless of value. Items that typically fall into this category include household goods and furnishings.

So-called wildcard exemptions, which you can apply to your nonexempt assets in the hopes of keeping them, also exist in some states. Use wildcard exemptions to exempt personal property of your choice up to a certain limit. You may use this exemption on items that would not normally be exempt, such as expensive jewelry or clothes, or use it to increase the amount for an already partially exempt item, such as an automobile, or use it to exempt a second automobile. Example: Your state has a $1,000 wildcard exemption, and you need another $1,000 of allowable exemption to keep your car—otherwise your trustee will sell the car for its proceeds. You can add the wildcard exemption toward exempting your car. If you needed less than that $1,000 to make your car exempt, you'd be able to apply any extra wildcard value to another nonexempt item. Bottom line: If you live in a state with a wildcard exemption, use it!

Homestead Exemptions. Homestead exemptions exist to protect your equity in your home. This home has to be your principle place of residence. If you are behind in your mortgage payments, you most likely won't be able to keep your home unless you file for Chapter 13 and reorganize your debts. A few states have unlimited homestead exemptions, so regardless of your home's value, residents of those states can keep their homes. Those states include Arkansas, the District of Columbia, Florida, Iowa, Kansas, Louisiana, Oklahoma, South Dakota, and Texas. But other restrictions might apply within those states, so consult an attorney if you find it difficult to understand your exemptions.

Keeping Nonexempt Property. If you exhaust your exemptions on a particular item that you really want to keep but you worry that your trustee will take it to sell, you have two options: You can pay the asset's cash value and keep it, or ask your trustee if he or she will accept an exempt asset of equal value instead of taking the nonexempt asset. Note, however, that trustees won't typically take any assets that cannot be sold for enough money to pay the selling costs and distribute proceeds to creditors. Your trustee will abandon such assets (and you can keep them!).

Example: You don't want to lose your grand piano, which cannot be exempted, and you're not a professional musician. It's valued at $7,500, and there are no liens on it. You can pay that amount to the trustee or you can give him an asset that you've exempted of equal value. This can be a hard negotiation to make because the price tag is large (you may not find an exempt item worth that much to make a deal). Alternatively, if you want to keep your stamp collection and it's worth $1,200, see if you can give your trustee exempted jewelry that can be sold for the same price. However, you may not have to negotiate anything on the stamp collection, because your trustee won't take the effort and money to sell it. If your trustee leaves assets alone because he or she cannot justify selling it to raise money for creditors, your trustee has abandoned that asset.

The lesson here: Be careful how you negotiate nonexempt property. Paying for valuable nonexempt items with money you don't really have may not be in your best interests.

Schedule D. Creditors Holding Secured Claims

This schedule lists creditors who hold claims secured by your assets. Example: Your mortgage lender holds a claim to your house; your car loan lender holds a claim to your car. If you've put up any assets as collateral for loans or for judgments against you, or if people or companies have filed liens against your property in the hopes of getting paid, you must include them here.

In Re and **Case No.** Enter your name and case number as you did on the previous forms.

Check this box if debtor has no creditors holding secured claims to report on this Schedule D. If you have no secured creditors, fill in or put an "X" in this box and move on to Schedule E.

Creditor's Name and Mailing Address Including Zip Code. Enter all your secured creditors and give the last four digits of the account numbers linked to those creditors. Try to keep your listings in alphabetical order.

Codebtor. If you share this debt with someone else who can be forced legally to pay your debt to a listed secured creditor, such as a cosigner, co-owner, ex-spouse, or coparty in a lawsuit, you must indicate that here by typing in an "X."

Husband, Wife, Joint, or Community. Mark accordingly as you did before.

Date Claim Was Incurred, Nature of Lien, and Description of Market Value of Property. Enter the date the debt began, such as the day you signed your first mortgage, your second mortgage, your car loan, and so on. Enter every single debt to each asset, even if you may

Form B6D
(12/03)

In re __John Smith_____, Case No. _____
                                Debtor

SCHEDULE D. CREDITORS HOLDING SECURED CLAIMS

State the name, mailing address, including zip code and last four digits of any account number of all entities holding claims secured by property of the debtor as of the date of filing of the petition. The complete account number of any account the debtor has with the creditor is useful to the trustee and the creditor and may be provided if the debtor chooses to do so. List creditors holding all types of secured interests such as judgment liens, garnishments, statutory liens, mortgages, deeds of trust, and other security interests. List creditors in alphabetical order to the extent practicable. If all secured creditors will not fit on this page, use the continuation sheet provided.

If any entity other than a spouse in a joint case may be jointly liable on a claim, place an "X" in the column labeled "Codebtor", include the entity on the appropriate schedule of creditors, and complete Schedule H - Codebtors. If a joint petition is filed, state whether husband, wife, both of them, or the marital community may be liable on each claim by placing an "H", "W", "J", or "C" in the column labeled "Husband, Wife, Joint, or Community."

If the claim is contingent, place an "X" in the column labeled "Contingent". If the claim is unliquidated, place an "X" in the column labeled "Unliquidated". If the claim is disputed, place an "X" in the column labeled "Disputed". (You may need to place an "X" in more than one of these three columns.)

Report the total of all claims listed on this schedule in the box labeled "Total" on the last sheet of the completed schedule. Report this total also on the Summary of Schedules.

☐ Check this box if debtor has no creditors holding secured claims to report on this Schedule D.

CREDITOR'S NAME, AND MAILING ADDRESS INCLUDING ZIP CODE, AND ACCOUNT NUMBER (See instructions above.)	CODEBTOR	Husband, Wife, Joint, or Community			DATE CLAIM WAS INCURRED, NATURE OF LIEN, AND DESCRIPTION AND MARKET VALUE OF PROPERTY SUBJECT TO LIEN	CONTINGENT	UNLIQUIDATED	DISPUTED	AMOUNT OF CLAIM WITHOUT DEDUCTING VALUE OF COLLATERAL	UNSECURED PORTION IF ANY
		H	W	J C						
Account No. **0999**					6/98					
Crown Mortgage **1775 Halston Street** **New York, NY 10245**	-				Mortgage Home **2500 Magnolia Street** **Queens, NY 10137**					
					Value $ **160,000.00**				153,000.00	0.00
Account No. **1285**					2004					
Ford Motor Credit **P.O. Box 542000** **Omaha, NE 68154**	-				Auto Loan **2004 Ford Explorer**					
					Value $ **16,000.00**				21,150.00	5,150.00
Account No.										
					Value $					
Account No.										
					Value $					

___0___ continuation sheets attached

| | Subtotal (Total of this page) | 174,150.00 | |
| | Total (Report on Summary of Schedules) | 174,150.00 | |

have multiple debts to the same asset, such as four claims against your house. Also enter the type of lien, such as a tax lien, that you have. (See chapter 9 for a list of types of liens to indicate here.) Describe each asset used as collateral by giving the location of the asset. Use the same descriptions you used in Schedules A and B. For market values, also refer to your entries in Schedules A and B.

Contingent, Unliquidated, Disputed. Type an "X" under the column(s) that describes the secured claim. A contingent claim is one that depends on a future event, such as a default on a loan you've cosigned with someone else. An unliquidated claim is one whose debt is uncertain. Example: You are involved in a court case that is still pending (you don't know the outcome yet) and you don't know how much you may have to pay as a result of the ruling. A disputed claim is one that has you and your creditor in disagreement over the amount. If you think you owe your construction worker $200 for remodeling your kitchen, and he says it's more like $1,500, record $1,500 as the amount of the claim. You may not need to mark these columns at all, and you may need to mark more than one X for a given asset.

Amount of Claim Without Deducting Value of Collateral. Enter the amount that you owe on the secured asset to fully own that asset. So, if you owe $250,000 on a home you bought for $300,000, you would type $250,000. Ask your lenders for these values if you cannot find them among your financial paperwork. If a lender and collections agency is after you for payment on the same asset, list the debt for the lender and use ditto marks (") for the collections agency.

Subtotal. Add up the subtotals for every page you have for Schedule D and enter those values in the boxes at the bottom of the Amount of Claim columns on every page.

Total. Compute the grand total and enter that amount into the last box on the last page of your Schedule D. If your Schedule D is only one page, you will do this on the first page.

Unsecured Portion, If Any. If you owe more on any secured asset that is more than the market value of the asset, indicate that difference here. Example: Your house is worth $180,000 today, but you still owe $200,000 on it (this is called being underwater on your mortgage), so you would write "$20,000" (200,000 minus 180,000) in this column. Likewise, if the market value of the asset exceeds (is more than) what you owe on the asset, type "0." So if your house is worth $200,000 today and you owe $180,000, you'd type in "0" because your creditor is fully secured by the value of the home.

Schedule E. Creditors Holding Unsecured Priority Claims (Debts)

This schedule, which is self-explanatory, shows any and all priority creditors who deserve to be paid first out of the sale of your nonexempt assets. Remember: Priority debts are debts that bankruptcy law stipulates should be paid first (they have high priority). Such debts include child support, taxes, alimony, contributions to employee benefits plans, and so on. The schedule lists the categories of priority claims, and you have to fill in or mark an "X" in the box beside any of these claims you have. If you have none, fill in or check the box that says "Check this box if debtor has no creditors holding unsecured priority claims to report on this Schedule

Form B6E
(04/04)

In re **John Smith**   Case No. _____
                                                                    ,
                                              Debtor

SCHEDULE E. CREDITORS HOLDING UNSECURED PRIORITY CLAIMS

A complete list of claims entitled to priority, listed separately by type of priority, is to be set forth on the sheets provided. Only holders of unsecured claims entitled to priority should be listed in this schedule. In the boxes provided on the attached sheets, state the name, mailing address, including zip code, and last four digits of the account number, if any, of all entities holding priority claims against the debtor or the property of the debtor, as of the date of the filing of the petition. The complete account number of any account the debtor has with the creditor is useful to the trustee and the creditor and may be provided if the debtor chooses to do so.

If any entity other than a spouse in a joint case may be jointly liable on a claim, place an "X" in the column labeled "Codebtor", include the entity on the appropriate schedule of creditors, and complete Schedule H-Codebtors. If a joint petition is filed, state whether husband, wife, both of them or the marital community may be liable on each claim by placing an "H", "W", "J", or "C" in the column labeled "Husband, Wife, Joint, or Community".

If the claim is contingent, place an "X" in the column labeled "Contingent". If the claim is unliquidated, place an "X" in the column labeled "Unliquidated". If the claim is disputed, place an "X" in the column labeled "Disputed". (You may need to place an "X" in more than one of these three columns.)

Report the total of claims listed on each sheet in the box labeled "Subtotal" on each sheet. Report the total of all claims listed on this Schedule E in the box labeled "Total" on the last sheet of the completed schedule. Repeat this total also on the Summary of Schedules.

☐ Check this box if debtor has no creditors holding unsecured priority claims to report on this Schedule E.

TYPES OF PRIORITY CLAIMS (Check the appropriate box(es) below if claims in that category are listed on the attached sheets.)

☐ **Extensions of credit in an involuntary case**

Claims arising in the ordinary course of the debtor's business or financial affairs after the commencement of the case but before the earlier of the appointment of a trustee or the order for relief. 11 U.S.C. § 507(a)(2).

☐ **Wages, salaries, and commissions**

Wages, salaries, and commissions, including vacation, severance, and sick leave pay owing to employees and commissions owing to qualifying independent sales representatives up to $4,925* per person earned within 90 days immediately preceding the filing of the original petition, or the cessation of business, which ever occurred first, to the extent provided in 11 U.S.C. § 507 (a)(3).

☐ **Contributions to employee benefit plans**

Money owed to employee benefit plans for services rendered within 180 days immediately preceding the filing of the original petition, or the cessation of business, whichever occurred first, to the extent provided in 11 U.S.C. § 507(a)(4).

☐ **Certain farmers and fishermen**

Claims of certain farmers and fishermen, up to $4,925* per farmer or fisherman, against the debtor, as provided in 11 U.S.C. § 507(a)(5).

☐ **Deposits by individuals**

Claims of individuals up to $2,225* for deposits for the purchase, lease, or rental of property or services for personal, family, or household use, that were not delivered or provided. 11 U.S.C. § 507(a)(6).

☐ **Alimony, Maintenance, or Support**

Claims of a spouse, former spouse, or child of the debtor for alimony, maintenance, or support, to the extent provided in 11 U.S.C. § 507(a)(7).

■ **Taxes and Certain Other Debts Owed to Governmental Units**

Taxes, customs duties, and penalties owing to federal, state, and local governmental units as set forth in 11 U.S.C § 507(a)(8).

☐ **Commitments to Maintain the Capital of an Insured Depository Institution**

Claims based on commitments to the FDIC, RTC, Director of the Office of Thrift Supervision, Comptroller of the Currency, or Board of Governors of the Federal Reserve System, or their predecessors or successors, to maintain the capital of an insured depository institution. 11 U.S.C. § 507(a)(9).

*Amounts are subject to adjustment on April 1, 2007, and every three years thereafter with respect to cases commenced on or after the date of adjustment.

                                   __1__ continuation sheets attached

Form B6E - Cont.
(04/04)

In re **John Smith**   Case No. _____
                                                     ,
                        Debtor

SCHEDULE E. CREDITORS HOLDING UNSECURED PRIORITY CLAIMS
(Continuation Sheet)

Taxes and Certain Other Debts
Owed to Governmental Units

TYPE OF PRIORITY

CREDITOR'S NAME, AND MAILING ADDRESS INCLUDING ZIP CODE, AND ACCOUNT NUMBER (See instructions.)	CODEBTOR	Husband, Wife, Joint, or Community				DATE CLAIM WAS INCURRED AND CONSIDERATION FOR CLAIM	CONTINGENT	UNLIQUIDATED	DISPUTED	TOTAL AMOUNT OF CLAIM	AMOUNT ENTITLED TO PRIORITY
		H	W	J	C						
Account No. **xxxxx 4405** Internal Revenue Service P.O.Box 8610 Philadelphia, PA 19101						**1997 Tax Year** Back Taxes 1040 Income Taxes (Less than 3 years old)				32,000.00	32,000.00
Account No. **xxxxx4405** IRS P.O. Box 8610 Philadelphia, PA 19101						**1990 Tax Year** Back Taxes 1040 Taxes assessed 1995 (More than 3 years old)				1,500.00	0.00
Account No.											
Account No.											
Account No.											

Sheet _1_ of _1_ continuation sheets attached to
Schedule of Creditors Holding Unsecured Priority Claims

Subtotal (Total of this page)	33,500.00
Total (Report on Summary of Schedules)	33,500.00

Copyright (c) 1996-2004 - Best Case Solutions, Inc. - Evanston, IL - (800) 492-8037   Best Case Bankruptcy

E" and you're done with this schedule. Don't forget to type in your name and case number (if you have it) at the top of the form.

If you check any of the other boxes, you will have to give more detailed information about these claims on additional sheets to this schedule, which itemizes your priority claims. In our sample, John Smith owes taxes to the IRS. Give the name and location of the creditor, the date you incurred the debt, the amount of the lien, and how much of that lien is entitled to priority. You can make estimates here so long as you don't severely under- or overestimate values.

> **NOTE:** As we said earlier, 1040 taxes that are owed for more than three years and that have been assessed by the IRS are dischargeable. FICA or 941 taxes are not dischargeable.

Schedule F. Creditors Holding Unsecured Nonpriority Claims

You should be getting good at understanding the forms by now. This schedule lists your creditors that hold unsecured nonpriority claims (surprised?), so this section of your bankruptcy papers may take up the most room. This is where most people's debt lies—in unsecured nonpriority claims such as credit cards, medical bills, promissory notes to individuals, debts resulting after repossession or foreclosure of property, returned checks, and so on. The vast majority of Chapter 7 filers have pages in Schedule F listing their debts for which they are seeking bankruptcy. Follow the instructions given at the top of the first page of Schedule F and be sure to include every single unsecured nonpriority debt you have, even if that entails listing your great aunt or father for loans they gave you out of their love for you and that you still haven't paid back. Use the sample schedule provided here to see how the form should read. Don't forget to complete the subtotals at the bottom of each page and the grand total at the bottom of the last page of this schedule.

Remember: A codebtor is anyone who is attached to your debts and who can be forced legally to pay your debt in the event you cannot. Mark an "X" in the codebtor column for any debts that you share with another person. You will then list the codebtor as a creditor (because you owe that person your half of the deal).

Schedule G. Executory Contracts and Unexpired Leases

List any leases or contracts that you are still a party to and that are still current. Include car leases, business leases, and service or business contracts. Other examples include cell phone contracts, apartment rental agreements, insurance contracts, time-share leases, and copyright or patent licensing agreements. See sample Schedule G for how this schedule should look. You must decide whether you want to reaffirm (keep) these contracts or void them, which we will discuss later.

Schedule H. Codebtors

List all codebtors that you included in Schedules D, E, and F. Unless your codebtors also file for bankruptcy, they will be held responsible for your collective debt. If you have no codebtors, check or fill in the box at the top that says, "Check this box if debtor has no creditors."

If you are married but filing alone, your spouse is probably a codebtor for the majority of your assets (assuming you've been married awhile). You will list your spouse as a codebtor but you don't have to relist every single creditor again that you listed in previous schedules. You can write, in the right-hand column, "See creditors listed in Schedules D, E, and F except for . . ." and then indicate any creditors that you owe by yourself.

Form B6F
(12/03)

In re **John Smith** _____ , Case No. _____

_____ Debtor

SCHEDULE F. CREDITORS HOLDING UNSECURED NONPRIORITY CLAIMS

State the name, mailing address, including zip code, and last four digits of any account number, of all entities holding unsecured claims without priority against the debtor or the property of the debtor, as of the date of filing of the petition. The complete account number of any account the debtor has with the creditor is useful to the trustee and the creditor and may be provided if the debtor chooses to do so. Do not include claims listed in Schedules D and E. If all creditors will not fit on this page, use the continuation sheet provided.

If any entity other than a spouse in a joint case may be jointly liable on a claim, place an "X" in the column labeled "Codebtor", include the entity on the appropriate schedule of creditors, and complete Schedule H - Codebtors. If a joint petition is filed, state whether husband, wife, both of them, or the marital community maybe liable on each claim by placing an "H", "W", "J", or "C" in the column labeled "Husband, Wife, Joint, or Community".

If the claim is contingent, place an "X" in the column labeled "Contingent". If the claim is unliquidated, place an "X" in the column labeled "Unliquidated". If the claim is disputed, place an "X" in the column labeled "Disputed". (You may need to place an "X" in more than one of these three columns.)

Report the total of all claims listed on this schedule in the box labeled "Total" on the last sheet of the completed schedule. Report this total also on the Summary of Schedules.

☐ Check this box if debtor has no creditors holding unsecured claims to report on this Schedule F.

CREDITOR'S NAME, AND MAILING ADDRESS INCLUDING ZIP CODE, AND ACCOUNT NUMBER (See instructions above.)	CODEBTOR	H W J C	DATE CLAIM WAS INCURRED AND CONSIDERATION FOR CLAIM. IF CLAIM IS SUBJECT TO SETOFF, SO STATE.	CONTINGENT	UNLIQUIDATED	DISPUTED	AMOUNT OF CLAIM
Account No. **5424** **Citibank** **P.O. Box 6000** **The Lakes, NV 89163**	-		1999 **Credit Card**				4,000.00
Account No. **4128** **Citibank** **P.O. Box 6001** **Sioux Falls, SD 57188**	-		1999 **Credit Card**				3,000.00
Account No. **5433** **Household Bank** **P.O. Box 4155** **Carol Stream, IL 60197**	-		1998 **Credit Card**				4,377.00
Account No. **4465** **Providian** **P.O. Box 9180** **Pleasanton, CA 94566**	-		1999 **Credit Card**				1,000.00

__1__ continuation sheets attached

Subtotal
(Total of this page)   **12,377.00**

Form B6F - Cont.
(12/03)

In re **John Smith** _____, Case No. _____

Debtor

SCHEDULE F. CREDITORS HOLDING UNSECURED NONPRIORITY CLAIMS
(Continuation Sheet)

CREDITOR'S NAME, AND MAILING ADDRESS INCLUDING ZIP CODE, AND ACCOUNT NUMBER (See instructions.)	C O D E B T O R	Husband, Wife, Joint, or Community			C O N T I N G E N T	U N L I Q U I D A T E D	D I S P U T E D	AMOUNT OF CLAIM
		H	W J	C				
Account No. **0654**		**1999** **Credit Card**						
Sears P.O. Box 182149 Columbus, OH 43218	-							3,650.00
Account No.								
Account No.								
Account No.								
Account No.								

Sheet no. __1__ of __1__ sheets attached to Schedule of Creditors Holding Unsecured Nonpriority Claims

Subtotal (Total of this page)	3,650.00
Total (Report on Summary of Schedules)	16,027.00

In re   **John Smith**   Case No. _____

                                         Debtor

SCHEDULE G. EXECUTORY CONTRACTS AND UNEXPIRED LEASES

Describe all executory contracts of any nature and all unexpired leases of real or personal property. Include any timeshare interests. State nature of debtor's interest in contract, i.e., "Purchaser," "Agent," etc. State whether debtor is the lessor or lessee of a lease. Provide the names and complete mailing addresses of all other parties to each lease or contract described.

NOTE: A party listed on this schedule will not receive notice of the filing of this case unless the party is also scheduled in the appropriate schedule of creditors.

☐ Check this box if debtor has no executory contracts or unexpired leases.

Name and Mailing Address, Including Zip Code, of Other Parties to Lease or Contract	Description of Contract or Lease and Nature of Debtor's Interest. State whether lease is for nonresidential real property. State contract number of any government contract.

   0   continuation sheets attached to Schedule of Executory Contracts and Unexpired Leases

In re   **John Smith**   ,   Case No. _____

Debtor

SCHEDULE H. CODEBTORS

Provide the information requested concerning any person or entity, other than a spouse in a joint case, that is also liable on any debts listed by debtor in the schedules of creditors. Include all guarantors and co-signers. In community property states, a married debtor not filing a joint case should report the name and address of the nondebtor spouse on this schedule. Include all names used by the nondebtor spouse during the six years immediately preceding the commencement of this case.

☐   Check this box if debtor has no codebtors.

NAME AND ADDRESS OF CODEBTOR	NAME AND ADDRESS OF CREDITOR

   0   continuation sheets attached to Schedule of Codebtors

Form B6I
(12/03)

In re **John Smith** , Case No. _____
                                         Debtor

SCHEDULE I. CURRENT INCOME OF INDIVIDUAL DEBTOR(S)

The column labeled "Spouse" must be completed in all cases filed by joint debtors and by a married debtor in a chapter 12 or 13 case whether or not a joint petition is filed, unless the spouses are separated and a joint petition is not filed.

Debtor's Marital Status:	DEPENDENTS OF DEBTOR AND SPOUSE	
	RELATIONSHIP **None.**	AGE
Married		

EMPLOYMENT:	DEBTOR	SPOUSE
Occupation	**Clerk**	
Name of Employer	**Walgreen Drug Company**	
How long employed	**4 yrs.**	
Address of Employer	**3427 North Brambly Lane New York, NY 10142**	

INCOME: (Estimate of average monthly income)	DEBTOR	SPOUSE
Current monthly gross wages, salary, and commissions (pro rate if not paid monthly)	$ **3,150.00**	$ **N/A**
Estimated monthly overtime	$ **0.00**	$ **N/A**
SUBTOTAL	$ **3,150.00**	$ **N/A**
LESS PAYROLL DEDUCTIONS		
a. Payroll taxes and social security	$ **220.00**	$ **N/A**
b. Insurance	$ **60.00**	$ **N/A**
c. Union dues	$ **0.00**	$ **N/A**
d. Other (Specify)_____	$ **0.00**	$ **N/A**
_____	$ **0.00**	$ **N/A**
SUBTOTAL OF PAYROLL DEDUCTIONS	$ **280.00**	$ **N/A**
TOTAL NET MONTHLY TAKE HOME PAY	$ **2,870.00**	$ **N/A**
Regular income from operation of business or profession or farm (attach detailed statement)	$ **0.00**	$ **N/A**
Income from real property	$ **0.00**	$ **N/A**
Interest and dividends	$ **0.00**	$ **N/A**
Alimony, maintenance or support payments payable to the debtor for the debtor's use or that of dependents listed above	$ **0.00**	$ **N/A**
Social security or other government assistance (Specify) _____	$ **0.00**	$ **N/A**
_____	$ **0.00**	$ **N/A**
Pension or retirement income	$ **0.00**	$ **N/A**
Other monthly income (Specify) _____	$ **0.00**	$ **N/A**
_____	$ **0.00**	$ **N/A**
TOTAL MONTHLY INCOME	$ **2,870.00**	$ **N/A**

TOTAL COMBINED MONTHLY INCOME $ **2,870.00**   (Report also on Summary of Schedules)

Describe any increase or decrease of more than 10% in any of the above categories anticipated to occur within the year following the filing of this document:

Schedule I. Current Income of Individual Debtor(s)

This schedule is self-explanatory and requires you to indicate some information about your income and your job. It's important for your trustee to have an idea of how much money you make monthly and how much you receive as net income once income from other sources and/or deductions are taken into account. This allows the trustee to know what your paying power is and if you have enough disposable income to file for Chapter 13. Have a recent pay stub on hand for entering specific amounts for taxes, Social Security, and so on. Enter the amounts accordingly. Total your income at the bottom, and if you are including your spouse as a joint filer, total your combined monthly income. If you are filing alone, type "N/A" in every line under the column labeled Spouse.

Schedule J. Current Expenditures of Individual Debtor(s)

Use the worksheet you completed in chapter 2 as a guide for filling out Schedule J, which itemizes your living expenses in detail. Follow the instructions at the top and work your way down the list of expenses you may or may not incur each month. Under utilities, be sure to include cell phone, cable, trash disposal, or Internet connection as Other if you incur such bills and for which there is no line dedicated for these expenses.

For bills you don't pay monthly (you pay them annually, bi-monthly, or some such way), figure out how much they would cost monthly and use that figure. Example: If you get your utility bill every two months (bi-monthly) and it's usually around $50, your monthly average is $25. If you pay your car insurance every six months at $525, calculate what that means on a monthly basis (525 divided by 6 months = $87.50). Do not include credit card payments in installment payments. Installment payments refers to secured items you've purchased such as a car, furniture, and home equity loan, and for which you have collateral to back up the loan.

In re   **John Smith**   Case No. _____

Debtor

SCHEDULE J. CURRENT EXPENDITURES OF INDIVIDUAL DEBTOR(S)

Complete this schedule by estimating the average monthly expenses of the debtor and the debtor's family. Pro rate any payments made bi-weekly, quarterly, semi-annually, or annually to show monthly rate.

☐   Check this box if a joint petition is filed and debtor's spouse maintains a separate household. Complete a separate schedule of expenditures labeled "Spouse."

Rent or home mortgage payment (include lot rented for mobile home)	$ 1,600.00
Are real estate taxes included? Yes_____ No___X___	
Is property insurance included? Yes_____ No___X___	
Utilities: Electricity and heating fuel	$ 105.00
Water and sewer	$ 45.00
Telephone	$ 65.00
Other_____cable_____	$ 40.00
Home maintenance (repairs and upkeep)	$ 150.00
Food	$ 250.00
Clothing	$ 150.00
Laundry and dry cleaning	$ 60.00
Medical and dental expenses	$ 60.00
Transportation (not including car payments)	$ 150.00
Recreation, clubs and entertainment, newspapers, magazines, etc.	$ 50.00
Charitable contributions	$ 40.00
Insurance (not deducted from wages or included in home mortgage payments)	
Homeowner's or renter's	$ 90.00
Life	$ 0.00
Health	$ 0.00
Auto	$ 105.00
Other_____	$ 0.00
Taxes (not deducted from wages or included in home mortgage payments)	
(Specify)_____	$ 0.00
Installment payments: (In chapter 12 and 13 cases, do not list payments to be included in the plan.)	
Auto	$ 360.00
Other_____	$ 0.00
Other_____	$ 0.00
Other_____	$ 0.00
Alimony, maintenance, and support paid to others	$ 0.00
Payments for support of additional dependents not living at your home	$ 0.00
Regular expenses from operation of business, profession, or farm (attach detailed statement)	$ 0.00
Other_____	$ 0.00
Other_____	$ 0.00
TOTAL MONTHLY EXPENSES (Report also on Summary of Schedules)	$ 3,320.00

[FOR CHAPTER 12 AND 13 DEBTORS ONLY]
Provide the information requested below, including whether plan payments are to be made bi-weekly, monthly, annually, or at some other regular interval.

A. Total projected monthly income	$ N/A
B. Total projected monthly expenses	$ N/A
C. Excess income (A minus B)	$ N/A
D. Total amount to be paid into plan each _____	$ N/A
(interval)	

Enter a figure on every line, or use "0" or "N/A" for lines that do not apply to you, including the lines reserved for Chapter 12 and 13 filers toward the bottom.

For business debtors: If you operated a business or profession, you'll need to attach a detailed statement about your regular business expenses. Look for the line that reads: "Regular expenses from operation of business, profession, of farm (attach detailed statement)" toward the bottom of the page. You can use Worksheet B in the back of this book (Appendix A) to attach this detailed statement.

Schedule 21

This form is not part of your regular bankruptcy paperwork, but you will have to provide your full Social Security number on this form for your creditors and trustee. You'll find this form included on the web site.

Summary of Schedules

Once you've completed all the above schedules, you will create a summary of them here by entering your figures into the proper boxes. Follow the instructions on this form for entering the total values you've calculated on your schedules. In the Attached (Yes/No) column, you will type "Yes" down the entire column because you've included all of the forms. This page also tallies up the total number of pages you've used to complete your schedules. Don't forget to complete the information at the top with your full name, case number (if you have it), and the Chapter (7) under which you're filing. In most bankruptcy filings, you will place this summary at the beginning of your schedules, before the first page of Schedule A. When you ask your local court how it wants your papers ordered, you will know exactly where to place this form.

Declaration Concerning Debtor's Schedules

Follow the instructions on this form to confirm that the information you've provided in all of your forms is true and correct. Indicate the number of pages your summary schedules comprise. Sign and date the top half. If you have someone fill out your forms for you, he or she will have to complete the bottom half. If you completed your forms by yourself, use "N/A" for any lines that do not pertain to you. If your form contains a section for corporations and partnerships, type "N/A" on every line.

Form 7: Statement of Financial Affairs

The purpose of this form is to give information about your recent financial transactions. Several pages make up Form 7, but if you start at the beginning and work your way through the pages, it won't take you long. The questions are self-explanatory, and you'll find that you don't have anything to report for most of the questions. In those cases, you will fill in or mark "X" in the box labeled "None" beside the question. Take your time and be thorough. Go question by question—step by step.

Your trustee will look at this form to ensure you haven't made any problematic transactions lately that jeopardize your bankruptcy filing. For example, if you paid off a creditor just before filing (because he was your friend) at the expense of forgetting your other, more important creditors, your trustee will note this. Also, if you transferred property to someone else before filing, your trustee can take that property back and use it to pay off creditors. This

Form B 21 Official Form 21
(12/03)

FORM 21. STATEMENT OF SOCIAL SECURITY NUMBER

United States Bankruptcy Court
Southern District of New York

In re   **John Smith**
Debtor

Case No. _____

Address   **2500 Magnolia Street**
         New York, NY 10034

Chapter   **7**

Employer's Tax Identification (EIN) No(s). [if any]: _____
Last four digits of Social Security No(s).:   **xxx-xx-9878**

STATEMENT OF SOCIAL SECURITY NUMBER(S)

1. Name of Debtor (enter Last, First, Middle): **Smith, John**
(Check the appropriate box and, if applicable, provide the required information.)

     / **X** /Debtor has a Social Security Number and it is: ___**123-45-9878**___
            (If more than one, state all.)

     / /Debtor does not have a Social Security Number.

2. Name of Joint Debtor (enter Last, First, Middle): _____
(Check the appropriate box and, if applicable, provide the required information.)

     / /Joint Debtor has a Social Security Number and it is: _____
            (If more than one, state all.)

     / /Joint Debtor does not have a Social Security Number.

I declare under penalty of perjury that the foregoing is true and correct.

X _____

     John Smith   Date
     Signature of Debtor

X _____

     Signature of Joint Debtor   Date

Joint debtors must provide information for both spouses.
Penalty for making a false statement: Fine of up to $250,000 or up to 5 years imprisonment or both. 18 U.S.C. §§ 152 and 3571.

United States Bankruptcy Court
Southern District of New York

In re __John Smith_____,   Case No. _____

                                  Debtor

                                             Chapter_____7_____

SUMMARY OF SCHEDULES

Indicate as to each schedule whether that schedule is attached and state the number of pages in each. Report the totals from Schedules A, B, D, E, F, I, and J in the boxes provided. Add the amounts from Schedules A and B to determine the total amount of the debtor's assets. Add the amounts from Schedules D, E, and F to determine the total amount of the debtor's liabilities.

NAME OF SCHEDULE	ATTACHED (YES/NO)	NO. OF SHEETS	AMOUNTS SCHEDULED		
			ASSETS	LIABILITIES	OTHER
A - Real Property	Yes	1	160,000.00		
B - Personal Property	Yes	3	17,915.00		
C - Property Claimed as Exempt	Yes	1			
D - Creditors Holding Secured Claims	Yes	1		174,150.00	
E - Creditors Holding Unsecured Priority Claims	Yes	2		33,500.00	
F - Creditors Holding Unsecured Nonpriority Claims	Yes	2		16,027.00	
G - Executory Contracts and Unexpired Leases	Yes	1			
H - Codebtors	Yes	1			
I - Current Income of Individual Debtor(s)	Yes	1			2,870.00
J - Current Expenditures of Individual Debtor(s)	Yes	1			3,320.00
Total Number of Sheets of ALL Schedules		14			
		Total Assets	177,915.00		
		Total Liabilities		223,677.00	

United States Bankruptcy Court
Southern District of New York

In re   <u>John Smith</u>   Case No. _____

                                    Debtor(s)   Chapter   **7** _____

DECLARATION CONCERNING DEBTOR'S SCHEDULES

DECLARATION UNDER PENALTY OF PERJURY BY INDIVIDUAL DEBTOR

I declare under penalty of perjury that I have read the foregoing summary and schedules, consisting of __**15**__ sheets *[total shown on summary page plus 1]*, and that they are true and correct to the best of my knowledge, information, and belief.

Date _____   Signature _____

                                         John Smith

                                         Debtor

Penalty for making a false statement or concealing property: Fine of up to $500,000 or imprisonment for up to 5 years or both. 18 U.S.C. §§ 152 and 3571.

CERTIFICATION AND SIGNATURE OF NON-ATTORNEY BANKRUPTCY PETITION PREPARER (See 11 U.S.C. § 110)

I certify that I am a bankruptcy petition preparer as defined in 11 U.S.C. § 110, that I prepared this document for compensation, and that I have provided the debtor with a copy of this document.

Jennifer West-We The People   **123-45-6789**

Printed or Typed Name of Bankruptcy Petition Preparer   Social Security No.

                                                    (Required by 11 U.S.C. ß 110(c).)

239 W. 72nd St.
New York, NY 10023
Address

Names and Social Security numbers of all other individuals who prepared or assisted in preparing this document:

If more than one person prepared this document, attach additional signed sheets conforming to the appropriate Official Form for each person.

X _____   _____

Signature of Bankruptcy Petition Preparer   Date

A bankruptcy petition preparer's failure to comply with the provisions of title 11 and the Federal Rules of Bankruptcy Procedure may result in fines or imprisonment or both. 11 U.S.C. § 110; 18 U.S.C. § 156.

Form 7
(12/03)

United States Bankruptcy Court
Southern District of New York

In re **John Smith** _____ Case No. _____

                              Debtor(s)   Chapter   **7**   _____

STATEMENT OF FINANCIAL AFFAIRS

This statement is to be completed by every debtor. Spouses filing a joint petition may file a single statement on which the information for both spouses is combined. If the case is filed under chapter 12 or chapter 13, a married debtor must furnish information for both spouses whether or not a joint petition is filed, unless the spouses are separated and a joint petition is not filed. An individual debtor engaged in business as a sole proprietor, partner, family farmer, or self-employed professional, should provide the information requested on this statement concerning all such activities as well as the individual's personal affairs.

Questions 1 - 18 are to be completed by all debtors. Debtors that are or have been in business, as defined below, also must complete Questions 19 - 25. **If the answer to an applicable question is "None," mark the box labeled "None."** If additional space is needed for the answer to any question, use and attach a separate sheet properly identified with the case name, case number (if known), and the number of the question.

DEFINITIONS

"In business." A debtor is "in business" for the purpose of this form if the debtor is a corporation or partnership. An individual debtor is "in business" for the purpose of this form if the debtor is or has been, within the six years immediately preceding the filing of this bankruptcy case, any of the following: an officer, director, managing executive, or owner of 5 percent or more of the voting or equity securities of a corporation; a partner, other than a limited partner, of a partnership; a sole proprietor or self-employed.

"Insider." The term "insider" includes but is not limited to: relatives of the debtor; general partners of the debtor and their relatives; corporations of which the debtor is an officer, director, or person in control; officers, directors, and any owner of 5 percent or more of the voting or equity securities of a corporate debtor and their relatives; affiliates of the debtor and insiders of such affiliates; any managing agent of the debtor. 11 U.S.C. § 101.

---

1. Income from employment or operation of business

None ☐

State the gross amount of income the debtor has received from employment, trade, or profession, or from operation of the debtor's business from the beginning of this calendar year to the date this case was commenced. State also the gross amounts received during the **two years** immediately preceding this calendar year. (A debtor that maintains, or has maintained, financial records on the basis of a fiscal rather than a calendar year may report fiscal year income. Identify the beginning and ending dates of the debtor's fiscal year.) If a joint petition is filed, state income for each spouse separately. (Married debtors filing under chapter 12 or chapter 13 must state income of both spouses whether or not a joint petition is filed, unless the spouses are separated and a joint petition is not filed.)

AMOUNT	SOURCE (if more than one)
$28,350.00	**2004 Employment/Debtor**
$37,800.00	**2003 Employment/Debtor**
$37,800.00	**2002 Employment/Debtor**

2. Income other than from employment or operation of business

None ■

State the amount of income received by the debtor other than from employment, trade, profession, or operation of the debtor's business during the **two years** immediately preceding the commencement of this case. Give particulars. If a joint petition is filed, state income for each spouse separately. (Married debtors filing under chapter 12 or chapter 13 must state income for each spouse whether or not a joint petition is filed, unless the spouses are separated and a joint petition is not filed.)

AMOUNT   SOURCE

2

3. Payments to creditors

None
■ a. List all payments on loans, installment purchases of goods or services, and other debts, aggregating more than $600 to any creditor, made within **90 days** immediately preceding the commencement of this case. (Married debtors filing under chapter 12 or chapter 13 must include payments by either or both spouses whether or not a joint petition is filed, unless the spouses are separated and a joint petition is not filed.)

NAME AND ADDRESS OF CREDITOR	DATES OF PAYMENTS	AMOUNT PAID	AMOUNT STILL OWING

None
■ b. List all payments made within **one year** immediately preceding the commencement of this case to or for the benefit of creditors who are or were insiders. (Married debtors filing under chapter 12 or chapter 13 must include payments by either or both spouses whether or not a joint petition is filed, unless the spouses are separated and a joint petition is not filed.)

NAME AND ADDRESS OF CREDITOR AND RELATIONSHIP TO DEBTOR	DATE OF PAYMENT	AMOUNT PAID	AMOUNT STILL OWING

4. Suits and administrative proceedings, executions, garnishments and attachments

None
■ a. List all suits and administrative proceedings to which the debtor is or was a party within **one year** immediately preceding the filing of this bankruptcy case. (Married debtors filing under chapter 12 or chapter 13 must include information concerning either or both spouses whether or not a joint petition is filed, unless the spouses are separated and a joint petition is not filed.)

CAPTION OF SUIT AND CASE NUMBER	NATURE OF PROCEEDING	COURT OR AGENCY AND LOCATION	STATUS OR DISPOSITION

None
■ b. Describe all property that has been attached, garnished or seized under any legal or equitable process within **one year** immediately preceding the commencement of this case. (Married debtors filing under chapter 12 or chapter 13 must include information concerning property of either or both spouses whether or not a joint petition is filed, unless the spouses are separated and a joint petition is not filed.)

NAME AND ADDRESS OF PERSON FOR WHOSE BENEFIT PROPERTY WAS SEIZED	DATE OF SEIZURE	DESCRIPTION AND VALUE OF PROPERTY

5. Repossessions, foreclosures and returns

None
■ List all property that has been repossessed by a creditor, sold at a foreclosure sale, transferred through a deed in lieu of foreclosure or returned to the seller, within **one year** immediately preceding the commencement of this case. (Married debtors filing under chapter 12 or chapter 13 must include information concerning property of either or both spouses whether or not a joint petition is filed, unless the spouses are separated and a joint petition is not filed.)

NAME AND ADDRESS OF CREDITOR OR SELLER	DATE OF REPOSSESSION, FORECLOSURE SALE, TRANSFER OR RETURN	DESCRIPTION AND VALUE OF PROPERTY

6. Assignments and receiverships

None
■ a. Describe any assignment of property for the benefit of creditors made within **120 days** immediately preceding the commencement of this case. (Married debtors filing under chapter 12 or chapter 13 must include any assignment by either or both spouses whether or not a joint petition is filed, unless the spouses are separated and a joint petition is not filed.)

NAME AND ADDRESS OF ASSIGNEE	DATE OF ASSIGNMENT	TERMS OF ASSIGNMENT OR SETTLEMENT

None
■ b. List all property which has been in the hands of a custodian, receiver, or court-appointed official within **one year** immediately preceding the commencement of this case. (Married debtors filing under chapter 12 or chapter 13 must include information concerning property of either or both spouses whether or not a joint petition is filed, unless the spouses are separated and a joint petition is not filed.)

NAME AND ADDRESS OF CUSTODIAN	NAME AND LOCATION OF COURT CASE TITLE & NUMBER	DATE OF ORDER	DESCRIPTION AND VALUE OF PROPERTY

3

7. Gifts

None
■ List all gifts or charitable contributions made within **one year** immediately preceding the commencement of this case except ordinary and usual gifts to family members aggregating less than $200 in value per individual family member and charitable contributions aggregating less than $100 per recipient. (Married debtors filing under chapter 12 or chapter 13 must include gifts or contributions by either or both spouses whether or not a joint petition is filed, unless the spouses are separated and a joint petition is not filed.)

NAME AND ADDRESS OF PERSON OR ORGANIZATION	RELATIONSHIP TO DEBTOR, IF ANY	DATE OF GIFT	DESCRIPTION AND VALUE OF GIFT

8. Losses

None
■ List all losses from fire, theft, other casualty or gambling within **one year** immediately preceding the commencement of this case **or since the commencement of this case.** (Married debtors filing under chapter 12 or chapter 13 must include losses by either or both spouses whether or not a joint petition is filed, unless the spouses are separated and a joint petition is not filed.)

DESCRIPTION AND VALUE OF PROPERTY	DESCRIPTION OF CIRCUMSTANCES AND, IF LOSS WAS COVERED IN WHOLE OR IN PART BY INSURANCE, GIVE PARTICULARS	DATE OF LOSS

9. Payments related to debt counseling or bankruptcy

None
☐ List all payments made or property transferred by or on behalf of the debtor to any persons, including attorneys, for consultation concerning debt consolidation, relief under the bankruptcy law or preparation of the petition in bankruptcy within **one year** immediately preceding the commencement of this case.

NAME AND ADDRESS OF PAYEE	DATE OF PAYMENT, NAME OF PAYOR IF OTHER THAN DEBTOR	AMOUNT OF MONEY OR DESCRIPTION AND VALUE OF PROPERTY
We The People-New York 239 W. 72nd St. New York, NY 10023	**02/09/04**	**$229.00 Breakdown Cost; $199.00 Typing Petition; $15.00 Copy Cost; $15.00 Process Server**
We The People-USA 1501 State Street Santa Barbara, CA 93105		

10. Other transfers

None
■ List all other property, other than property transferred in the ordinary course of the business or financial affairs of the debtor, transferred either absolutely or as security within **one year** immediately preceding the commencement of this case. (Married debtors filing under chapter 12 or chapter 13 must include transfers by either or both spouses whether or not a joint petition is filed, unless the spouses are separated and a joint petition is not filed.)

NAME AND ADDRESS OF TRANSFEREE, RELATIONSHIP TO DEBTOR	DATE	DESCRIBE PROPERTY TRANSFERRED AND VALUE RECEIVED

11. Closed financial accounts

None
■ List all financial accounts and instruments held in the name of the debtor or for the benefit of the debtor which were closed, sold, or otherwise transferred within **one year** immediately preceding the commencement of this case. Include checking, savings, or other financial accounts, certificates of deposit, or other instruments; shares and share accounts held in banks, credit unions, pension funds, cooperatives, associations, brokerage houses and other financial institutions. (Married debtors filing under chapter 12 or chapter 13 must include information concerning accounts or instruments held by or for either or both spouses whether or not a joint petition is filed, unless the spouses are separated and a joint petition is not filed.)

NAME AND ADDRESS OF INSTITUTION	TYPE OF ACCOUNT, LAST FOUR DIGITS OF ACCOUNT NUMBER, AND AMOUNT OF FINAL BALANCE	AMOUNT AND DATE OF SALE OR CLOSING

4

12. Safe deposit boxes

None ▪ List each safe deposit or other box or depository in which the debtor has or had securities, cash, or other valuables within **one year** immediately preceding the commencement of this case. (Married debtors filing under chapter 12 or chapter 13 must include boxes or depositories of either or both spouses whether or not a joint petition is filed, unless the spouses are separated and a joint petition is not filed.)

NAME AND ADDRESS OF BANK OR OTHER DEPOSITORY	NAMES AND ADDRESSES OF THOSE WITH ACCESS TO BOX OR DEPOSITORY	DESCRIPTION OF CONTENTS	DATE OF TRANSFER OR SURRENDER, IF ANY

13. Setoffs

None ▪ List all setoffs made by any creditor, including a bank, against a debt or deposit of the debtor within **90 days** preceding the commencement of this case. (Married debtors filing under chapter 12 or chapter 13 must include information concerning either or both spouses whether or not a joint petition is filed, unless the spouses are separated and a joint petition is not filed.)

NAME AND ADDRESS OF CREDITOR	DATE OF SETOFF	AMOUNT OF SETOFF

14. Property held for another person

None ▪ List all property owned by another person that the debtor holds or controls.

NAME AND ADDRESS OF OWNER	DESCRIPTION AND VALUE OF PROPERTY	LOCATION OF PROPERTY

15. Prior address of debtor

None ☐ If the debtor has moved within the **two years** immediately preceding the commencement of this case, list all premises which the debtor occupied during that period and vacated prior to the commencement of this case. If a joint petition is filed, report also any separate address of either spouse.

ADDRESS	NAME USED	DATES OF OCCUPANCY
123 Oak Street New York, NY 10001	**John Smith**	**01/1999-02/2002**

16. Spouses and Former Spouses

None ☐ If the debtor resides or resided in a community property state, commonwealth, or territory (including Alaska, Arizona, California, Idaho, Louisiana, Nevada, New Mexico, Puerto Rico, Texas, Washington, or Wisconsin) within the **six-year period** immediately preceding the commencement of the case, identify the name of the debtorís spouse and of any former spouse who resides or resided with the debtor in the community property state.

NAME
Lisa Smith (Former Spouse)

17. Environmental Information.

For the purpose of this question, the following definitions apply:

"Environmental Law" means any federal, state, or local statute or regulation regulating pollution, contamination, releases of hazardous or toxic substances, wastes or material into the air, land, soil, surface water, groundwater, or other medium, including, but not limited to, statutes or regulations regulating the cleanup of these substances, wastes, or material.

"Site" means any location, facility, or property as defined under any Environmental Law, whether or not presently or formerly owned or operated by the debtor, including, but not limited to, disposal sites.

"Hazardous Material" means anything defined as a hazardous waste, hazardous substance, toxic substance, hazardous material, pollutant, or contaminant or similar term under an Environmental Law

5

None ■   a. List the name and address of every site for which the debtor has received notice in writing by a governmental unit that it may be liable or potentially liable under or in violation of an Environmental Law. Indicate the governmental unit, the date of the notice, and, if known, the Environmental Law:

SITE NAME AND ADDRESS	NAME AND ADDRESS OF GOVERNMENTAL UNIT	DATE OF NOTICE	ENVIRONMENTAL LAW

None ■   b. List the name and address of every site for which the debtor provided notice to a governmental unit of a release of Hazardous Material. Indicate the governmental unit to which the notice was sent and the date of the notice.

SITE NAME AND ADDRESS	NAME AND ADDRESS OF GOVERNMENTAL UNIT	DATE OF NOTICE	ENVIRONMENTAL LAW

None ■   c. List all judicial or administrative proceedings, including settlements or orders, under any Environmental Law with respect to which the debtor is or was a party. Indicate the name and address of the governmental unit that is or was a party to the proceeding, and the docket number.

NAME AND ADDRESS OF GOVERNMENTAL UNIT	DOCKET NUMBER	STATUS OR DISPOSITION

18 . Nature, location and name of business

None ■   a. If the debtor is an individual, list the names, addresses, taxpayer identification numbers, nature of the businesses, and beginning and ending dates of all businesses in which the debtor was an officer, director, partner, or managing executive of a corporation, partnership, sole proprietorship, or was a self-employed professional within the **six years** immediately preceding the commencement of this case, or in which the debtor owned 5 percent or more of the voting or equity securities within the **six years** immediately preceding the commencement of this case.

     If the debtor is a partnership, list the names, addresses, taxpayer identification numbers, nature of the businesses, and beginning and ending dates of all businesses in which the debtor was a partner or owned 5 percent or more of the voting or equity securities, within the **six years** immediately preceding the commencement of this case.

     If the debtor is a corporation, list the names, addresses, taxpayer identification numbers, nature of the businesses, and beginning and ending dates of all businesses in which the debtor was a partner or owned 5 percent or more of the voting or equity securities within the **six years** immediately preceding the commencement of this case.

NAME	TAXPAYER I.D. NO. (EIN)	ADDRESS	NATURE OF BUSINESS	BEGINNING AND ENDING DATES

None ■   b. Identify any business listed in response to subdivision a., above, that is "single asset real estate" as defined in 11 U.S.C. § 101.

NAME	ADDRESS

     The following questions are to be completed by every debtor that is a corporation or partnership and by any individual debtor who is or has been, within the **six years** immediately preceding the commencement of this case, any of the following: an officer, director, managing executive, or owner of more than 5 percent of the voting or equity securities of a corporation; a partner, other than a limited partner, of a partnership; a sole proprietor or otherwise self-employed.

     *(An individual or joint debtor should complete this portion of the statement **only** if the debtor is or has been in business, as defined above, within the six years immediately preceding the commencement of this case. A debtor who has not been in business within those six years should go directly to the signature page.)*

19. Books, records and financial statements

None ■   a. List all bookkeepers and accountants who within the **two years** immediately preceding the filing of this bankruptcy case kept or supervised the keeping of books of account and records of the debtor.

NAME AND ADDRESS	DATES SERVICES RENDERED

6

None ■ b. List all firms or individuals who within the **two years** immediately preceding the filing of this bankruptcy case have audited the books of account and records, or prepared a financial statement of the debtor.

NAME	ADDRESS	DATES SERVICES RENDERED

None ■ c. List all firms or individuals who at the time of the commencement of this case were in possession of the books of account and records of the debtor. If any of the books of account and records are not available, explain.

NAME	ADDRESS

None ■ d. List all financial institutions, creditors and other parties, including mercantile and trade agencies, to whom a financial statement was issued within the **two years** immediately preceding the commencement of this case by the debtor.

NAME AND ADDRESS	DATE ISSUED

20. Inventories

None ■ a. List the dates of the last two inventories taken of your property, the name of the person who supervised the taking of each inventory, and the dollar amount and basis of each inventory.

DATE OF INVENTORY	INVENTORY SUPERVISOR	DOLLAR AMOUNT OF INVENTORY (Specify cost, market or other basis)

None ■ b. List the name and address of the person having possession of the records of each of the two inventories reported in a., above.

DATE OF INVENTORY	NAME AND ADDRESSES OF CUSTODIAN OF INVENTORY RECORDS

21 . Current Partners, Officers, Directors and Shareholders

None ■ a. If the debtor is a partnership, list the nature and percentage of partnership interest of each member of the partnership.

NAME AND ADDRESS	NATURE OF INTEREST	PERCENTAGE OF INTEREST

None ■ b. If the debtor is a corporation, list all officers and directors of the corporation, and each stockholder who directly or indirectly owns, controls, or holds 5 percent or more of the voting or equity securities of the corporation.

NAME AND ADDRESS	TITLE	NATURE AND PERCENTAGE OF STOCK OWNERSHIP

22 . Former partners, officers, directors and shareholders

None ■ a. If the debtor is a partnership, list each member who withdrew from the partnership within **one year** immediately preceding the commencement of this case.

NAME	ADDRESS	DATE OF WITHDRAWAL

None ■ b. If the debtor is a corporation, list all officers, or directors whose relationship with the corporation terminated within **one year** immediately preceding the commencement of this case.

NAME AND ADDRESS	TITLE	DATE OF TERMINATION

7

23 . Withdrawals from a partnership or distributions by a corporation

None
■ If the debtor is a partnership or corporation, list all withdrawals or distributions credited or given to an insider, including compensation in any form, bonuses, loans, stock redemptions, options exercised and any other perquisite during **one year** immediately preceding the commencement of this case.

NAME & ADDRESS OF RECIPIENT, RELATIONSHIP TO DEBTOR	DATE AND PURPOSE OF WITHDRAWAL	AMOUNT OF MONEY OR DESCRIPTION AND VALUE OF PROPERTY

24. Tax Consolidation Group.

None
■ If the debtor is a corporation, list the name and federal taxpayer identification number of the parent corporation of any consolidated group for tax purposes of which the debtor has been a member at any time within the **six-year period** immediately preceding the commencement of the case.

NAME OF PARENT CORPORATION	TAXPAYER IDENTIFICATION NUMBER

25. Pension Funds.

None
■ If the debtor is not an individual, list the name and federal taxpayer identification number of any pension fund to which the debtor, as an employer, has been responsible for contributing at any time within the **six-year period** immediately preceding the commencement of the case.

NAME OF PENSION FUND	TAXPAYER IDENTIFICATION NUMBER

DECLARATION UNDER PENALTY OF PERJURY BY INDIVIDUAL DEBTOR

I declare under penalty of perjury that I have read the answers contained in the foregoing statement of financial affairs and any attachments thereto and that they are true and correct.

Date _____   Signature _____

John Smith
Debtor

Penalty for making a false statement: Fine of up to $500,000 or imprisonment for up to 5 years, or both. 18 U.S.C. §§ 152 and 3571

CERTIFICATION AND SIGNATURE OF NON-ATTORNEY BANKRUPTCY PETITION PREPARER (See 11 U.S.C. § 110)

I certify that I am a bankruptcy petition preparer as defined in 11 U.S.C. § 110, that I prepared this document for compensation, and that I have provided the debtor with a copy of this document.

Jennifer West-We The People _____   **123-45-6789** _____
Printed or Typed Name of Bankruptcy Petition Preparer   Social Security No.
                                                              (Required by 11 U.S.C. § 110(c).)

239 W. 72nd St.
New York, NY 10023 _____
Address

Names and Social Security numbers of all other individuals who prepared or assisted in preparing this document:

If more than one person prepared this document, attach additional signed sheets conforming to the appropriate Official Form for each person.

X _____   _____
Signature of Bankruptcy Petition Preparer   Date

A bankruptcy petition preparer's failure to comply with the provisions of title 11 and the Federal Rules of Bankruptcy Procedure may result in fines or imprisonment or both. 18 U.S.C. § 156.

Tips to Completing Your Statement of Financial Affairs

1. *Income from employment/business:* Your wages, salary, etc. If you and your spouse are filing jointly, you must state your income separately.

2. *Income from other than employment/business:* For example, interest, dividend income, Social Security and benefit payments, rent receipts, and income from the sale of assets. Include loans and cash advances from credit cards.

3a. *Payments to creditors:* List all payments to creditors made within the past 90 days that total more than $600 (that is, a total amount of $601 or more). For example, three separate payments of $300 each to Visa Credit Card made within 90 days of filing add up to $900 and must be listed. Include name and address of creditor, amount of payments, and dates of each payment.

3b. *Payments to insider creditors:* List all payments made to insider creditors within the one year of filing. Insider creditors means your relations and business partners.

4a. *Suits, executions, garnishments, and attachments:* List all lawsuits to which you are a party or were a party within one year of filing. List case name and number (Bank of America vs. Mark Hanson, 00 CH 0987), nature of lawsuit (foreclosure, etc.), Court and location (Circuit Court of Cook County, Richard J. Daley Center, Chicago, IL 60602), and status or disposition (Pending or Judgment entered May –, 20–).

4b. List any property (real or personal) that has been garnished, seized, or attached.

5. *Repossessions, foreclosures, and returns:* List all property that has been taken from you by a creditor within the past one year. For example, a bank that has foreclosed on your home or an automobile financing company that has repossessed your car should be listed.

6a. *Assignments and receiverships:* List any property that has been voluntarily returned or given to any person/entity/creditor within the past 120 days. Include name and address of the person holding the property, date they were given it, and the details of the transaction.

6b. List all property that has been in the hands of a custodian, receiver, or court-appointed official within the past one year. For example, property in the hands of a sheriff or marshal.

7. *Gifts:* List all gifts and charitable donations made within the past one year. You do not need to list usual and ordinary gifts that total less than $200. For example, do not list birthday gifts to a child if the total value of the gifts given during the past year do not exceed $200. But if you gave your child a birthday gift of $150 and a Christmas gift of $100, then you need to list both gifts with the details. List donations to churches, especially tithing.

8. *Losses:* List all losses from fire, theft, or other casualty—or gambling—within the past year. Describe the property, the value, and the circumstance surrounding the loss; include the date and the insurance, if any.

9. *Payments related to debt counseling or bankruptcy within past year:* List all payments made to an attorney or other person regarding filing for bankruptcy. List property transferred to any person in connection with debt consolidation. Example: We The People assists in preparing bankruptcy petitions.

10. *Other transfers:* List all property transferred outright or as security with the past year. For example, security deposits to landlords or utility companies. Include the identity of the person receiving the item, their relationship to you, date of transfer, description of the property, and value received by you for the transfer.

11. *Closed financial accounts:* List all checking, savings, CDs, credit union, brokerage accounts, and other financial accounts that have been closed, transferred, or sold within the past year. For example, you must list a checking account that you closed 11 months ago.

12. *Safe deposit boxes:* List all safe deposit boxes in which you have had any valuables within the past year. Include name and address of bank, identification of those having access to box, contents of box, and date of surrender of box.

13. *Setoffs within the past 90 days:* This is where a creditor takes an asset of yours and applies it to money that you owe the creditor. For example, a bank takes money that is in your checking account and applies it to money that you owe the bank. List name and address of creditor, date of setoff, and amount of setoff.

14. *Property held for another person:* List all property that is owned by someone else but is in your possession or control. Example: You are storing furniture belonging to a family friend in your home.

15. *Prior address of debtor:* List all previous addresses used by you within the past two years. If you are filing jointly with your spouse, you must also list any separate address that your spouse has. Because the court is asking for prior addresses, do not include your current address.

16. *Spouses and former spouses:* Give the name of your spouse or former spouse who lives or lived with you if you live in a community property state (Alaska, Arizona, California, Idaho, Louisiana, Nevada, New Mexico, Puerto Rico, Texas, Washington, or Wisconsin).

17. *Environmental information:* List any notices you may have received from a government unit indicating that you may be liable for a violation of environmental laws arising out of a business you operated.

17b. *Site address:* List the address of each site that received a notice from a government unit indicating that you may be liable for a violation of environmental laws arising out of a business you operated.

17c. *List proceedings:* List all judicial or administrative proceedings, including settlements, arising from any environmental law case. List case name and number (Environmental Protection Agency vs. Mark Hanson, 00 CH 0987), nature of lawsuit, court and location, and status or disposition (Pending or Judgment entered May —, 20—).

18. *Nature, location, and name of business:* Nature, location, and name of business owned within past six years. List ownership interest, names, and addresses of business. Examples: self-employment in your company, stock owned in a closely-held company, or a partnership. Complete items 19–25 only if you owned a business (or percent of a business) or were an officer, director, partner, or manager of a business.

19a. *Books, records, and financial statements:* List all bookkeepers and accountants used in the business for the past six years.

19b. *Audits:* List all firms or individuals who have audited books and records within the past two years.

19c. *Firms or individuals in possession of books or records:* List all firms or individuals who were in possession of books and records.

19d. *Parties to whom a financial statement was issued:* List all financial institutions and other parties to whom a financial statement was issued within the past two years.

20a. *Inventories:* List the dates of the last two inventories taken of your property, name of the person supervising the taking of the inventory, the dollar amount, and basis of the inventory.

20b. List the name and address of the person who has possession of these inventories.

21a. *Current partners, officers, directors, and shareholders:* For partnerships, list nature and percentage of partnership owned by each member of the partnership.

21b. For corporations, list all officers, directors, and shareholder who own more than five percent of the corporate stock.

22. *Former partners, officers, directors, and shareholders:* a) For partnerships, list each member who withdrew from the partnership within the past year. b) For corporations, list each officer or director who resigned or was fired within the past year.

23. *Withdrawals from a partnership or distributions by a corporation:* List all payments, withdrawals, compensation, and distributions (bonuses, loans, etc.) given to an insider within the past year.

24. *Taxpayer identification number:* List the name and federal taxpayer identification number of the parent corporation of any consolidated group of which you were a member any time within the six-year period immediately preceding the commencement of the case.

25. *Pension Funds:* If the debtor is not filing as an individual (generally filing other than a Chapter 7 or 13), list the name and federal taxpayer identification number of any pension fund you were responsible for contributing to at any time within the six-year period immediately preceding the commencement of the case.

is why transferring your interest in any large property, such as a home, to others, such as your children, is not a good idea if you plan to file for bankruptcy.

As always, be truthful and meticulous in this form. Don't leave any transactions out in hopes that your trustee doesn't find out about them. Refer to the sample Form 7: Statement of Financial Affairs for guidance. Don't forget to add dates and signature(s) to the last page, as well as any petition preparer you use. If you've completed your forms alone, type "N/A."

Form 8: Chapter 7 Individual Statement of Intention

Your secured assets take center stage on your Statement of Intention. This is where you must indicate what you plan to do with your secured assets. Your creditors can repossess any secured property, regardless of the exemptions, so use this form as your platform for negotiating with your creditors (and trustee) over how you plan to deal with your secured assets.

Under Property to Be Surrendered, list all secured assets you intend to release to your trustee so he or she can pay back the creditor and then use any extra proceeds to pay other creditors. Under Property to Be Retained, list all secured assets you intend to keep and give details about how you will keep it. This is where you must indicate whether the asset is

Official Form 8
(12/03)

United States Bankruptcy Court
Southern District of New York

In re   **John Smith**   Case No. _____

                     Debtor(s)   Chapter   **7** _____

CHAPTER 7 INDIVIDUAL DEBTOR'S STATEMENT OF INTENTION

1. I have filed a schedule of assets and liabilities which includes consumer debts secured by property of the estate.

2. I intend to do the following with respect to the property of the estate which secures those consumer debts:

     a. Property to Be Surrendered.

Description of Property	**Creditor's name**
-NONE-	

     b. Property to Be Retained   *[Check any applicable statement.]*

	Description of Property	Creditor's Name	Property is claimed as exempt	Property will be redeemed pursuant to 11 U.S.C. § 722	Debt will be reaffirmed pursuant to 11 U.S.C. § 524(c)
1.	**Home** **2500 Magnolia Street** **Queens, NY 10137**	**Crown Mortgage**			**X**
2.	**2004 Ford Explorer**	**Ford Motor Credit**			**X**

Date _____   Signature _____

                                        John Smith

                                        Debtor

CERTIFICATION AND SIGNATURE OF NON-ATTORNEY BANKRUPTCY PETITION PREPARER (See 11 U.S.C. § 110)

I certify that I am a bankruptcy petition preparer as defined in 11 U.S.C. § 110, that I prepared this document for compensation, and that I have provided the debtor with a copy of this document.

Jennifer West-We The People   **123-45-6789**

Printed or Typed Name of Bankruptcy Petition Preparer   Social Security No.

                                                  (Required by 11 U.S.C. § 110(c).)

239 W. 72nd St.

New York, NY 10023

Address

Names and Social Security numbers of all other individuals who prepared or assisted in preparing this document:

If more than one person prepared this document, attach additional signed sheets conforming to the appropriate Official Form for each person.

X _____   _____

Signature of Bankruptcy Petition Preparer   Date

A bankruptcy petition preparer's failure to comply with the provisions of title 11 and the Federal Rules of Bankruptcy Procedure may result in fines or imprisonment or both. 11 U.S.C. § 110; 18 U.S.C. § 156.

Key Words to What You Intend to Do . . .

Reaffirm. Agree to keep the debt and continue to make payments on it. Example: You reaffirm you car loan to keep your car.

Redeem. Agree to buy the debt at fair market value. Example: You buy your car at current market value. If your car is worth less than what you still owe on it, redeeming it allows you to keep it and pay it off for less than what you would have paid if you had reaffirmed the debt.

Surrender. Agree to give up the debt and let the trustee do what he or she wants with the asset (the collateral you've used to secure the debt). Example: You let your trustee take your car, sell it, and distribute the proceeds to creditors after the car lender is paid off. If you owe more on your car than your car is currently worth, let the trustee take it. You can purchase a cheaper vehicle.

Exempt. Void nonpurchase money security interests. This makes the debt unsecured. Example: You get a loan by putting your home or car up as collateral. The lender has a security interest in your asset. We will explain how this works in chapter 5; it is a powerful tool to use when creditors have liens on assets that you already own. But voiding or reducing these liens requires more complex paperwork than your original petition. You can also refer to chapter 9's definition of liens for more information.

claimed as exempt, is being redeemed, or is being reaffirmed. Mark an "X" under the corresponding column.

Some districts allow you to retain a secured asset without formally reaffirming or redeeming, in which case you type "I intend to retain the property by keeping current on payments with creditor" beside the creditor's name. This assumes, of course, that you are current on your payments and that you have negotiated with the creditor. You won't need to check anything under the Exempt, Redeem, or Reaffirm columns. Many courts, however, will require you to officially either reaffirm, redeem, or surrender. Because of the pros and cons related to making this decision (in jurisdictions where you can), you may want to consult with an experienced bankruptcy attorney about electing this method. You do not want to end up with a burdensome debt that costs you more money in the end than other options available to you, such as redeeming the asset for its current market value.

Don't forget to date and sign this form, adding any signatures you need from a bankruptcy petition preparer. If you've filed without help, don't forget to put "N/A" in any blank sections that do not pertain to you.

Local Requirements

Whew! You're almost done with the hardest part to your paperwork. While we've given you step-by-step instructions for the bulk of the official forms, you will have to obtain any local forms from your court, fill them out, and add them to your set of papers. Also required by

CITIBANK
P.O. BOX 6000
THE LAKES, NV 89163

CITIBANK
P.O. BOX 6001
SIOUX FALLS, SD 57188

COLORADO CAPITAL, INVES.
305 NE LOOP STE. 820
HURST, TX 76053

CROWN MORTGAGE
1775 HALSTON STREET
NEW YORK, NY 10245

FORD MOTOR CREDIT
P.O. BOX 542000
OMAHA, NE 68154

HOUSEHOLD BANK
P.O. BOX 4155
CAROL STREAM, IL 60197

INTERNAL REVENUE SERVICE
P.O. BOX 8610
PHILADELPHIA, PA 19101

IRS
P.O. BOX 8610
PHILADELPHIA, PA 19101

PROVIDIAN
P.O. BOX 9180
PLEASANTON, CA 94566

SEARS
P.O. BOX 182149
COLUMBUS, OH 43218

SHERMAN ACQUISITION
P.O. BOX 740281
HOUSTON, TX 77274

United States Bankruptcy Court
Southern District of New York

In re   **John Smith**   Case No. _____

Debtor(s)   Chapter   **7** _____

DISCLOSURE OF COMPENSATION OF ATTORNEY FOR DEBTOR(S)

1.   Pursuant to 11 U.S.C. § 329(a) and Bankruptcy Rule 2016(b), I certify that I am the attorney for the above-named debtor and that compensation paid to me within one year before the filing of the petition in bankruptcy, or agreed to be paid to me, for services rendered or to be rendered on behalf of the debtor(s) in contemplation of or in connection with the bankruptcy case is as follows:

     For legal services, I have agreed to accept... $ _____   **0.00**

     Prior to the filing of this statement I have received... $ _____   **0.00**

     Balance Due.. $ _____   **0.00**

2.   The source of the compensation paid to me was:

     ■ Debtor   ☐ Other (specify):

3.   The source of compensation to be paid to me is:

     ■ Debtor   ☐ Other (specify):

4.   ■ I have not agreed to share the above-disclosed compensation with any other person unless they are members and associates of my law firm.

     ☐ I have agreed to share the above-disclosed compensation with a person or persons who are not members or associates of my law firm. A copy of the agreement, together with a list of the names of the people sharing in the compensation is attached.

5.   In return for the above-disclosed fee, I have agreed to render legal service for all aspects of the bankruptcy case, including:
     a.   Analysis of the debtor's financial situation, and rendering advice to the debtor in determining whether to file a petition in bankruptcy;
     b.   Preparation and filing of any petition, schedules, statement of affairs and plan which may be required;
     c.   Representation of the debtor at the meeting of creditors and confirmation hearing, and any adjourned hearings thereof;
     d.   [Other provisions as needed]
         Negotiations with secured creditors to reduce to market value; exemption planning; preparation and filing of reaffirmation agreements and applications as needed; preparation and filing of motions pursuant to 11 USC 522(f)(2)(A) for avoidance of liens on household goods.

6.   By agreement with the debtor(s), the above-disclosed fee does not include the following service:
     Representation of the debtors in any dischargeability actions, judicial lien avoidances, relief from stay actions or any other adversary proceeding.

CERTIFICATION

     I certify that the foregoing is a complete statement of any agreement or arrangement for payment to me for representation of the debtor(s) in this bankruptcy proceeding.

Dated: _____   _____

United States Bankruptcy Court
Southern District of New York

In re   **John Smith** _____   Case No. _____

                                        Debtor(s)   Chapter   **7** _____

VERIFICATION OF CREDITOR MATRIX

The above-named Debtor hereby verifies that the attached list of creditors is true and correct to the best of his/her knowledge.

Date: _____   _____

                                             John Smith
                                             Signature of Debtor

Mailing Matrix

Don't let the word "matrix" confuse you; think "list." You must submit a list of your creditors—names and addresses—to your court so it can send out notices to your creditors and inform them of your bankruptcy.

every bankruptcy court is a mailing matrix, which is a list of all your creditors.

To finish our look at a sample bankruptcy petition, we've added John Smith's mailing matrix and two local forms that he had to submit (a matrix Verification and a Disclosure of Compensation). If you have any assistance in typing your forms or hire an attorney, your local court may have specific forms to fill out to list these people and their contact information. Ask your local court exactly how best to supply your matrix (some ask that you supply your list on a computer disk, for example). You can also contact a We The People office for this information in your area, if we have a store nearby. We will also be able to help you locate and understand your local forms—right down to how you should submit your paperwork to the court.

Conclusion

By now, you are done with the forms! Now that your forms are complete, you are ready to submit your entire petition to the court, and you are at the point where the bankruptcy court can take charge of your case and administer the legal end of the process.

We'll take you through the logistics of the bankruptcy courts in the next chapter and describe what you can expect when you file your papers and await the court's response. Do not attempt to get rid of any assets while you wait for the court to deal with your case. The process is straightforward and follows a definite path so you can prepare for all that's about to happen. Having said that, don't file your papers and then leave town or take a vacation. You need to be available and ready to deal with your filing and respond to any of the court's requests for information or your presence. Filing a bankruptcy petition puts a series of events in motion that includes your participation. Should you decide *Oops, I really don't want to file for bankruptcy* after you've already submitted your papers, you have a way out that we'll discuss in the next chapter.

For now, pat yourself on the back and keep your head up!

CHAPTER 5

How Chapter 7 Works

Bankruptcy procedures follow a defined course the moment you file your papers with your bankruptcy court. Technically, you place your financial affairs under control of the courts, but this is a good thing if creditors hound you and you know you can't run from them any longer. Filing for bankruptcy raises a huge Stop! sign that allows you to breathe and take care of your financial affairs with the guidance of the court. You can go about your daily living and let the court direct your bankruptcy from this point forward.

Bankruptcy courts are unique—they don't work like other courts. If you're picturing the kinds of courts portrayed on television and in the movies, with sharp-looking attorneys, robed judges, frightened witnesses, barrel-chested bailiffs, jury boxes, and austere courtrooms, you're not thinking about bankruptcy courts. For most Chapter 7s, you can handle your entire bankruptcy proceeding and your interaction with the bankruptcy court all by yourself. You probably won't see a judge or a courtroom, and your experience will leave you wondering why the word "court" is even used.

We know what you can expect and what you should be prepared for when it comes to the bankruptcy courts. We share that information here, telling you how your bankruptcy will likely proceed from start to finish in the hands of the courts. When you're going through a bankruptcy, you don't want to encounter an unexpected event or problem for which you don't have any preparation. Over the years we've watched our customers successfully handle the courts and emerge from their bankruptcy feeling good about themselves and the process, and they frequently have a new respect for how the system works. If this is your first time dealing with the courts, you're in luck: Bankruptcy courts are pretty painless, and as we've said throughout this book, if you're an honest and diligent person, you have very little to worry about.

> Once you file for bankruptcy, you don't have to stop living normally while you await the court process. Just don't do anything extravagant or outrageous, such as selling one of your valuable assets and using that money to buy tickets on a Caribbean cruise.

> Federal courts have exclusive jurisdiction over bankruptcy cases. Bankruptcy cases cannot be filed in state court. Each of the 94 federal judicial districts handles bankruptcy matters.

A Review of How Chapter 7 Works

A Chapter 7 case begins with the **filing of petition,** schedules of assets and liabilities, and a statement of financial affairs with the bankruptcy court serving the area where you live. A husband and wife may file one joint petition. Currently, the courts are required to charge a **$209 filing fee** to cover court costs. In most courts (again, check with your specific court's procedures), the fee is paid by either a U.S. Postal Service money order or a bank cashier's check in full upon filing, payable to the U.S. Bankruptcy Court. Courts also accept cash if you have exact change (but don't mail cash!). Personal checks and credit cards are not accepted unless they come from a law firm or attorney. If a joint petition is filed, only one $209 filing fee is charged. Upon the filing of the petition, an impartial **trustee is appointed** by the court to administer the case and liquidate your nonexempt assets. The **automatic stay goes into effect,** which stops your creditors from initiating or continuing any lawsuits, wage garnishments, or even telephone calls demanding payment. A meeting day is set for your meeting of the creditors, and you'll receive an official case number.

In order to complete the official bankruptcy forms (see chapter 4), which must be filed with the court, you will need to compile the following information:

- A list of all creditors including addresses, amounts owed, and account numbers
- A list of all debtor's property
- A detailed list of debtor's monthly income and living expenses

Creditors will receive notice of the filing of the petition from the court, including the day and time of your meeting of the creditors. You (and your spouse if filing jointly) must attend this **meeting of the creditors** (341A in the Bankruptcy Code), which takes places no less than 20 days after you file and no more than 40 days after you file, if you're filing Chapter 7. Creditors may appear and ask questions regarding the debtor's financial affairs and property. Be aware that if you are married and filed individually, your spouse can be responsible for the debts he or she signed for.

Your appointed trustee will direct this meeting and question you on your filed paperwork. It is important for you to cooperate with the trustee and provide any financial records or documents that your trustee requests. In order to preserve their independent judgment, bankruptcy judges are prohibited from attending the creditors' meeting. If the debtor has assets that cannot be exempted (kept), your trustee could take those assets and sell them. The money received at the sale will then be used to pay creditors. If, as is often the case, all of your assets are exempt, there will be no distribution to creditors (this would be called a no-asset bankruptcy). We will discuss how creditors' meetings function and how you should prepare for your meeting in the next chapter.

In all reaffirmations agreements, you must be current on your payment upon filing the agreement with the court. You cannot be three months behind on a car loan, for example, and reaffirm that debt.

Discharge

Approximately 45 to 60 days after your meeting of the creditors, you will receive a **notice of a discharge,** which extinguishes your obligations to pay many debts. Unsecured debts (debts with no asset attached to them) may generally be defined as obligations based purely on future ability to pay, as opposed to secured debts, which are based on the creditor's right to seize pledged property upon default. Creditors whose unsecured

The bankruptcy law regarding the scope of a Chapter 7 discharge is complex. Know your rights. Should you have any doubts about the appropriateness of bankruptcy in your particular case, you should seek the advice of an attorney. Generally speaking, most debts in a Chapter 7 Bankruptcy are discharged. Those exceptions include alimony and support obligations; certain taxes; debts incurred by fraud, embezzlement, larceny, or willful malicious injury; debts arising from driving while intoxicated; and certain educational loans. In the event of fraud (lying) during bankruptcy proceedings, such as the hiding of assets or your failure to obey a lawful order of the court, the discharge can be denied or revoked. Bankruptcy fraud is a felony under federal criminal law and may result in arrest, fine, or imprisonment.

debts are discharged may no longer initiate or continue any legal or other action against you to collect the obligations. Because secured creditors retain some rights that may permit them to seize pledged property, even after a discharge is granted, it is often advantageous for you to reaffirm a debt when property, such as a car, has been pledged to the creditor. A reaffirmation is an agreement between you and the creditor whereby you will pay the money owed even though you filed for bankruptcy. In return, the creditor promises that as long as payments are made, the creditor will not repossess (take back) the car or other property.

In some courts, it may not be necessary to formally sign a reaffirmation agreement if you remain current on your payments. In Colorado, for example, you do not need to use reaffirmation agreements for car loans. Technically, the car loan is discharged in the bankruptcy, but your lender still has a secured interest in the car if you fail to stay current in payments. If you fail to pay, the car will be repossessed.

All written agreements to reaffirm a debt must be filed with the court and, if you are not represented by an attorney, must generally be approved by the judge before you are discharged. (More on this below.)

Filing Your Petition

Submitting your paperwork to the court is easy. Because you've already interacted with the court in some way to acquire any local forms and special instructions, you should already know where you need to go to file your completed petition. You cannot file in any court; you must file in your local federal bankruptcy court in the district where you've been living (for

CHAPTER 7 ORDER OF EVENTS

1. Filing of petition
2. Filing fee paid
3. Trustee appointed by court
4. The automatic stay goes into effect
5. Notice of meeting of creditors to you and your creditors
6. Meeting of creditors takes place
7. Trustee administers your case
8. Discharge and case closed, or dismissal and case closed

> Appendix B contains the list of all bankruptcy courts in the United States. You'll find
> addresses and contact information. You can also find these courts' web sites by going to
> www.uscourts.gov and clicking on "Bankruptcy Courts." Bankruptcies are governed by federal
> laws, so the bankruptcy courts are federal courthouses. The federal court system is divided
> into districts. Some states have only one judicial district; larger states have more. To find your
> court, locate your state and see how many districts are listed within your state. If there is only
> one, then that court is your bankruptcy court. If there are more than one, call the court that's
> closest to you geographically and ask which district pertains to you. Generally, if you pick the
> court in the nearest city, that will be your court.

the most part) for the previous 180 days (six months). If you own a business and are declaring your business as bankrupt, you can file where your principle place of business has been located during the previous 180 days or where the business's main assets have been located during that time. If you live in a rural or remote area, chances are the nearest sizeable city will be your district for court-filing.

How Many Copies to Make

Unless your court only asks for one original copy because it can create digital copies now, you need several copies of your completed petition—and it never hurts to make more than is required for your own safe-keeping. Although you will ask your court how many copies it requires you to provide, which is typically four (4) plus your original, it's helpful to have other sets for other purposes, including:

- one set for the court clerk to give or send back to you with an official stamp on it
- one set for you to keep in case a set gets lost, such as in the mail

No matter what the minimal number of copies your court suggests you make of your petition, always have a clean and complete petition on hand if and when you need to make more copies of any or all parts of your petition. For example, the court may ask you to send copies of a particular form, such as your Statement of Intention, to your trustee and listed secured creditors. If you've never been overly cautious about paperwork in the past, now is the time to be supercautious.

The following is a checklist for you to do before you actually file:

- ☑ Double-check your paperwork, making sure you (and your spouse, if filing jointly) have signed, dated, and marked each and every form where required.
- ☑ Look for blank spaces; be sure you've at least marked "N/A" or "none" in any places that do not pertain to you.
- ☑ Check to ensure you've made an adequate number of copies; consider making more copies than are required for your own safe-keeping.
- ☑ Check the order of your papers.
- ☑ Check the presentation of your papers; if your court prefers you to two-hole punch your set of papers from the top, do so. If it has specific instructions for paying the filing fee and attaching it to your set of papers, follow those instructions.

Common to some bankruptcy courts is the two-hole punch plus bluebacks assembly of your paperwork. Bluebacks are long blue sheets of paper also known as manuscript covers. You can find these papers in stationery or office supply stores. You will two-hole punch your bankruptcy paperwork by setting your hole-puncher at 8½″ for your petition and at 9″ for the bluebacks you use. Your original petition is clipped; your copies are stapled. But again, check with your local court's guidelines before assembling your paperwork for official filing. Bluebacks are not required in many courts. Your particular court's preferences may vary slightly.

☑ Follow all of your local court's rules for making life easy for your bankruptcy court clerk!

Filing your paperwork is as easy as dropping your documents in the mail or visiting the courthouse. To avoid the chance of your petition getting lost in the mail or arriving in a battered and messy envelope, physically going to the court is best. You will not have to do anything more than park your car, enter the building, and locate the clerk's office for handing it over. The clerk may look at your documents briefly to ensure everything is in order. You can correct minor mistakes that are brought to your attention. The clerk may give you (or mail you) a so-called deficiency notice that indicates areas where you're missing items, such as a form or schedule. Respond to deficiency notices in a timely manner by submitting the missing part with a cover letter that clearly states you are responding to the deficiency notice and that the requested materials are enclosed. Deficiency notices are easier to respond to than requests to make formal amendments to your paperwork, so don't ignore them. Be sure to promptly complete your paperwork at the court's request and within the court's specified time frame, which is usually 15 days. If you do opt to mail in your documents, use an envelope large enough to accommodate your documents perfectly (usually a 9-inch × 12-inch envelope is perfect). Include a self-addressed stamped envelope with enough postage for the court to mail back a stamped copy of your entire petition. If you want to mail your paperwork by certified mail, return receipt requested, or any other way besides standard first-class mail, ask your local court what kind of mail it can accept. (Most courts will accept certified mail.)

A sequence of events automatically occurs once you file your petition, the first of which is the automatic stay.

The Automatic Stay Says Stop!

The automatic stay is the magic wand of bankruptcy. The moment you file your bankruptcy petition at the clerk's office (or it gets received by the clerk's office), the law imposes an automatic stay that takes effect immediately. It's officially called the Order for Relief. The automatic stay prohibits all creditors—including collections agencies and government agencies—from any attempts to collect from you or take any action against you or your property. This includes starting or continuing any legal actions (lawsuits) against you. Creditors must be advised that the automatic stay is in effect, so even though the court will send out a notice about your bankruptcy to your creditors (using the mailing matrix you've provided), you may have to notify some creditors the day you file in order to stop any immediate actions against you. The court needs time, up to two weeks, to get its official notices out to your creditors. Making sure the court has every address to every creditor in your paperwork is essential; otherwise, a creditor will be left out and the associated debt with that creditor may not become discharged. The court will not double-check your mailing matrix or ensure you've included every creditor. You are responsible for taking care of the mailing list for the court to use. Your creditors will receive an official notice from the bankruptcy court of the following:

- Your case number
- Your date of filing
- The existence of the automatic stay
- The name of the trustee assigned to your case
- The date set for the meeting of creditors
- The deadline (if any) for filing objections to the discharge of your debts or any specific debt
- Where a creditor can file claims

Notices from different bankruptcy courts will vary, and they will also vary depending on what Chapter you're filing. For Chapter 7 filings, creditors generally have 60 days from the creditors' meeting to file formal objections to the discharge of your debts or a particular debt.

Notifying Your Creditors

If you are in dire need of stopping particular creditors from pursuing you once you file your petition, you need to notify those creditors immediately and inform them of your bankruptcy proceeding and case number. The bankruptcy court will notify your creditors, but it may take up to two weeks for the paperwork to be processed and for those notices to arrive in your creditors' mailboxes. You have a right to notify your creditors as soon as you file. This puts a temporary end to creditors calling, harassing, garnishing your wages, repossessing your car, foreclosing your home, cutting off your utilities, and so on. The automatic stay is a powerful tool in bankruptcy, and although a creditor can later get the automatic stay lifted to collect a debt, the creditor will have to follow the court's instructions and process, which entails filing certain documents, going to court, and getting the judge's permission.

If there is a lawsuit pending against you, you will have to send a Plea of Stay in Bankruptcy to the court clerk to notify them of your bankruptcy filing.

Call or write to the creditors you wish to silence as soon as possible. If you do call, follow it up with a letter that provides the following information (which should also be included in any phone call): your case number, your date of filing, the court name, and a reminder of the automatic stay and its protections. A sample of such a letter is provided here. (See Figure 5.1.)

The Automatic Stay and the Place Where You Live. If you are late or unable to pay your mortgage or rent, which is quickly leading to a home foreclosure or an eviction from your rented unit, the automatic stay will buy you time and prevent these actions from happening—temporarily.

The Automatic Stay and Your Wages. If a creditor has garnished your wages, the automatic stay stops this from continuing. However, if the wage garnishment is in relation to paying

John Doe
3356 Boathouse Way
Key West, FL 33040

March 10, 20XX

Acme Builder's Emporium, Inc.
4153 Latigo Bay Drive
Miami, FL 33130

Dear Acme Builder's Emporium:

Please be advised that I have filed for personal bankruptcy under Chapter 7 of the U.S. Bankruptcy Code as of March 9, 20XX. My case number is 77-3411-88 and I have filed in the Southern District of Florida, Miami Division. Under the Bankruptcy Code, you may not do any of the following:

- Pursue me in any way—legally or not—as a means to collect any debt
- Enforce a lien on any of my property
- Repossess any of my property
- Garnish any of my wages or
- Discontinue any services or benefits that I currently have

Any failure to comply to this Order of Relief (or automatic stay) can result in court-enforced penalties. Thanks.

Sincerely,

John Doe

Figure 5.1

Automatic Stay Will Not Stop . . .

- Criminal cases from proceeding against you
- Cases against you for child support, alimony, or paternity tests
- The IRS from pursuing your default on taxes (but the IRS cannot record a lien against your property)
- Any creditors that successfully file motions to have the judge lift the stay and continue their attempts to collect from you
- Actions against your codebtors
- Acts under any government regulatory powers
- Acts taken to perfect interests in property
- Setoff of certain debts relating to certain contracts, such as commodity securities
- Acts by lessor (a person leasing property) of nonresidential real property to obtain possession of the property
- Presentation of a negotiable instrument (example: a check), sending notice, and protesting the instrument's dishonor

child support, you will still need to keep those payments current. Child support and alimony cannot be affected by a bankruptcy.

If you need to file quickly because you need the automatic stay to take effect as soon as possible, you can file a minimal set of papers (typically, your two-page Voluntary Petition and Mailing Matrix) that your local bankruptcy court requires and then file the rest of the paperwork to make your petition complete within the next 15 days. Emergency filing is helpful for people who face foreclosures, evictions, or the loss of necessary living needs, such as your heat, your driver's license, or even your job. Some courts will allow you to submit your Matrix a few days after your Petition, but the most important part of emergency filing is completing your entire bankruptcy petition (all the paperwork) within 15 days of your initial filing. If you fail to do so, you risk your case being dismissed.

Home Ownership and Bankruptcy

If you are behind on your mortgage payments, the chance of losing your home is greater if you file a Chapter 7 bankruptcy. Your mortgage lender will ask the bankruptcy court to lift the automatic stay to begin or resume foreclosure proceedings. You can, however, successfully negotiate with your lender to catch-up on your payments, and even arrange to change payments terms, to keep your home. In a Chapter 13 bankruptcy, you will not lose your house if you immediately resume making the regular payments called for under your agreement and repay your missed mortgage payments through your plan.

If you are current on your mortgage payments, you will not lose your house if you file for Chapter 13 bankruptcy, as long as you continue to make your mortgage payments. In Chapter 7 bankruptcy, whether or not you will lose your house depends on the amount of equity you have in the property and the amount of any homestead exemption (which varies state-to-state) to which you are entitled.

> ### ERIC'S STORY
>
> **I was down to nothing** when I filed for Chapter 7. I should have filed sooner because dealing with the creditors to the point they were on their way to seize my car, my furniture, and even foreclose my home wasn't fun. I don't know why I waited so long; I suppose the shame and humiliation I felt about my financial situation kept me from thinking clearly and doing what I needed to do.
>
> I didn't know anything about the automatic stay before filing, but it made a huge difference in my life. All I had to say when creditors called was that I had officially filed and they would be receiving their notice from the court shortly. I gave them my case number and told them that they couldn't continue to keep contacting me in any way.
>
> Once I was freed from the burden of answering creditors' harassing phone calls and their threats of lawsuits, my mind had room to think long and hard about my financial life and how I would use the bankruptcy to get rid of my mistakes and prepare me for a new life. I worked with the exemptions and dealt with my secured property smartly. The way bankruptcy works, you can keep most of your assets or find ways of using the laws to protect the ones you fear losing. I was surprised by the protections provided by the law. I didn't lose my home or my car and am working my way back to the financial living!

Renting and Bankruptcy

If you are current on your rent payments and file for bankruptcy, it's unlikely your landlord would ever find out. But if you are behind on your rent, there's a good chance that your landlord will begin eviction proceedings to get you out. Your inclination may be to file for bankruptcy just to get the automatic stay in place to stop the eviction. This will work, but not for very long. Expect your landlord to come into court to have the stay lifted, which is likely to be granted.

As you move through your bankruptcy proceeding and reconfigure your financial life, you will have to decide if where you live is too expensive and if you should consider moving to a place with lower rent. (Once you file, you may have more money available to catch up on back rent.)

Changing or Correcting Your Petition

You can change any of your paperwork while your case is in the hands of the court and before you receive your official discharge. This includes corrections, additions, and deletions. Bankruptcy courts have different rules for making changes, and some will charge you a nominal fee for any kind of change. If you need to amend your paperwork before your meeting of the creditors is held, the court may want to resend a new notice to your creditors (especially if you amend any

Copies to the Court

In Chapters 7 and 13, you typically must file an original plus four (4) copies. In Chapters 11 and 12, you must file an original plus six (6) copies.

paperwork that reflects them). If you add new creditors to your paperwork, you may have to send those newly added creditors notice of your meeting and notice that you've amended your paperwork to include them.

If you feel you need to change any of your papers once you file initially, ask your court's clerk how to make those changes and how it can affect your case. One minor change may require you to amend several papers, so be sure to find out exactly what forms you'll have to change given your specific court's rules.

Adding or Deleting Property on Schedule A or B. If you forgot to include some assets on either of these two forms, you'll need to make the proper changes to your papers. Also, if you've received any of the following assets after you've filed—or become entitled to receive such assets—you must report them to the court within 180 days of your initial filing:

- Assets you inherit or become entitled to inherit
- Assets you receive as a result of a divorce
- Any death benefits or life insurance proceeds

Adding or Deleting Exempt Property on Schedule C. Adding or deleting assets from your exemption list unfortunately requires you to file a new Schedule C. And you will have to make other amendments to other papers as well.

Changing Your Intentions for Secured Property. If you change your mind about how you want to deal with a secured asset, you'll have to file an amended Form 8. Ask your local court how best to do this.

Filing an Amendment. Following your local court's rules and policies for making amendments is the only way to ensure that your changes become accepted and that delays in your bankruptcy proceeding are minimized. You can ask a We The People office near you, or you can seek this information from your court clerk or a local bankruptcy attorney. You'll want to be sure you complete all the necessary papers, including any special cover letters required by your court, and to submit the proper number of copies.

Courts customarily request that you send amendments with the following enclosed:

1. Amendment Cover
2. Proof of Mailing with a list attached of recipients who have been formally notified of your amendment, which must include your trustee
3. Amendment Papers, such as new forms or schedules

You local court may have its own form that has the Cover Sheet on one side and the Proof of Mailing on the other side, which is how the Southern District of New York deals with amendments (see sample).

Send notices and copies of your amendment to your trustee and anyone else affiliated with the amendment. For example, if you are adding a codebtor to Schedule H, you will send your amendment to your trustee and to your newly listed codebtor. If you are adding a creditor to Schedule F, you will send your amendment to your trustee and to your newly listed creditor. Other tips include the following:

UNITED STATES BANKRUPTCY COURT
Southern District of New York

Filer's Name: _____ Atty Name (if applicable): _____

Street Address: _____ CA Bar No. (if applicable): _____

_____ Atty Fax No. (if applicable): _____

Filer's Telephone No.: _____

In re:

Case No

Chapter 7 _____ 11 _____ 13 _____

AMENDED SCHEDULE(S)

A filing fee of $26.00 is required to amend any or all of Schedules "D" through "F." An addendum mailing list is also required as an attachment if creditors are being added to the creditors list. Is/are creditor(s) being added?   Yes _____   No _____

Indicate below which schedule(s) is(are) being amended.

A _____ B _____ C _____ D _____ E _____ F _____ G _____ H _____ I _____ J _____

Statement of Financial Affairs _____   Statement of Intention _____   Other __

NOTE: IT IS THE RESPONSIBILITY OF THE DEBTOR TO MAIL COPIES OF ALL AMENDMENTS TO THE TRUSTEE AND TO NOTICE ALL CREDITORS LISTED IN THE AMENDED SCHEDULE(S) AND TO COMPLETE AND FILE WITH THE COURT THE PROOF OF SERVICE ON THE BACK OF THIS PAGE.

I, XXXXXXXXXXX, the person(s) who subscribed to the foregoing Amended Schedule(s) do hereby declare under penalty of perjury that the foregoing is true and correct.

FOR COURT USE ONLY

DATED: _____

_____

_____

SEE REVERSE SIDE

B-1008 *Revised 2/99*

Figure 5.2a

PROOF OF SERVICE

I hereby certify that a copy of the Amendment(s) was(were) mailed to the Trustee and that notice was given to the additional creditors listed.

DATED: _____   _____

_____

(SEE ATTACHED MAILING LIST.)

B-1008 *Revised 2/99*

Figure 5.2b

Don't be afraid to change your paperwork. Although you've signed your papers under penalty of perjury that everything is true and correct in them, you do yourself more harm if you ignore mistakes and/or omissions and fail to amend your documents. If your trustee discovers inaccuracies or omissions in your papers, you will be ordered to make the necessary changes and it will delay your case (you may also have to return for another meeting of the creditors so your trustee can confirm with you the corrected paperwork). Moreover, if your trustee discovers serious problems with your paperwork that you failed to correct (example: the inclusion of a large asset or a preferred creditor), you risk the dismissal of your entire case. The lesson: Be honest and forthright with your paperwork from beginning to end—even if that includes admitting mistakes and fixing them. You will not be penalized for making the proper changes.

- Sign your original set of documents before you hole-punch it all.
- Two-hole punch your amendment package as you did your original set of paperwork: Set the hole-punch at 8½″ for the papers and 9″ for the bluebacks (if your court uses bluebacks).
- Make four copies of your amendment package in addition to your original.

Signing your papers before you hole-punch and make copies allows the court to know exactly which copy is the original. You can amend multiple forms and schedules at the same time and send one entire package together with one Proof of Mailing and one Amendment Cover Sheet. Courts charge additional fees for filing amendments (example: In the Southern District of New York, it costs $26 for any amendment made to any or all of Schedules D through F), so the incentive to get your paperwork accurate when you initially file is huge. Depending on the amendment you make to your paperwork, your trustee may schedule another meeting of the creditors if one has already taken place.

You cannot amend your paperwork once you've been discharged. For problems that occur with your paperwork after your discharge, see chapter 7 in this book.

Changing your address. Use a Change of Address form from your local court. A sample of one is shown here. You should not have to inform anyone else, but again, ask your court. Some may require that you notify your trustee.

If you discover problems with your paperwork once the court discharges you, and you know you need to report such problems to the court (example: you receive a very large inheritance soon after your discharge that you weren't aware of during your bankruptcy), we have solutions for you detailed in chapter 7.

I Changed My Mind! I Don't Want My Bankruptcy to Proceed

There are plenty of reasons why people decide they don't want to declare bankruptcy after all—and after they've officially filed. Some reasons include: striking it rich or receiving a large sum of money; realizing that you're using bankruptcy for the wrong reasons or that your major debts don't qualify as dischargeable; fearing you'll lose an asset that the trustee will

IN THE UNITED STATES BANKRUPTCY COURT
Southern District of New York

In the Matter of :

}
}   Case No.
}
}   Chapter 7
}
Debtor(s)   }

Notice of Change of Address

Debtor's Social Security Number:
My (Our) Former Mailing Address and Telephone Number was:

Name:
Street:

City,State,Zip:

Telephone #:   **(debtor(s) telephone number)**

Please be advised that effective _____, 20_____,
my (our) new mailing address and telephone number is:

Name: **(debtor(s) name(s))**

Street: **(debtor(s) new address)**

City,State,Zip: **(debtor(s) new city,state,zip)**

Telephone #:   **(debtor(s) new telephone number)**

_____

_____
Debtor(s)

Figure 5.3

surely take away; or just not wanting to file for bankruptcy and deciding you would rather resort to other tactics first to try to settle your financial problems.

After you initially file for bankruptcy, you cannot simply ask the court to dismiss your case. You must file a formal request and hope that the court grants it. Some bankruptcy courts aren't kind about dismissing cases once they are filed, so if you experience trouble getting your case dismissed, you'll need to hire an attorney to help you.

If and when you decide you don't want your bankruptcy case to proceed, contact your court clerk (or you can try calling your trustee's office) about the procedure for getting a voluntary dismissal. You will need to inquire about the required paperwork, time frames or limits, and information about the general process.

Reaffirming An Asset (Keeping a Debt That Has an Asset Attached)

A reaffirmation agreement is an agreement between you and a creditor in which you agree to keep a debt (that would otherwise be discharged) so long as you continue to make payments on it. You cannot reaffirm any asset for which your payments are not current. To repeat: You must be current on your payments at the time you reaffirm.

Reaffirmation agreements are voluntary (you decide you want one or more than one), but they are also legal documents, so you become obligated to pay for all or a portion of a certain debt. In other words, both the creditor's lien on the asset and your personal liability survive the bankruptcy as if you never filed. In order for these agreements to be effective and enforceable, they must be filed in your bankruptcy case according to specified rules and procedures. You do not have to reaffirm any debt. However, if you choose not to reaffirm, the secured creditor is then entitled to repossess its collateral and sell it to satisfy the debt. If a debtor and creditor choose to enter into a reaffirmation agreement, it must be done before the discharge is granted.

Courts don't usually like reaffirmation agreements because they go against the purpose of bankruptcy: You keep a debt that bankruptcy is designed to discharge. Among the most common reaffirmation agreements made are those for cars, which would otherwise be repossessed by the creditor or seized and sold by the trustee if they had more value than you can exempt. If you reaffirm your car, you can continue making payments on it—and keep the car. (You cannot use bankruptcy to discharge your debt on the car, avoid reaffirming it, and keep the car!) Again, in some states you do not need to officially reaffirm your car loan if you remain current in your payments. Check your local rules.

When you reaffirm an asset, you and your creditor agree to certain terms in a written, formal agreement and submit it to the court. These agreements and their associated paperwork usually come your way via the creditor. Courts can also provide this paperwork. Once the creditor receives notice of your bankruptcy filing, the creditor will contact you, asking you if you want to reaffirm the secured asset. If you say yes, the creditor will send you the agreement to sign, which outlines the amount you owe and how you intend to pay it. The agreement must contain a clear and conspicuous statement, which advises you that the agreement may be rescinded or cancelled at any time prior to your discharge or within 60 days after the agreement is filed with the court, whichever occurs later.

Your official reaffirmation agreement will be accompanied by an Application of Reaffirmation Agreement and an Order Approving Reaffirmation Agreement. If you are represented by an attorney, the attorney must also file a declaration or affidavit stating the agreement (a) is a fully informed and voluntary agreement by you, and (b) does not impose an undue hardship on you or a dependent of you. The court must approve of this agreement. If you default on any of your payments, the creditor can repossess the asset. The creditor can also demand that you pay the debt in full or get current in your payments if you're behind before agreeing to the reaffirmation. If the asset is not worth as much as you owe—which can be the case when it comes to cars that have devalued over time yet you remain stuck with paying the original sticker price—try negotiating with the creditor. You may be able to strike a deal whereby you reaffirm the debt, pay only the current market value of the item, and keep it.

If you file for bankruptcy without an attorney and reaffirm any debt, you will more than likely have to attend a discharge hearing. A discharge hearing takes place in front of a judge in court: It is brief and allows the judge to remind you of your responsibilities as a debtor to reaffirmed assets and the consequences of reaffirming debt. The judge will explain that you still owe the full debt and that failure to make payments may result in losing the asset. Chapter 7 filers who reaffirm debt generally receive their notice of official discharge within four weeks of this hearing. This may be the only time you ever have to go before a judge, and it's painless because the judge does all the talking while you do all the listening. The judge might, however, ask a few questions to determine whether or not the reaffirmation is a good idea in your situation. If the judge thinks that such an agreement would place too much of a burden on you financially, you may have to reconsider your decision to reaffirm.

Any reaffirmation agreement you sign with a creditor becomes valid only when it gets filed with the court. It is in your best interest to make payments as defined by the agreement after the court officially stamps the agreement and sends you your copy. You can cancel a reaffirmation agreement at any time before your discharge or within 60 days after you file your agreement with the court—whichever occurs later. If you wish to cancel a reaffirmation agreement, you should send a letter to the creditor within that time period. No court order is required. The creditor will then probably repossess that asset (or in the case of a house, enforce a foreclosure).

Four Key Points When Reaffirming

- It is very difficult to reaffirm any debts for which you are behind in payments (some courts don't allow any reaffirmation agreements to happen on debts that are behind in payments; other courts are more flexible).

- Reaffirm debts that are important to your daily living.

- Don't reaffirm any debts that cost you more to repay than what they are currently worth on the market.

- Get to know your local bankruptcy court's policies about reaffirming secured debt. In some districts, you don't have to use reaffirmation agreements to keep a debt, and can simply continue making payments on the debt. This is the case when it comes to car loans in many states. (Also note that questions loom in the courts as to whether continuing payment of a discharged debt constitutes a reaffirmation of the debt.)

If a debt is reaffirmed and the reaffirmation agreement is not terminated within the 60 day period described above, the debt is not discharged and you will remain personally liable to pay that debt.

Your House. No written reaffirmation agreement is necessary if you wish to reaffirm a mortgage on your house. Under 11 USC 524 (c)(b) of the Bankruptcy Code, if you are representing yourself in your bankruptcy (*pro se*), you do not need a judge to approve a reaffirmation of a home mortgage. Many home mortgage companies do not require reaffirmation agreements, because they already have a secured interest in the house and can foreclose with or without a valid contract under the terms of the mortgage if payment is not current.

If the trustee is not selling your house to obtain cash for any equity above your exemptions, and if the secured creditor has no right to foreclose your mortgage or elects to give up that right at this time, you can simply continue to pay your mortgage. In that event, as long as you make payments in a timely manner and comply with all other provisions of your mortgage, the lender cannot foreclose.

All reaffirmation agreements must be made within 45 days of filing your Statement of Intention, the document where you indicated what you planned to do with secured assets.

Redeeming Assets
(Buying Assets at Current Market Value)

As we mentioned in chapter 4, you can keep assets on which a creditor holds a lien by paying for it or giving the creditor what he or she wants to let you keep it. You redeem assets that are exempt or that your trustee has abandoned because the asset wasn't valuable enough for your trustee to sell it. Redeeming assets allows you to pay for their current market value and not have to pay back the entire debt if it exceeds that.

You can keep certain kinds of collateral—tangible, personal property intended primarily for personal, family, or household use—by paying the lienholder the amount of its so-called allowed secured claim, which typically means the lesser of the amount owed or the value of the property. This means you can often get liens released on personal household possessions for less than the underlying debt on those secured possessions. Example: You owe $4,500 on a living room set that is only worth $2,500 now. You can redeem that debt by paying the creditor $2,500 instead of the full $4,500. This payment must be paid within 45 days of your bankruptcy filing.

In most cases, you have to pay for the asset in one lump-sum payment, unless you are able to work a payment plan with the creditor. Agreeing on the value of assets to be redeemed can be problematic and may require the help of the court to intervene and resolve the dispute.

> To review: Some creditors may have liens on certain assets. As a lienholder, a creditor has a special right to sell that asset—called collateral—and use the proceeds to satisfy its claim. The asset thus secures the debt, so the lienholder is said to have a secured claim. Bankruptcy usually leaves a creditor's lien in place, which means the creditor can take back that collateral, sell it, and satisfy its claim.

Like reaffirming assets, redeeming assets requires you to complete an official Redemption Agreement. You and your creditor agree on the value of the asset and sign a document that states what you negotiated.

Surrendering Property

Secured assets that you are willing to let your creditor repossess become surrendered property. You are then freed of that debt. Your Statement of Intention indicates which assets you are surrendering. Those creditors who decide to take back those assets to satisfy their claim will have to make arrangement with you to pick up the goods. Creditors who decide that the assets are not worth repossessing and reselling will leave you alone, and the property is yours to keep. You don't have to worry about getting the assets back to the creditors. They will contact you if they want to retrieve them.

Eliminating Liens
(Exempting Secured Assets)

Previously, we mentioned the possibility of eliminating your liens. If you can totally eliminate a lien through your bankruptcy, this is an excellent way to reduce or eliminate a debt and keep the asset. Also called lien avoidance or exempting secured assets, this is a procedure whereby you ask the bankruptcy court to avoid (get rid of or reduce) liens on your exempt assets that you owned before the liens were attached to the assets. How does this work? Let's say a creditor has a lien on your fancy watch, which can be claimed as exempt for up to $750 in your state, and that you own it outright. The watch is worth $1,200 so you claim it as exempt and ask the court to reduce the lien to $450. If the watch was only worth $500, less than your allowable exemptions, you ask the court to wipe out the entire lien.

The value of the asset and the amount of the exemption determines how much of a lien can be avoided. If the asset is worth less than your exemption or you can exempt it entirely, the court will eliminate the entire lien and you can keep the asset without paying anything. If the asset is worth more than your allowable exemption, the court will reduce the lien to the difference between the exemption limit and the asset's value or the amount of the debt, whichever is less.

To ask the court to avoid or reduce a lien, you must file a motion, which requires some paperwork. Check with your local court to see if it has a form for filing such a motion. You can try to do this yourself or you can seek the help and guidance of an attorney who is experienced in dealing with these forms and motions. (Remember: A motion is your formal request to the court.) On your Statement of Intention, you request your lien avoidance by checking the "Property is claimed as exempt" column and filing this motion.

Rules to Eliminating Liens

Asking the court to avoid or reduce a lien on any of your assets requires the following:

- You owned the asset before the lien became attached to it.
- The asset is claimed as exempt.
- The lien falls into one of the following categories: judicial lien (example: you lost a lawsuit and the amount you owe on the judgment has resulted in a lien against your car) or a nonpossessory nonpurchase-money security interest. This is a lien caused by you borrowing money (a loan) and pledging assets you already own as collateral (such as a family heirloom) as security for the loan.

To eliminate or reduce these types of liens, only the following categories of exempt property can apply: household goods, furnishings, clothing, appliances, books, musical instruments, or jewelry used for personal, family, or household use; health aids prescribed for you or a dependent; animals or crops for your personal, family, or household use up to the first $5,000 of the lien; and implements, professional books, or tools used in a trade up to the first $5,000 of the lien.

Lien avoidance is advantageous to you in your bankruptcy. Use it wherever possible. We repeat: It's best to find an experienced attorney to help you file these motions and ask the court to void or reduce your liens. Should you decide that you don't want the attached asset to the lien, you can still get the court to avoid the lien and then sell the property to get the money that you do need. File motions for lien avoidance on any assets that qualify for this procedure. The procedure may require some paperwork (and a consultation with an attorney), but the pros outweigh the cons.

Meeting of the Creditors

We'll go over all the dynamics involved in your meeting of the creditors in the next chapter (there are no serious dynamics to worry about; for routine Chapter 7 bankruptcies, it's a 90-second event). After this meeting, creditors and trustees have a defined time to raise objections. If the deadline for objecting to your discharge passes without any objections, the court will issue the discharge order.

If you have no assets from which creditors can be paid, your trustee will prepare a report of no distribution and finish the administration of your case. Your case will eventually be closed by the clerk's office once you've been given your discharge.

If you have nonexempt assets from which creditors can be paid, the trustee will collect the assets, sell them, and hold the proceeds for distribution to creditors. In the meantime, the court will set a deadline for filing claims and notify all creditors to file their proofs of claim before the deadline. Your trustee can object to those claims if he or she believes any to be invalid or excessive and, after the creditor is given notice of the objection and an opportunity to be heard, the court rules on the trustee's objection. When the deadline for filing claims has passed and all disputed claims have been resolved, the trustee will distribute the proceeds of your sold assets to creditors. When the assets have been completely administered, the court will close the case.

Handling Objections

You want your bankruptcy to proceed without complications—and most do. But sometimes there's little you can do to prevent objections from either your creditors or your trustee. What you have to do, then, is be ready to handle those objections successfully. You will know if someone has objected to a debt or the automatic stay if the court sends you a notice, which is called a Notice of Motion or a Notice of Objection. You will then have to decide how to proceed and respond.

Objections from Creditors to Lift the Automatic Stay

As we've seen, the automatic stay is a powerful tool in your bankruptcy proceeding. It lasts from the day you first file to the close of your case, and it prevents creditors for pursuing you, so any creditor that feels the automatic stay should not affect its perusal of you will file an objection with the court.

Creditors cannot bring their objections with them to your creditors' meeting, nor can they try to object to your discharge or automatic stay with you personally. They must file their objections formally with the court and await the court's control over the matter.

Creditors who file objections to the automatic stay often do so when they have claims to debts that cannot be affected by your bankruptcy. Example: A car or home lender may ask the court to lift the stay so it can continue repossession or foreclosure proceedings. Likewise, a landlord who wants to evict you for unpaid rent can ask the court to lift the stay and continue eviction proceedings. Once a creditor formally asks the court to lift the stay (called a Motion to Lift Stay), the court schedules a hearing on the motion and sends you a written notice. You'll have a defined period of time to file a written response, and you will be asked to appear in court. If you don't show up (and if you don't respond), the court will rule on the objection anyways. If you do respond, the court will take into consideration any defense you provide either in writing or in person. Responding both in writing and in person increases your chances of fighting the objection. Successful objections from some creditors can lift the stay within a couple of weeks from your filing date; some take longer to resolve and give you more time.

You can expect creditors holding secured claims to file motions to the court for the stay to be lifted. A court will refuse objections if you can prove that keeping the stay protects the asset, which you intend to keep through redeeming it or exempting it, or that by lifting the stay for one creditor, you harm other creditors. This can happen, for example, if a creditor gets the stay lifted to repossess an asset. If the asset is worth more than what you owe on it, your trustee would rather take it to sell and use a portion of those proceeds to pay other creditors.

The automatic stay secures your utility connections for 20 days. After that, they can discontinue service unless you prove your ability to pay. You may have to pre-pay or pay a security deposit if you intend to resume your utility services beyond the 20 days. Otherwise, you risk being left in the dark.

Objections from Creditors or Your Trustee on Your Exemptions

Creditors have 30 days to object to your exemptions following the meeting of the creditors. Trustees also have this time limit, but sometimes they can get away with filing objections successfully after the 30-day limit. The ability of a trustee to file objections after the time limit depends on the particular court and the bankruptcy judge in charge of hearing the objection. Like objecting to the automatic stay, creditors and trustees must formally file their objections with the court. You and your trustee will receive copies of the objection filing.

Reasons for objections include the following:

- You've claimed an exemption that's not covered by law.
- You've undervalued an asset in the hopes of retaining it.
- You've applied your exemptions incorrectly, such as doubling an exemption for you and your spouse where doubling is not permitted.

Trustees are most likely to object to any asset that you've severely undervalued or to which you've misapplied exemptions. Keep in mind that trustees want to take valuable nonexempt property and sell it to raise money for creditors (and themselves). If you severely undervalue assets in the hopes that your trustee avoids noticing them and thus abandons them, your bankruptcy case faces grave complications. Your trustee will think you're trying to defraud him or her, and you'll end up losing more than you intended, possibly your entire bankruptcy case.

Creditors, on the other hand, are most likely to raise objections related to how you incurred the debt to begin with. Because credit card companies are typically the losers in bankruptcy cases, they may try to prove that you incurred credit card debt knowing you were going to file for bankruptcy. To limit the chances of credit card companies proving you're a fraudulent consumer (that is, you fraudulently represented yourself when you acquired the credit because you didn't have the means to pay) and thus a fraudulent bankruptcy filer, you must avoid raising the red flags. We've mentioned some of these red flags already, but they bear repeating: Don't run up credit card debt or take out cash advances shortly before filing for bankruptcy. Don't use your credit cards to pay off other serious debts that cannot be discharged through bankruptcy (example: using your Visa or Mastercard to pay the IRS its dues over the Internet). And don't use the card when it's clear that you cannot afford to pay your debts. Any suspicious activity on your credit cards, which results in more debt shortly before your filing, will result in complications to your case.

You can respond to objections raised by your trustee or creditors in writing and by attending the hearing that the court schedules. If you fear you might lose an asset you cannot bear to lose or that your bankruptcy case hinges on this one objection, you may want to get an attorney to help you defend yourself in court.

Be brave, responsive, and self-assertive in your defense to any objections. Always remember: You have a right to represent yourself in your own bankruptcy case, so don't let objections filed officially and that require real judges to resolve, intimidate you. You may not feel like you've got the advantage over your trustee's objections, but you'll never know unless you take a stand and defend yourself. If you let your trustee and creditors pursue objections and you refuse to respond, you jeopardize your case and may lose assets you had hoped to keep.

> We've said that most Chapter 7 filers don't ever have to go before a judge or defend themselves in a courtroom. If major objections are raised in your case and for which you are requested to attend a hearing, you will have to go to court. At this time, depending on the gravity of the objections and what you stand to lose as a result (including the legitimacy of your entire case), you may want a bankruptcy attorney at your side to help you defend yourself. Objections can be complicated and time sensitive.

Chapter 13 Filers

Chapter 13 bankruptcies are a bit more complex than Chapter 7. Refer to chapter 3 for our overview of Chapter 13 bankruptcy. You must submit a repayment plan to the court that outlines how you will repay your debts. Creditors also have an opportunity to object to the proposed plan, but if no one objects to it, the court will enter an order confirming the plan as filed. Once the plan is confirmed, the trustee will distribute the proceeds of your plan payments to creditors until you complete the plan or the court dismisses or converts the case. When you've met the goals of your plan (that is, finished paying off your debts), the court will issue an order discharging you and your trustee will prepare a final report.

The Bankruptcy Code sets guidelines for debtors who want to convert their cases to other Chapters. For example, you can convert a Chapter 7 case to either a Chapter 11 reorganization case or a case under Chapter 13, as long as you meet the eligibility standards under the Chapter to which you seek to convert and as long as the case has not previously been

> A fee of $645 is charged for converting, on request of the debtor, a case under Chapter 7 to a case under Chapter 11. There is no fee for converting from Chapter 7 to Chapter 13. (You can also convert any Chapter to a Chapter 7 for $15.) You may, upon the suggestion of your trustee, have to convert to Chapter 13 or risk your case getting dismissed. This can happen, for example, if your trustee thinks you make too much money to avoid paying off debt, and especially if your debts are primarily consumer (not business). Your trustee will then raise an objection and ask the court to rule. If you don't agree to converting your Chapter 7 to a Chapter 13 debt adjustment, your Chapter 7 case will be dismissed.

converted to Chapter 7 from either Chapter 11 or Chapter 13. Thus, you cannot convert your case repeatedly back and forth.

Getting Your Discharge

Bankruptcy courts usually issue discharges to a Chapter 7 filer when the expiration date for filing objections to the discharge has been reached. Creditors and trustees have 60 days after the meeting of the creditors to file their objections with the court; they only have 30 days, however, to file objections to your exemptions. If an objection to your discharge is filed on time, the court will enter the discharge if and when it overrules the objection.

In routine Chapter 7 cases with no objections raised, you can expect to receive your discharge approximately 45 to 60 days after the meeting of the creditors. This discharge extinguishes your obligations to pay many debts. Remember: Unsecured debts may generally be defined as obligations based purely on future ability to pay as opposed to secured debts, which are based on the creditors' right to seize pledged property upon default. Creditors whose unsecured debts are discharged may no longer initiate or continue any legal or other action against you to collect the obligations.

You will receive a copy of your discharge order in the mail from the clerk's office. The clerk's office will also send out copies of the discharge to your trustee and all of your creditors.

Denial of Discharge

If you are denied a discharge, your bankruptcy case is effectively dismissed and you are back where you started—with creditors free to come after you again. There are several reasons why the court can deny a debtor a discharge, which are explained in section 727(a) of the Bankruptcy Code. People who are denied a discharge have done something wrong, such as defrauded a creditor, lied on their bankruptcy papers, hidden assets, or disregarded the rules and procedures of bankruptcy. A denial of discharge is not the same as the court determining that a debt is nondischargeable. A nondischargeable debt reflects only one particular debt, and not your entire inventory of debts. If the court determines that a particular debt or debts are nondischargeable, you remain responsible for those debts and must pay them.

Case Dismissed

A dismissed case is one that has ended before you get any discharge. If your case is dismissed, you are back where you started again and the automatic stay is lifted (exposing you to creditors hounding you down and threatening repossession or foreclosure). The court will dismiss any case that involves a debtor who fails to do something required of him or her. Throughout this book we've warned you about acts that will get your case dismissed, such as missing your creditors' meeting, refusing to answer your trustee's questions, or failing to produce records requested by the court and trustee. You can attempt to appeal an order to dismiss your case, but you will have to explain why you failed to do what was required of you. Seeking the help of an attorney in such a situation would be a good idea.

Effects of Discharge

A discharge in bankruptcy has the following effects:

- It voids any judgment that determines your personal liability on a debt.
- It prohibits creditors from taking any action to collect a debt as a personal liability of yours. However, if a debt is secured by a lien on any property of yours (such as a lien on your car or a mortgage on your house), the discharge does not prevent the creditor from exercising its rights under the lien, such as through repossession or foreclosure. Generally speaking, you must pay a secured debt according to its terms to prevent a secured creditor from exercising its right under that lien. Also, while the discharge relieves you of the personal liability on a debt, it does not relieve anyone else who was liable with you on the same debt (such as, for example, someone who has cosigned a loan for you).

Exceptions to Discharge

1. Taxes for which a tax return is due less than three years before the date which your bankruptcy petition is filed, and certain other taxes and customs duties.
2. Certain fines and penalties payable to any governmental units.
3. Any debts not listed in the schedules of creditors that you filed with your bankruptcy petition, unless the creditor had notice or actual knowledge that you filed for bankruptcy at the time you did so.
4. Alimony, maintenance, or support to a spouse, former spouse, or a child in connection with a separation agreement, divorce decree, or other order of a court or record.
5. Educational loans made, insured, or guaranteed by a governmental unit (unless you can prove financial hardship).
6. Debts arising from a judgment against you as a result of your operation of a motor vehicle while legally intoxicated, and any surcharge due as a result of a conviction for driving while intoxicated.
7. Debts that were or could have been scheduled in a prior bankruptcy case in which you waived or were denied a discharge.
8. Debts for willful or reckless failure of bank officers and directors that lead to a bank failure.
9. Debts arising from fraud, false pretenses, or false representations.
10. Debts arising from embezzlement or larceny.
11. Debts arising from willful and malicious injury by you to another person or entity or to their property. (With certain exceptions, debts listed in (9) through (11) are automatically discharged unless the creditor files a complaint within 60 days of the first date set

for your meeting of creditors, requesting a determination that the debt is not dischargeable, and then obtains a judgment that the debt is not dischargeable.)

Dispute

By contrast, if there is a dispute between you and a creditor as to whether a particular debt is excepted from discharge under (1) through (7) of this section, either you or the creditor may file a complaint in court requesting a judgment resolving the dispute. Unlike the debts listed in (9) through (11) above, there is no time limit for requesting a determination as to whether a particular debt is dischargeable under (1) through (7). A case may be reopened for that purpose.

Knowing Exactly What's Discharged

Unfortunately, knowing what has been discharged and has not when you receive your notice of discharge can be confusing. The court will not send you an itemized list of debts you no longer owe. So how do you know? You should already have an idea of the kinds of debts that are dischargeable and those that are not (your final discharge notice will contain such information in general terms). What you can assume: All the debts you listed in your bankruptcy papers are eliminated unless a creditor or trustee has successfully objected to a particular discharge (or it falls into a category of nondischargeable debts listed above).

If a creditor attempts to collect on discharged debts, you will have to write a letter reminding the creditor of your discharge and give the date as well as a copy of your discharge notice. If a creditor persists in attempting to collect a discharged debt from you—despite your letter—you can file a complaint against the creditor in the bankruptcy court. If the judge finds that the creditor has violated your discharge, the creditor can be held in contempt of court, fined, and made to pay.

Although a creditor whose debt has been discharged cannot take any action to collect it from you, you will always have the right (but not any obligation) to voluntarily repay any debt that has been discharged. We'll go into more detail of dealing with cranky creditors in chapter 7.

Property Taxes

Property taxes are not dischargeable unless they became due more than a year before you file for bankruptcy. Even if your personal liability for paying the property tax out of your pocket is discharged, the tax lien on your property is unaffected. From a practical standpoint, this discharge is not a discharge at all, because you will have to pay off the lien before you can transfer clear title to the property.

Other Taxes

Other types of taxes that are not dischargeable are business related taxes such as FICA or 941 taxes, excise taxes, and customer duties. As a general rule, Federal, State, and Local taxes are not dischargeable. There are some exceptions, such as tax debt more than three years old where no lien had been filed prior to filing bankruptcy. However, the taxing authority can probably be able to enforce any tax lien that has been placed on your property.

Child Support and Alimony

Alimony (also called spousal support or maintenance) and child support obligations are not dischargeable.

Businesses Gone Bust

Small businesses are a driving force in the American economy; they are the engine for economic growth and play a significant role in people's lives. More small businesses have been started by a larger variety of people during the 1990s and 2000s than in the 50 years prior. In 2003, there were approximately 23.7 million businesses in the United States; small firms with less than 500 employees represent 99.7 percent of these 23.7 million businesses. Part of the American Dream involves starting a small business and having the freedom and flexibility of being one's own boss. The millions who run small business do so for the benefit of others as well.

But small businesses come with a high risk of failure—one-third in the first two years and 50 percent in the first five years. In 2003, estimates for businesses with employees indicate there were 572,900 new firms and 584,800 closures (both about 10 percent of the total). About 35,037 declared bankruptcy. This isn't necessarily a bad thing, as it is a reality of today's business climate and economy. Many entrepreneurs who go bust simply take the time to reorganize their financial lives and brainstorm their next big venture.

You've read stories in the newspaper about big companies, such as the airlines, that file for Chapter 11 bankruptcy and attempt to reorganize their debts while maintaining business as usual. This can be too much of a challenge for small businesses, however, as most find the best way out is to terminate the business entirely. With small businesses that don't intend to continue onward, a Chapter 7 bankruptcy is useful for liquidating the business. If you're a sole-proprietor, incorporated, or have formed a limited liability company (LLC), you can file your company through a Chapter 7 bankruptcy and be discharged of most of your business debts. However, you will have to choose between filing personally and/or filing your business. If you (or you and your spouse) are the sole-proprietors of a business and you file a personal bankruptcy, your business's assets will be pulled into your personal bankruptcy. And those assets will be nonexempt because businesses cannot claim exemptions. Business bankruptcies work a little differently from personal bankruptcies. It can be hard to escape filing personally when a business is involved. Many entrepreneurs start their small business with personal loans and have intertwined their business and personal life to the point that it's a challenge to distinguish the two. If, however, you are part of a partnership, the agreement you've made with your partner(s) will dictate how the company deals with your bankruptcy.

Form 7, your Statement of Financial Affairs, is where you need to be specific about your business's assets and answer specific questions related to your business, if in fact, you are filing a business bankruptcy. Questions 19 through 25 on this form provide your trustee with information about your books, records, financial statements, inventory, partners, pension funds, and so on. If you are a business debtor, you must pay

What's a Business Debtor?

You are a business debtor if, any time during the last six years prior to filing for bankruptcy, you

- operated a business (including a profession); or
- were self-employed.

attention to and complete this form. Use Worksheet B to itemize business-related expenses that will become attached to Schedule J.

Business debtors must supply other information throughout their forms. For example, Schedule E will list creditors holding unsecured priority claims, which can include wages, salaries, and commissions that a business owner owes to employees or independent contractors. Any wages, vacation pay, or sick leave that an employee earned within 90 days of an employer's bankruptcy filing or within 90 days of the business closing shop must get recorded here and prioritized among the list of debts owed. Likewise, an employer's missing contributions to employee benefits plans (within 180 days of the filing or cessation of the business) will be listed as a priority debt.

We've been going through the bankruptcy process assuming readers are individuals filing Chapter 7 cases; if you own a business and need more guidance with filling out your forms, feel free to contact a We The People office, another bankruptcy petition preparer, or an attorney for help. For complex legal matters and answers to questions about filing a business bankruptcy, you should seek the advice of a competent bankruptcy attorney who specializes in business bankruptcies.

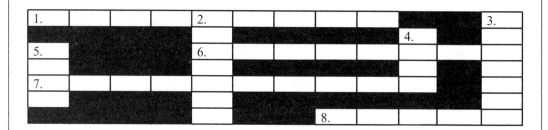

BANKRUPTCY CROSSWORD PUZZLE

ACROSS

1. Protection of your home

6. Person you owe money to

7. Get rid of your debts, file _____

8. Another name for cash

DOWN

2. Debt with collateral

3. Telling a lie to the court is committing _____

4. You get an automatic_____ when you file

5. Money you owe is a _____

Figure 5.4

Retirement Plans

Building a retirement fund should be part of your lifetime goals, but if during your lifetime you have to file for bankruptcy, losing a retirement fund that took years to build can be devastating. The more money you have in a retirement fund, the more you have to lose. You may be able to protect your retirement fund through bankruptcy under a federal law called the Employee Retirement Income Security Act (ERISA) or by using your exemptions. Consult with your pension plan administrator or benefits coordinator for more information about the kind of plan you have and how any federal or state laws can protect your plan. If you fear losing your retirement fund in your bankruptcy, find a lawyer to help you navigate the system so you can use any and all laws to prevent that loss.

Conclusion

Your encounter with the courts is minimal in a routine Chapter 7 bankruptcy. And unlike most other court proceedings, bankruptcy proceedings put you in the driver's seat—for the most part. What we mean by this is you have options. The scope of bankruptcy law contains a variety of choices for you to make so that you can release your debts but continue to retain certain assets for daily living. How you choose to use your exemptions and what you decide to do with your secured property ultimately characterize your bankruptcy and make your particular case unique. Moreover, your negotiations with your trustee over your assets—as well as your secured creditors—can determine the end result of your case and what you stand to lose and/or gain.

The trustee-debtor relationship is special; it is not like an attorney-client relationship, a defendant-judge relationship, nor any other kind of typical court-related relationship. How you interact with your trustee decides how your case proceeds and whether or not you can expect a fresh start as soon as possible. Because your meeting of the creditors and this interaction with your trustee are important, we've dedicated the next chapter to giving you all the information you need to get through this meeting successfully.

CHAPTER 6

Attending Your Creditors' Meeting

Do you remember going to the Department of Motor Vehicles for the first time to get your driver's license? You were anxious and nervous about passing the test and walking out with a piece of paper that represented your license. But now you don't like going to the DMV because you know it entails long lines, frustrated people, and lots of democratic red tape. Anyone who wants to drive a car legally must pay a visit to the DMV. You can't send your mother or spouse to do it for you, and you can't talk to the DMV over the phone or e-mail in your responses to questions the DMV has for you. Dealing with the DMV is a right of passage for people seeking licenses to drive. Similarly, creditors' meetings are a right of passage for people seeking relief from their debts. And you can't send anyone else but yourself to do the work for you in those meetings. As digital as our world has become, you can't call in, write in, fax in, nor e-mail in to your creditors' meeting. For those that don't like face-to-face meetings, this can be daunting. But how else did you get your license? How else will you get the financial relief you're seeking?

Getting worked up before you attend your creditor's meeting is useless. Creditors' meetings are part of your bankruptcy proceeding, and frankly, they aren't that difficult to get through. It's similar to going to the DMV (but faster and you don't get your picture taken): You arrive with your papers in order, wait your turn, present yourself in front of someone, answer a few questions, and then you are done. Going to your creditors' meeting drums up similar emotions to that first DMV visit, but it shouldn't. Trouble is, you're not likely to have to do this more than once in your life (unlike subsequent visits to the DMV to maintain your

☺ **Encouragement Alert!** The key to succeeding at this point in your bankruptcy case is honesty. If you are honest and do your best to answer questions in your creditors' meeting, you have nothing to worry about. Look at it this way: You're almost done! A lot of the hard work is already behind you, and soon enough, you'll be debt-free and able to move on in your new life. Go ahead and pat yourself on the back for making it this far. Also never forget: You have a right to represent yourself, so don't let the fact you don't have an attorney in a pinstripe suit by your side discourage you or diminish your courage in any way.

driving privilege), so you don't have the opportunity to get used to creditors' meetings. Take it from us, while creditors' meetings do entail some bureaucracy, waiting, responding to questions, and official formalities, attending your creditors' meeting is far less painful than going to the DMV. In fact, you will find that getting through this important step to your bankruptcy is faster and easier than ever going to the DMV.

Call It the 341 Meeting

Usually, the only formal proceeding at which you must appear is the meeting of creditors, which is usually held at the offices of the U.S. trustee (not a courtroom). Your attendance at this meeting cannot be waived. This meeting is informally called a 341(A) meeting because section 341 of the Bankruptcy Code requires that the debtor attend this meeting so that creditors can question you about your debts and assets. Don't let the 341 frighten you. The numbers are meaningless for you—unless you want to sound cool.

According to the Bankruptcy Code, "in a Chapter 7 liquidation or a Chapter 11 reorganization case, the United States trustee shall call a meeting of creditors to be held no fewer than 20 and no more than 40 days after the order for relief. In a Chapter 13 individual's debt adjustment case, the United States trustee shall call a meeting of creditors to be held no fewer than 20 and no more than 50 days after the order for relief."

> Creditors' meetings are the only time you need to present yourself in front of someone official if you're filing a Chapter 7. Never forget: This is the government running a meeting. You can't get fired or be charged extra for acting nervous or stuttering. If you're honest and patient throughout the process, you'll be fine. If you're confident and organized, you'll be even finer.

The meeting permits the trustee or representative of the U.S. Trustee's Office to review your petition and schedules with you face to face. You are required to answer questions under penalty of perjury (you must tell the truth) concerning your acts, conduct, assets, liabilities, financial condition, and any matter that may affect your bankruptcy proceeding or your right to a discharge. This information enables the trustee or representative of the U.S. Trustee's Office to understand your circumstances and facilitates the efficient administration of the case.

It Only Takes a Few Minutes

If you include parking your car and waiting in the audience for your name to be called, then your creditors' meeting shouldn't take more than an hour. Yes, we said "audience." Did you think you'd be the only one awaiting a meeting with an appointed trustee? Your trustee didn't get out of bed that morning just to deal with your case. To the contrary, in the space of an hour for Chapter 7 or an hour and a half for Chapter 13, your trustee in charge of the meeting has to run a docket with up to 20 or more cases. You can imagine that in the space of that time, some will go extremely fast and others will take some time. Do not stress yourself out waiting for this meeting. Your individual time with your trustee will be less than the time it takes for you to drive, park, and wait. You can bring a book or magazine with you to read while you wait for your turn.

An average meeting can take from three to five minutes depending on your case. Most are routine and take only several minutes. Creditors have become a rarity. In the past, you could count on three or four per meeting. It is rare for even one creditor to show up at most meetings. It's still called a meeting of creditors, but you're the one taking center stage. If your creditors do show up, we have some advice for you at the end of this chapter.

Who's Involved in a 341 Meeting?

No judges. No bailiffs. No court reporters. These meetings are conducted in regular meeting room settings. (See Figure 6.1.) Some districts conduct these meetings in the courthouse but not in a courtroom. Other districts conduct 341 meetings in office buildings that house dozens of other professionals and private businesses. The exact kind of setting you can expect will depend on your district. If you're truly worried about what to expect, there's no harm in calling your local bankruptcy court and asking about the next 341 meeting. All of these meetings are open to the public, so you can go and spy on someone else's 341 meeting before your own (unless the next date for these meetings is scheduled the same day as yours). Take a field trip and go see for yourself. In small cities, 341 meetings might be scheduled once a month, while in larger metropolitan areas they take place every day of the week. Call your local bankruptcy court to find out when and where the meetings are held (and ask when is the best time to show up).

United States Trustee

The U.S. Trustee's Office is part of the U.S. Department of Justice. It is completely separate from the Bankruptcy Court. The U.S. Trustee's Office is a watchdog agency, charged with monitoring all bankruptcies, appointing and supervising all trustees, and identifying fraud in bankruptcy cases. The office cannot give you legal advice, but it can give you information about the status of a case. You may also contact the U.S. Trustee's Office if you are having a problem with an individual trustee, or if you have evidence of any fraudulent activity.

The administrative functions were placed within the Department of Justice through the creation of the U.S. Trustee Program (USTP). The USTP's mission statement reads:

> The USTP acts in the public interest to promote the efficiency and to protect and preserve the integrity of the bankruptcy system. It works to secure the just, speedy, and economical resolution of bankruptcy cases; monitors the conduct of parties and takes action to ensure compliance with applicable laws and procedures; identifies and investigates bankruptcy fraud and abuse; and oversees administrative functions in bankruptcy cases.

For example, assume you're a debtor who lives in Santa Monica, California. The U.S. Trustee for your region—region 16—is responsible for bankruptcy cases filed in the Central District of California. The headquarters is located in downtown Los Angeles, and you'd have to visit that office for your 341 meeting. While there is a U.S. Trustee in charge of your region (the chief of the trustee program in your region), you won't be meeting with that particular trustee; instead, you'll be meeting with a private trustee who gets assigned by the regional U.S. Trustee to oversee your case.

The duties of a United States Trustee include the following:

- Appointing and supervising the private trustees who collect and disburse funds to creditors in bankruptcy cases under Chapters 7, 12, and 13

341(A) Meeting of the Creditors Cast of Characters

Trustee with
Administrative Assistant

Some Creditors

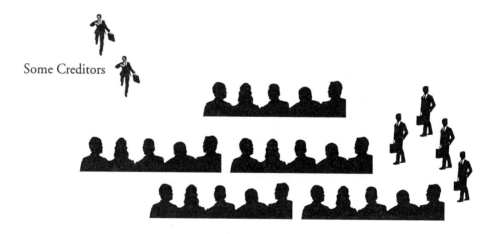

Debtors, some with attorneys, some without

Figure 6.1

> Review: A bankruptcy trustee is appointed in all Chapter 7, 12, and 13 cases, and in some Chapter 11 cases. The trustee administers the bankruptcy estate and ensures that creditors get as much money as possible. In a Chapter 7 case, the trustee collects and sells nonexempt assets. In a Chapter 13 case, the trustee collects money from the debtor and distributes it to creditors according to the debtor's repayment plan. The trustee can require that you provide information and documents either before, after, or at the section 341 meeting. You should always cooperate with the trustee, because failure to cooperate with the trustee could be grounds to have your discharge denied.

- Assuring compliance with the Bankruptcy Code with respect to information disseminated in cases through reports, schedules, disclosure statements, reorganization plans, and other filings
- Reviewing fee applications of professionals, like attorneys and accountants, who serve in Chapter 11 business reorganization cases
- Monitoring bankruptcy cases for fraud and abuse and referring criminal matters to U.S. Attorneys for prosecution in accordance with the USTP Mission Statement

U.S. Trustees that manage regions also serve as and perform the duties of a regular, private trustee in a case when required.

A major reason for the enactment of the Bankruptcy Reform Act of 1978 was to remove the bankruptcy judges from the responsibilities for day-to-day administration of cases.

Debtors, creditors, and third parties litigating against bankruptcy trustees were concerned that the court, which previously appointed and supervised the trustee, may not be able to judge fairly when it came to legal actions against trustees. To address these concerns, judicial and administrative functions within the bankruptcy system were split into two. This ensures a fair and balanced system.

The Executive Office for U.S. Trustees, located in Washington, D.C., oversees the U.S. Trustee Program's substantive operations and handles the program's administrative functions. One person serves as Director of the Executive Office for U.S. Trustees under authority derived from the Attorney General. (See Figure 6.2.)

Where Do Trustees Come From?

The Attorney General is charged with the appointment of U.S. Trustees and Assistant U.S. Trustees; the U.S. Trustees in the 21 national regions are charged with appointing their private panel of trustees. They operate in all states except North Carolina and Alabama.

Despite what you might think, private trustees are not schooled for years specifically for serving the role of a bankruptcy trustee. Trustees are not necessarily attorneys, either. They are professionals who, by their type of work and experience, qualify for the role of trustee and get appointed by their regional U.S. Trustee.

If you live in Alabama or North Carolina, the system is the exact same, but the trustee has a different name: administrator. The 341 administrator is appointed by the bankruptcy Administrator's office (not the Office of the Trustee) and they ask the same kinds of questions that a 341 trustee would ask in other states.

Bankruptcy Courts' Trustee Program

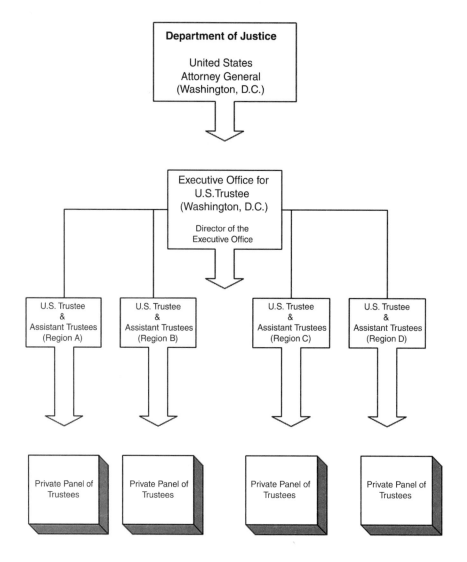

Department of Justice

United States
Attorney General
(Washington, D.C.)

Executive Office for
U.S. Trustee
(Washington, D.C.)

Director of the
Executive Office

U.S. Trustee
&
Assistant Trustees
(Region A)

U.S. Trustee
&
Assistant Trustees
(Region B)

U.S. Trustee
&
Assistant Trustees
(Region C)

U.S. Trustee
&
Assistant Trustees
(Region D)

Private Panel of
Trustees

Private Panel of
Trustees

Private Panel of
Trustees

Private Panel of
Trustees

Note: A similar structure exists in North Carolina and Alabama, but "Administrator" is used in place of "Trustee." There are 94 federal judicial districts that handle bankruptcy matters, and 21 federal U.S. Trustee offices nationwide.

Figure 6.2

How a Trustee Gets Paid

In Chapter 7 cases, a trustee gets paid a flat fee for every case (around $60). Because most Chapter 7 cases are no-asset cases, a trustee who manages several cases quickly can rack up a lot of money. If there are nonexempt assets available in the debtor's estate, the trustee is entitled to a percentage of those funds upon the sale of those assets. A trustee will take 25 percent of the first $5,000 disbursed to creditors, 10 percent of the next $45,000, and so on. See below for more information about the sale of your assets.

Trustees serve one-year renewable terms. Usually as bankruptcy attorneys (and part-time trustees), they keep regular offices that are not necessarily near a courthouse or judicial setting. While most do come from a background in law, some are CPAs by trade. All take on the role of trustee as a credit to their professional life and for the prestige that comes with the job. They have the potential for financial gain, too.

Trustees are not paid by the court. The trustees report to the court, but their fees are paid from the bankruptcy filing fees or, if the estate has assets, from the assets of the estate.

Will a Moving Van Come Pick Up My Stuff?

The thought of having nonexempt assets seized makes a lot of bankruptcy filers worry about when the moving van will show up at their doorsteps and begin hauling out their personal items. It doesn't work like that.

First of all, seizing and selling assets costs money. A trustee isn't going to bother taking your extra television sets if they will generate only $100 (maybe) on a quick sale but it costs him $500 to arrange for the seizure and sale. Any assets worth taking must be carefully evaluated before a trustee will take them and sell them. Then, the trustee has to get a judge to approve of the seizure. In other words, the trustee cannot come and take any assets without a bankruptcy judge's permission. So, the transactional cost of seizing and selling assets makes sense only when it comes to high-ticket items. A Steinway grand piano? Unless you're a classic pianist or can exempt that from your bankruptcy, a trustee likely will try to sell your piano (some of which do appreciate over time, so they are not the same as your used assets). But the majority of your assets—even nonexempt ones—won't be worth the taking.

No moving van will show up at your house, and you won't return from your creditors' meeting to an empty house, either.

What Happens Play by Play?

The day has come for you to attend your meeting. It has been a month since you first filed your petition, and you've got your notice that says where you need to go and when. You organize your papers, dress appropriately, and venture out to your 341 meeting. You park, find the meeting room, sign an attendance sheet (maybe), and wait for some direction. Here's what you'll likely do:

→ Hear the trustee call the meeting to order and introduce him or herself. The trustee will explain how the meeting will proceed and what to expect. He or she will give any important instructions and direct people to where they should sit when their number and name are called. A typical statement made is as follows:

> "My name is _____, and I have been appointed by the Office of the United States Trustee, a component of the United States Department of Justice, to serve as interim trustee in the cases scheduled for this morning/afternoon. I will preside at these meetings and examinations of the debtors. Debtors are here today because the Bankruptcy Code requires that they be examined under oath with respect to the petitions they have filed. All persons appearing must sign the appearance sheet. All persons questioning the debtor must state their name and whom they represent for the record, and speak clearly. All examinations will be electronically recorded and testimony is under penalty of perjury."

Then, he or she will call the first number and name.

➔ Wait your turn.

➔ When your number and name are called, you will proceed to the front of the room where the trustee and his or her assistant sit. You will present original government-issued photo identification and confirmation of your Social Security number. Any document used to confirm your identity and Social Security number must be an original (copies may not be accepted; however, under the discretion of the trustee, a copy of a W-2 Form, an IRS Form 1099, or a recent payroll stub may be accepted). This helps ensure an accurate court record and deters identity theft. Acceptable forms of picture identification (ID) include a valid state driver's license, U.S. government identification card, state-issued picture identification card, passport (and current U.S. visa, if not a U.S. citizen), military identification card, and resident alien card.

Acceptable forms of proof of Social Security number include Social Security card, medical insurance card, current pay stub or statement, W-2 form for the most recent tax year, IRS Form 1099, and a Social Security Administration (SSA) Statement. When debtors state that they are not eligible for a Social Security number, the trustee will need to inquire further in order to verify identity. In this situation, proof of an Individual Tax Identification Number (ITIN) issued by the IRS for those people not eligible for a Social Security number would be acceptable documentation.

If you don't have either proof of your Social Security card or a standard photo ID, contact your local court to ask what's acceptable.

➔ Take an oath under penalty of perjury. The trustee must administer the oath to you individually if you are filing with your spouse; your spouse will take the oath as well. The trustee will require you to raise your right hand and respond affirmatively to the following: "Do you solemnly swear or affirm to tell the truth, the whole truth, and nothing but the truth?"

➔ Answer questions. After administering the oath, the trustee must ask you to verify that the signatures appearing on the petition and schedules are yours and that you reviewed the documents before signing them. Trustees must examine your documents offered for proof of identity and Social Security number and compare them with the information on the petition.

The trustee must note for the record that proof of identity and Social Security number has been provided. He or she will say something like: "I have viewed the original drivers license [or other type of original photo ID] and original Social Security card [or other original document used for proof] and they match the name and Social Security number on the petition."

If the trustee determines that the names or Social Security numbers do not match the information on the petition, the trustee must ask you to explain why the name or Social Security number on the document used for proof does not match the name or number on the petition and try to determine if it is a typographical error or a possible misuse or falsification. The trustee will not read the Social Security number into the record, unless it does not match the one on the petition.

Your trustee must establish on the record that you acknowledge an awareness of

- the potential consequences of seeking a discharge in bankruptcy, including the effects that this action may have on your credit history;
- the ability to file a bankruptcy petition under a different Chapter of the Bankruptcy Code;
- the effect of receiving a discharge of debts under Chapter 7 of the Bankruptcy Code; and
- the effect of reaffirming a debt, including your knowledge of the provisions.

If you have an attorney representing you, your attorney's office will send you an information sheet about bankruptcy before your creditors' meeting date. If you are representing yourself, you will find all the information you need about bankruptcy in this book. Some trustees will send an information pamphlet to you before your meeting, which is made by your particular district and may even be called "the green pamphlet" or some such depending on the color of paper used. The trustee simply wants to know that you understand the basics of bankruptcy and make sure you know how it will affect your credit rating. If you respond in the negative, the trustee must provide a copy of the information sheet and either move you to the end of his line of debtors that day or have you return on another day. The meeting cannot be concluded until the information has been conveyed. (If you're reading this book, you'll have an awareness of all these issues.) These information sheets are usually available in the meeting rooms.

If you assert the Fifth Amendment privilege in response to a particular question, the trustee will proceed with the meeting and continue to question you. At the conclusion of the questioning, the trustee will adjourn or continue the meeting and immediately notify the U.S. Trustee.

After the trustee has completed the examination, the trustee will inquire if there are any creditors or parties in interest present who wish to ask questions. Your creditors are not likely to show up, and this part of the process won't take long. If someone does show up to challenge your bankruptcy, the trustee will take charge of this person's inclusion in your meeting. Creditors cannot take more than a reasonable period of time to make inquiries at the meeting since they can use other avenues to obtain more detailed information. The trustee is trained to halt any examination that appears to be primarily aimed at harassing you. The trustee's job is to balance the informational needs of the creditor with the time available to complete the entire day's appointments. If your case requires more time, it may need to be adjourned temporarily in order to finish more routine cases. A lengthy case can be reconvened at the end of the day, or, if necessary, adjourned to or continued on another day.

The trustee may be required to complete a record of the proceeding, such as a minute sheet, for your case. If required, a copy must be submitted promptly to the U.S. Trustee and filed with the clerk of the bankruptcy court, if the clerk so requests. The trustee will keep a copy in your file.

All Meetings Are Recorded

All 341 meetings must be recorded electronically. The trustee is responsible for ensuring that the recording equipment is operating properly. He or she should announce that testimony is being recorded and that parties are required to speak clearly. The spelling of the names of any parties formally entering their appearance on the record should be obtained in case a transcript is requested at a later date. The trustee must provide the recording to the U.S. Trustee upon conclusion of the day's meetings. The U.S. Trustee keeps the recordings for a period of two years. You have a right to a copy of your taped session; on the day of your creditors' meeting, your trustee will give instructions for obtaining a copy.

> If a non-English speaking debtor is unable to communicate with the trustee, or the trustee plans to take any adverse action against a non-English speaking debtor, such as filing an objection to a case with the court, the trustee will consult with the U.S. Trustee.

When a trustee becomes aware of a debtor's disability, including hearing impairment, the trustee must notify the main U.S. Trustee office so that reasonable accommodations can be made. As far as non-English speaking debtors go, there is no statutory obligation to provide language interpreters at 341 meetings. However, trustees are instructed to attempt to communicate with a non-English speaking debtor by seeking the assistance of third parties such as attorneys and family members. All parties who offer to interpret must be placed under oath. Such an oath is: "Do you solemnly swear or affirm that you will truthfully and impartially act as an interpreter for the debtor during this meeting?"

Your trustee must conduct the meeting in an orderly, yet flexible, manner and provide for the questioning of you as to matters affecting your financial affairs and conduct. The trustee's demeanor toward all parties should be appropriate and professional. Despite the attendance of lawyers, you'll find that they don't do much at all during these meetings. The trustee is solely interested in you and your answers. The trustee may not even allow the lawyers to sit beside their clients. During the meeting, you are, for the most part, speaking directly with the trustee.

Your Big Fat Check from Uncle Sam

You'll see that among the questions typically asked at creditors' meetings is one about your tax return. Your trustee will ask how much of a return you received the previous year and if you expect another one this year. If you do expect a big tax return and you are filing for bankruptcy during the tax season—between January and April 15th—your trustee will take your refund (assuming your refund is pending at the time you filed for bankruptcy).

We tell our customers that it's legal to delay your filing until after you get and spend your tax refund, as long as you spend the money on necessities, such as rent, food, and so on. Obviously, if you are desperate to file for bankruptcy and need the automatic stay to take effect as soon as possible, you won't be able to time your bankruptcy filing in consideration of your refund. But if you are not in dire need of this protection, with a little planning you can save quite a bit of money.

Common Questions Asked at the Creditors' Meeting

- What is your full name and address?
- Do you own or rent your home?
- What is your spouse's name?
- What was your wife's maiden name?
- Have you made any voluntary or involuntary transfers of real property or personal property within the last year?
- Are any of your debts from credit card use?
- Have you returned or destroyed your credit cards?
- Is Schedule A a complete list of all your real estate property?
- Is Schedule B a complete list of all your personal property?
- Is Schedule C a complete list of all your exempt property?
- Is Schedule D a complete list of all your secured creditors?
- Is Schedule F a complete list of all your unsecured creditors?
- Are you suing anyone?
- Is anyone suing you?
- Are you currently expecting a tax refund?
- Did you receive a tax refund last year?
- Are you current on your payments on the Ford (or whatever you're keeping for a car)?
- Have you made any recent large payments to creditors or relatives?
- Do you expect to receive any inheritance or insurance proceeds?
- Are you currently employed and, if so, by whom?
- Has your job and income changed since you first filed your petition?
- Did anyone help you prepare your bankruptcy papers? If yes, who?
- How much did you pay for the preparation of your bankruptcy petition? (For example, in the case of We The People the charge is $199, excluding any copy charges.)

If You Cannot Show Up for Your Meeting

Unlike scheduling a teeth-cleaning or a doctor's appointment, you don't have much choice about when and where your creditors' meeting takes place. Except in rare circumstances, you must appear in person before the trustee. Should you require an alternative for your scheduled meeting, the trustee will consult with the U.S. Trustee regarding the general procedures for approving your alternative appearance. Note that this happens only when extenuating circumstances prevent you from appearing in person.

Extenuating circumstances may include the following:

- military service
- serious medical condition
- incarceration

In such instances, your appearance may be secured by alternative means, such as telephonically. Arrangements are then made for an independent third party authorized to administer oaths to be present at the alternate location to administer the oath and to verify your identity and state your Social Security number on the record. Examples of individuals who may serve in this capacity include employees of the U.S. Trustee or bankruptcy trustees situated in your locale, court reporters, notaries, or others authorized by law to administer oaths in the jurisdiction where you will appear.

Because of the widespread abuse of identities and the trend for identity thieves to use fictitious Social Security numbers—including those used in bankruptcy filings—the bankruptcy process and how a debtor must present him or herself before a trustee is designed to protect you. To that end, don't count on getting any special passes to attend your creditors' meeting telephonically unless you do qualify for extenuating circumstances.

If you fail to show up for your scheduled meeting, your case may be dismissed. You also face being held in contempt of court for willful failure to cooperate.

What to Wear, What to Bring

Torn T-shirts and flip-flops are not appropriate attire for your creditors' meeting—neither is a tuxedo or three-piece suit. Use good judgment when dressing for your appearance. You want to look professional, organized, prepared, and practiced in your filing a bankruptcy. While you won't (hopefully) be an expert in the bankruptcy process from experience (in other words, this is the one and only time you'll deal with a bankruptcy), you want to come across as someone who has done your homework and who knows what's expected of you. Being clean and groomed will also affect your overall appearance, giving you an honest, serious look.

Appearances matter, and people still judge others based on appearance alone, so think about how you look before you leave for your meeting. Your trustee will be dressed in a suit, and so will the lawyers around the room. This doesn't mean you, too, have to don a formal suit, but it can immediately put you at more equal footing with the trustee if you're feeling extremely intimidated by the prospects of a stranger asking you personal financial questions.

Take a copy of every paper you have filed with the bankruptcy court. Some courts, not all, require that you bring financial records, tax returns, and checkbooks. Most clerks of the court are responsive and helpful. Although the clerks cannot give legal advice, they are required, as part of their general duties as public servants, to give you general information about the court requirements.

A few days before your meeting, find time to call your assigned trustee, whose name and phone number appear on the formal notice you received from the court. Inform your trustee (or his or her office) that you are filing on your own behalf (you don't have a lawyer) and ask what records you should bring. You want to be careful about documents or paperwork that your particular trustee requests but which are not typically required. It doesn't hurt to bring along copies of documents that describe your debts and property, such as deeds, titles, contracts, bills, and licenses. That way, if your trustee needs these items and asks for them during the meeting, you can provide them at that time and not have to return on a later date and thus further delay your bankruptcy proceeding.

The night before your creditors' meeting, thoroughly review the papers you filed with the bankruptcy court. If you discover any mistakes, make a careful note of them. Before you

---

Important Tip

Do not act like your 341 meeting is a time to seek legal advice from the trustee. While many trustees do have law degrees and practice bankruptcy law, they cannot give any legal advice. Some trustees will refuse to answer any questions if they can be construed as legal advice. Likewise, creditors who probe trustees on how to proceed with collecting their money will also find trustees unhelpful. Just as you've done your homework before attending your 341 meeting, any creditors who decide to show up must do their homework. Creditors who attempt to openly challenge your case before the trustee won't get very far. The trustee will prevent the creditors from pursuing their losses and will direct them to make the appropriate filing with the court.

---

answer any questions at the meeting, advise the trustee of the errors. Admitting mistakes and acting on them voluntarily is much better than discovering them during the question process. You will probably have to amend your papers after the meeting. Don't be nervous at the prospect of answering questions. If you were careful in the preparation of your papers, all should go well.

Be Prepared, Organized, and Ready

Delays in the processing of debtors at their 341 meetings happen when debtors don't arrive with paperwork thoroughly completed. Less prepared debtors can prolong the meeting and make everyone who is scheduled on the same day frustrated. Because offices of trustees find that debtors who represent themselves are more likely to cause delays, trustees will schedule *pro se* debtors at the end of their calendar, which can be at the end of the hour or session. Trustees will also order their meetings by whether or not you are a continuation or a new case. Continuation cases are those in which people have already attended their first 341 meeting and have been called back for another round. A trustee who orders someone to surrender her car, for example, can request her to return a month after her initial meeting to show proof that she surrendered her vehicle or risk her case being dismissed.

Things to Bring to Your 341 Meeting

- Valid identification and proof of Social Security card
- Every piece of paper you've filed with the bankruptcy court
- List of mistakes, if any, that you have found in reviewing your papers
- Any financial records or documents requested by your trustee
- Prepared answers to the questions you're likely to face (see box above)
- Good mood
- Patience and determination

Don't allow the fact that you're representing yourself in your bankruptcy to intimidate you. If you're prepared, organized, and ready to go the morning of your meeting, you have nothing to worry about. Look sharp and act collected. Don't make the trustee ask that you speak louder or clearer. Speak up! You don't want to frustrate or annoy your trustee. Think of your trustee as someone you need to have on your side for your bankruptcy to proceed smoothly.

Review your documents the night before your meeting. Check all names and numbers, verifying their accuracy. Below is a checklist for you to use the night before your meeting.

If Your Trustee Acts Unkindly

Trustees don't have bad reputations, but some debtors experience mean trustees or harassing creditors at their meetings. The majority of debtors find the 341 meeting painless and procedural, but if your trustee or a creditor becomes abusive, here are some tips:

- Refuse to answer any more questions until you are treated civilly. You can even stop the meeting by simply telling the trustee you want a hearing before the bankruptcy court judge to clear up the scope of the trustee's authority.

- If your trustee demands that you surrender your credit cards on the spot, you have a right to refuse and ask the trustee to consult with the judge. The bankruptcy law does not authorize the seizure of credit cards at 341 meetings.

- Do not be afraid to assert your rights, as you perceive them, at your creditors' meeting.

- Do not be afraid to express your views to the bankruptcy judge if it comes to that. No harm comes from appearing before the judge, as long as you obey the judge's decisions and treat the judge respectfully.

A trustee might treat you unkindly because you are representing yourself, and there's nothing you can do to prevent that treatment. If your trustee is exceedingly abusive, adversarial, or acting like a bully you recall from middle school, assert your rights to go before a bankruptcy judge. But this won't likely happen. Realize that trustees are human, too, and they can harbor ill-feelings that you can't do anything about. They also can have bad days and be moody for reasons that have nothing to do with you and your bankruptcy case.

Be strong and stay focused. This is when being organized and prepared is essential—you can prove to your trustee that a *pro se* bankruptcy can proceed as easily as one assisted by an attorney. Trustees are not supposed to treat self-representing debtors nastily, but they sometimes do. Tell yourself that it's okay to feel intimidated. You are doing the best you can under the circumstances.

If Creditors Show Up

Creditors should receive a notice from the bankruptcy court, which states the date, time, and place of your meeting. Although the creditor may be represented by an attorney at the meeting, that is not required. Creditors may appear directly or by in-house non-lawyer representatives. But overall, creditors' appearances are rare. They are not required to attend these hearings and, in general, do not waive their rights by failing to appear. If they do attend, they are probably curious about your intentions and whether you are using bankruptcy to discharge your debts to them.

Keep in mind that a 341 Meeting is held for the benefit of creditors and parties in interest (including the trustee). It is their opportunity to question you regarding your debts and assets. It also provides them with the chance to learn about your financial situation in greater detail through questioning by other creditors. Prior to the meeting, the trustee can ask the debtor to provide documents to corroborate the information contained in the petition, statements, and schedules. Such documents may include but are not limited to tax returns, financial statements, loan documents, trust deeds, titles, insurance policies, and wage and bank statements.

TOM'S STORY

I was terrified of going to my 341 meeting. My debts were huge and I had fears of all my creditors showing up and fighting against me for every dollar. I was told not to worry about facing creditors because they weren't likely to show up, but why else would they call it a "creditors' meeting"? I didn't sleep for the three nights before my meeting!

I was very organized and prepared for my creditors' meeting. I had all my paperwork in order and there were no mistakes. I even had compiled all my most important financial documents in a neat folder in case the trustee asked unexpected questions. The night before my scheduled meeting, I felt a little better about the situation and wanted to get it over with.

The setting of my meeting surprised me. I had expected something very formal and stiff, but it wasn't like that at all. I was in the lobby of a high-rise building downtown. I didn't see any signs of the court, or a judge in a gown. There were lots of other people there like me, awaiting their turn and worrying about how much parking would cost if they weren't called soon.

Not a single creditor showed up to contest my bankruptcy filing. But someone else did: My ex-wife! She was horrifying. She tried to yell and scream about money I owed her and a boat we had sold during our divorce. I owed her nothing. I think she even scared the trustee, who had to calm her down and act as a referee when I reacted to her false accusations. I was shocked she had bothered to show up. Our divorce had not been amicable, but this was ridiculous. She was bringing stuff into the conversation that had nothing to do with my bankruptcy. In fact, much of my bankruptcy was a result of her, and I was trying my hardest not to resent her for that. I was embarrassed. I was surprised by her audacity. I was scared of my ex-wife!

My trustee responded to the situation like a king. He knew the right things to say and took control of everything quickly. My ex-wife wasn't allowed to go on and on and rant like she used to when we were married. The trustee explained to her that the purpose of the meeting was not to harass or attack me. It was for creditors to question the state of my financial affairs and get an idea of my ability to pay off debts. When the meeting was adjourned, my wife walked away mad but the trustee said that she wasn't likely to ruin my chances of getting a discharge. He said she was out of line.

Four months after that dreadful day, I got my discharge and my bankruptcy case was closed. My wife called to wish me luck in my new financial life and apologized for her behavior that day.

The meeting is usually valuable to secured creditors, who can question you about the status of your collateral (for instance, whether your home is properly insured) and ask your trustee to abandon collateral in which there is no equity and which, therefore, cannot be liquidated for the benefit of other creditors. In addition, the meeting is a convenient time for creditors to negotiate with you about the return of collateral or the resumption of payments. Creditors want to know if you could pay at least 50 cents on the dollar, and if not, they won't waste their time objecting to the discharge.

We mentioned this above, but it bears repeating: Creditors must show up at these meetings just as prepared as you. They won't get anything accomplished if they arrive with the intention of talking to the trustee and getting the trustee to go after you for their losses. Creditors are entitled to question you at 341 meetings—but they cannot seek any legal advice from the trustee. Because popular creditors like large credit card companies and retailers like Home Depot and Nordstrom's know how bankruptcy court works, these companies avoid the creditors' meetings and file the appropriate documents with the courts for raising objections. However, if you've given a Promissory Note to someone who isn't a huge company and who doesn't know how to formally approach the Bankruptcy Court in pursuit of his loss, you will likely find that person appear on the day of your meeting to inquire about your note. Personal loans made to you from friends, family, or business colleagues can be the hardest debts to confront during a bankruptcy.

Unsecured creditors might show up, if, let's say, a week before your filing, you ran up charges on your credit card and took out a large cash advance as well, knowing that you were going to file for bankruptcy. Similarly, if you've taken cash advances from a credit card, the credit card company is going to want to know what you did with the money. Information contained in your bankruptcy papers that differs from your credit application will also be questioned. If there's any way a credit card issuer can prove you applied for credit under false pretenses, either because you lied about your income or provided other false information, the trustee can side with the credit card company and object to the discharge of those debts.

Like the trustee, your creditors have 30 days to file an objection with the court. (See below.)

Earlier, we mentioned that some retail giants like Sears, Circuit City, and Best Buy have, in the past, gotten a reputation in some communities for showing up at creditors' meetings to argue that any purchases made on their store cards represent security for the credit they extend to card holders. In other words, the credit on the card is secured by the items purchased with the card, and thus, people who have debt on those cards cannot discharge those debts unless they reaffirm or give back the goods. Courts do not like this argument and tend to treat store cards like credit cards, which are routinely discharged. It is highly unlikely that you will face any creditors in your meeting, even ones from these retail giants, but should this happen, understand that you cannot be forced to reaffirm any debt.

> Never blame mistakes in your paperwork on someone else, such as an attorney or legal document preparer. You are ultimately responsible for the information in your papers! This is why carefully reviewing every piece of paperwork the night before your meeting is crucial.

If Your Trustee Questions a Discrepancy

The secondary reason for questioning you about your financial affairs during your creditors' meeting is to ensure you are an honest person and that your bankruptcy filing is a good faith effort to cast bad financial history away and start over again. United States Trustees work closely with their Department of Justice colleagues from the FBI and other federal agencies to hunt down fraud and abuse of the bankruptcy system. Your trustee is supervised carefully by the regional U.S. Trustee and assistants to ensure that no person gets away with committing fraud to the benefit of the debtor.

During your questioning, a trustee will suspect any answers that do not corroborate your bankruptcy papers. If you've made mistakes in your paperwork, be open and honest about those mistakes, even if that requires more paperwork and questioning.

Beware of undervaluing assets. If you own valuable nonexempt assets that appear to be undervalued in your papers, expect a barrage of questions from your trustee. For example, if you value your real estate at $175,000 and your trustee has reason to believe that its true market value is at least four times that amount, you will have to explain how you arrived at your figure. Also, you will face questions about why you claimed certain assets to be exempt. Because the process of claiming exemptions (including understanding what the term "exemptions" means) requires some knowledge and instruction, trustees can act authoritatively and think you cannot negotiate your own exemptions without a lawyer. If you encounter a trustee who does not like the fact you've chosen to file your own bankruptcy without a lawyer and you're claiming exempt assets, explain to your trustee how you selected your exemptions. You can kindly inform him that you've done your homework and are up to speed about your rights to claim exemptions.

> A 30-day window remains open after your creditors' meeting during which your trustee and creditors can object to your exemptions. They must file their objections in writing to the bankruptcy court. Copies of their formal objections must also go to you, your trustee, and your lawyer if you have one. In rare cases, a trustee can file any objections after this 30-day period, but a judge ultimately decides whether it can be considered.

Lastly, beware of any actions you take just before or after you file for bankruptcy. For example, if you transfer interest in your house to your children as you contemplate bankruptcy, your trustee will have a problem with this action and make it difficult to process your case quickly.

The only thing a trustee can do to antagonize your case is to object to your exemptions within 30 days of your creditors' meeting. You'll then go before a judge to explain your case.

The most common reasons for a trustee or creditor to raise objections are as follows:

- You've claimed an exemption that is not recognized by the law.

- Before your bankruptcy filing, you sold nonexempt assets and used that money to buy exempt assets. Trustees see this as a way of cheating creditors.

- You've undervalued your assets in the hopes of keeping those assets.

- You've filed a joint bankruptcy with your spouse and you've doubled exemptions where that is not permitted.

- You haven't filed jointly but you've been married a long time and you say that only your spouse owns assets. (Example: If you are married and your wife owns a condominium and several assets, the trustee will ask how long you've been married, and whether she acquired her assets before the marriage.)

The court will schedule a hearing upon the submission of objection papers. This is when the trustee or creditor must prove that your exemptions are improper. If you don't show up at this hearing, the judge will base his or her decision on the paperwork and the applicable laws. In some districts, you will be required to attend this hearing, but if your bankruptcy court's local laws do not require your attendance and you don't intend to appear, you should at least respond to the objections in writing and defend your exemptions. No-shows who are up against their trustee or a bankruptcy attorney representing a creditor are likely to lose.

Closing the Creditors' Meeting

When the trustee and creditors are done questioning you, the trustee will dismiss you ("I have no other questions"). If you are reaffirming some debts with no other secured debts and have no nonexempt assets, your case is effectively over. Within six months you'll receive the court's final notice of discharge and the close of your case in the mail.

Conclusion

A Chapter 7 creditors' meeting isn't all that bad. It's a once in a lifetime experience for most, and in a worst-case scenario, you have to go before a judge or come back another day to finish your meeting (if, let's say, something was wrong with your paperwork). Organized, prepared, and mentally brave debtors find creditors' meetings a breeze. Of course, we can't sugar coat this entirely: Some debtors will find these meetings excruciating or emotionally painful. Mean trustees who discriminate against self-filing bankruptcy filers do exist, and the best you can do is hold your head up high and act informed and responsible.

Once your creditors' meeting is over (and you know you don't have to come back again at a future date), you've turned a corner and are well on your way to the finish line. You can see that finish line and now moving on becomes possible. You also know that crossing the finish line enters you into a new phase in your life. It's life after bankruptcy, and it requires a new way of thinking and a set of tools so you never go back to your life before bankruptcy (which got you there in the first place).

CHAPTER 7

Life After Bankruptcy

Hurray! Once you receive the final discharge from the court, you can breathe another sigh of relief and welcome the fresh start that you've been given. The court will send you a notice of your discharge and the close of your case in about four to six months after your creditors' meeting, if everything goes smoothly. In routine bankruptcy cases, prepared debtors who file no-asset Chapter 7s will get their discharge and begin to rebuild their lives on the other side of bankruptcy. This entails rebuilding credit and changing one's financial attitudes and aptitudes. Once you become debt free you want to remain debt free.

First, however, you need to be wary of possible leftover business to your bankruptcy filing that can emerge after your discharge. Even though you're not technically required to report your economic activities to the court, certain situations can happen that have the potential to reopen your case or become residual problems to solve in your post-bankruptcy life. For example, if you receive or become eligible to an inheritance, insurance proceeds, or proceeds from a divorce within 180 days of your filing, the court must be notified. Similarly, if you discover property or creditors you failed to include in your bankruptcy papers, you will have to report them formally or risk getting into trouble with the law.

So, despite your discharge, you may still need to manage these potential situations, including creditors that continue to harass you, a trustee who decides to reopen your case, and discrimination against you because of your bankruptcy. Both private and pubic employers cannot discriminate against you solely because of your bankruptcy, but that doesn't mean you won't encounter complications or frustrations with your employment that is easily disguised as anything but discrimination. While the majority of the work involved in a bankruptcy is now behind you, you need to remain focused and alert to the goal: becoming free of debt and moving toward a brighter financial future.

This chapter will give you the tools for dealing with these unlikely situations that you can face after you've been discharged, including unfair discrimination for which no law exists to protect you. We'll also give you some tips to living in your new financial life and learning how to build wealth—regardless of your income. Wealth is in closer reach than most people think, because wealth is built more upon attitudes toward money than on how much one makes.

Oops! You Forgot to Include Some Assets and Creditors

The reason you want your bankruptcy papers to be as perfect as can be when you file is you don't want to leave an asset or a creditor out that gets discovered at a later date. Newly discovered assets and creditors after the court discharges your debts can complicate your case and haunt you if your trustee decides to reopen your case and proceed to file actions with the court against you.

If you leave assets or a creditor out of your bankruptcy filing while your case is still open, you can amend your paperwork as we described in chapter 5. But if you don't discover an omission (something you left out) until your case is closed, the situation is different. You may not have been aware of this omission until afterward. And now you wonder if this debt remains your responsibility, and if you have to declare your newly discovered asset.

You Discover Or Acquire Assets

Judges must approve a trustee's motion to reopen your case, and a trustee who files a complaint with the court, asking for authorization to take your asset and sell it, won't try to reopen your case unless you discover a nonexempt asset that is worth selling. Remember: Nonexempt property refers to assets that you cannot keep, such as an off-roading vehicle you use when you go on vacation, a fancy (and quite valuable) telescope, or a signed Picasso painting. Your trustee will want to try and sell these items to help pay back your creditors. Whether this asset was omitted from your paperwork or you acquired it after your discharge, it's a good idea to notify your trustee. Judges can also reopen cases and deal with matters without appointing a trustee unless assets are added to the bankruptcy case and should be managed by the trustee.

You are legally responsible to notify your trustee if (a) you receive or become entitled to receive assets within 180 days of filing for bankruptcy or (b) you failed to list some of your nonexempt assets in your paperwork.

Even if you think your asset is exempt and your case is closed, it's wise to report to the trustee and be open and honest about it. You don't want your trustee to learn of your asset, become angry, and ask the court to cancel your bankruptcy discharge.

Typically, a request to revoke a debtor's discharge must be filed within one year after the granting of the discharge or, in some cases, before the date that the case is closed. It's up to the court to determine whether such allegations are true and, if so, to revoke the discharge. A discharge can be revoked under certain circumstances. For instance, a trustee, creditor, or the U.S. Trustee may request that the court revoke a debtor's discharge in a Chapter 7 case based on allegations that the debtor obtained the discharge fraudulently; the debtor failed to disclose the fact that he or she acquired or became entitled to acquire assets that would constitute assets of the bankruptcy estate; or the debtor committed one of several acts of impropriety described in section 727(a)(6) of the Bankruptcy Code.

Assets you must report include the following:

- **Assets from a divorce settlement**
- **Proceeds from a life insurance policy or death benefit plan**
- **Any inheritance you receive as a result of someone's death**

For Assets Acquired after Your Bankruptcy Case Is Closed. Reporting assets you acquire after your discharge, which must be reported to the court, entails forms and expertise best suited for an attorney. In some courts, a trustee who learns of your newly acquired assets will file a motion to

---

MONICA'S STORY

"**Three months after my bankruptcy** case closed, my mother called to tell me that a long-lost cousin had purchased stocks in a major company for me when I was born. I didn't know about these stocks and hadn't gotten any money from them—ever. They sat in a bank account far from me and only came to my attention when my mother called (because a death in the family unearthed a lot of family secrets). I was terrified that this new situation would ruin my discharge. I was told that the stocks were worth about $15,000 now if they were sold. My trustee had already given me a hard time about my case, and I didn't like him that much. The thought of him reopening my case and revoking my discharge just because one phone call changed my financial situation, didn't seem fair.

But I did the right thing: I contacted my trustee promptly to report the stocks and I gave him clear instructions to the bank account and cited the exemption law that I thought could protect this asset. He must have been happy with my honesty, because he didn't reopen my case or sound angry. I have yet to touch the stocks, too afraid to do anything with them. I think I'll keep them as a reminder of my past and use them only in an emergency in the future."

---

reopen your case and have those assets added to your schedule. If you need to report an asset, start by notifying your trustee or ask your local bankruptcy court's clerk how best to deal with this situation. Local court rules may vary.

For Assets Missing in Your Paperwork after Your Bankruptcy Case Is Closed. If you discover assets that should have been part of your paperwork, write a letter to your trustee in which you explain how you discovered this asset, any relevant details about the asset, and whether you think it can be exempt from your bankruptcy, citing the exemption specifically from the bankruptcy code. End the letter by asking the trustee to inform you of how he or she intends to proceed given this new piece of information.

You Discover Other Creditors

Creditors you failed to include in your paperwork don't automatically become your responsibility after your bankruptcy case is closed. Whether your omitted creditors knew of your bankruptcy or not, the debts you have with them will probably be considered discharged as if these creditors were listed. Technically, the statute says you are out of luck when it comes to unlisted creditors, but in no-asset cases, courts have ruled that unlisted debts become discharged as well. To avoid civil litigation (getting into trouble), you should file a motion to reopen your case so you can add omitted creditors to your schedule. This transaction is routinely done, but may entail your hiring an attorney.

Listing every single creditor in your bankruptcy papers is challenging for those with dozens of creditors, or those who have creditors that are hard to identify. The more creditors you have, the greater likelihood that some will be missed. This doesn't go to say you should have tried to miss them in your paperwork—but that it's okay and there are ways to deal with them afterward.

In a No-asset Case. If your bankruptcy was a no-asset case, any debts held of creditors excluded in your bankruptcy papers may be considered discharged—but there is no guarantee. If such creditors allege that they missed their opportunity to protest the discharge because you committed a fraud or a willful and malicious act, such as assault or libel, your trustee might have grounds for reopening the case and dealing with these creditors.

Alternatively, the missed creditors can attempt to go after you in state court, at which time you can defend yourself in that court or ask that the case go back to the bankruptcy court. If you find yourself dealing with this kind of situation, a competent bankruptcy attorney would be helpful.

In an Asset Case. Asset cases present a complicated scenario: Money has already been distributed to the creditors you did include in your paperwork (from the nonexempt assets your trustee sold). So the creditors that were left out are not happy about being excluded from those proceeds, and they should be entitled to a share of your bankruptcy estate. If your trustee decides to reopen your case, and you worry that you might end up with this debt, hire a lawyer to assist you.

The Threat of Your Case Reopening to Schedule Omitted Assets

Reopening a bankruptcy case isn't easy. A trustee cannot do it without the approval of the court. Reopening a case is costly and time consuming; a trustee has to file a formal complaint with the court, ask for authorization to sell the new assets and distribute the proceeds. A judge will deny the trustee's request if the newly discovered assets are not worth the trouble of reopening the case or if too much time has passed. How much time is too much time? Impossible to tell. Every judge is different, so you cannot assume that one judge will act in the same way as another. The same goes for trustees: One trustee may give you a hard time about your new asset while another will do nothing and allow you to keep it.

The more honest and trustworthy your trustee perceives of you, the greater the chance that you won't have problems dealing with new assets that come your way after your case is closed. Remember: Part of a trustee's job is to ensure that you are using bankruptcy for the right reasons and are not trying to pull a fast one on the courts and hide property that clearly should be part of your bankruptcy. If you are worried about how your trustee will act upon hearing about your postbankruptcy asset, consult with an attorney who can help you in your defense. Example: You forgot to include the 10-acre parcel of land that your grandfather left you in upstate New York, a place you've never been but that holds a lot of family value. You guess that it's a valuable piece of property, and you have no idea how you forgot about it (maybe because it's never on your mind, and with all the debt you've experienced, doing something with the land has been off your radar for years).

If your trustee succeeds in reopening your case, and you fear losing your discharge entirely or the valuable asset you've found, you have two options: Go to an attorney to help you defend your case in court, or agree to whatever the trustee wants.

Attemps to Collect after Your Discharge

If a creditor attempts collection efforts on a discharged debt, you can file a motion with the court, reporting the action and asking that the case be reopened to address the matter. The bankruptcy court will often do so to ensure that the discharge is not violated. Getting a discharge means creditors are legally prohibited from attempts to collect from you, including filing lawsuits. This is called a discharge injunction, and violating the injunction is civil contempt. So if a creditor violates this discharge injunction, the court can punish the creditor with a fine.

Nondischarged Debts

You are responsible for these debts regardless of your bankruptcy. In chapter 5 we discussed how to know which debts are discharged and which ones are not. Debts like child support, certain student loans, and taxes due within the past three years remain your responsibility after your bankruptcy case is closed.

You have a few options for dealing with creditors who attempt to collect nondischarged debts:

- Negotiate a payment schedule you can handle, or even a lower balance if you can pay off that debt sooner. This is similar to dealing with creditors before resorting to bankruptcy, discussed in chapter 2. Some creditors can be tough to negotiate with, however. If you begin to have a very difficult time dealing with the creditor, seek the advice of an attorney to assist you in your negotiations.

- Ignore the attempts to collect and wait until you can afford to pay them. However, if a creditor wins a judgment against you for failure to pay, you risk having your wages garnished (taken away) by a certain percentage. Creditors can take 25 percent of your wages to pay for nondischarged debts. Depending on the kind of debt involved, that percentage can be higher (examples: child support payments can reach 60 percent of your wages; the IRS can try to take all of your wages to pay for back taxes). If you find that you face financial hardship as a result of this garnishment, you'll have to file a document in state court and attend a hearing. You may still have to accept the garnishment.

If a creditor takes you to court over a debt you think should have been discharged, you must respond and either answer the creditor's complaint or file a motion to dismiss the creditor's case. If you land back in the bankruptcy court, your affirmative defense is that the debt was discharged in your bankruptcy case. A judge will have to rule on the complaint. This is the time to consider having a lawyer by your side.

Discharged Debts

The best way to deal with attempts to collect from you is to start with a letter to the creditor that details the discharged debt and states the closing date of your bankruptcy case. A sample letter is included here. (See Figure 7.1.)

Enclose a copy of your discharge notice. If there's a question as to whether this debt was discharged, assume that it was if (a) it was included in your paperwork, (b) there were no formal objections raised to its discharge, and (c) it doesn't fall into one of the nondischargeable debts categories. Any further protests from the creditor can be settled by the bankruptcy court once you file a motion and report the action by the creditor against you.

Attempts to Discriminate against You after Your Bankrupcy

Laws exist to prevent discrimination against you as a result of your bankruptcy, but you may find enough gray areas to question the power of these laws. Bankruptcy law provides express

John Doe
3356 Boathouse Way
Key West, FL 33040

March 10, 20XX

Acme Builder's Emporium, Inc.
4153 Latigo Bay Drive
Miami, FL 33130

Dear Acme Builder's Emporium:

Please be advised that I received a bankruptcy discharge from my debts on July 16, 2005. I've received numerous letters and phone calls regarding charges to my account between November of 2003 and May of 2004, for which I am no longer responsible. Enclosed is a copy of my discharge.

Sincerely,

John Doe

Figure 7.1

prohibitions against discriminatory treatment of debtors by both governmental units and private employers. A governmental unit or private employer may not discriminate against you solely because you were a debtor, were insolvent before or during the case, or have not paid a debt that was discharged in the case. The key word here is solely. And this is where the gray area surfaces.

Preventing Governmental Discrimination

All government entities, including federal, state, and local, cannot terminate an employee; discriminate with respect to hiring; or deny, revoke, suspend, or decline to renew a license, franchise, or similar privilege. This means the government cannot deny you a job or fire you, deny you a driver's license or passport, kick you out of public housing, or terminate any public benefits you receive. The government can, however, deny you a contract whose application takes your credit into consideration. For example, you can be denied a small business loan through a lender as a result of the bankruptcy's mark on your record (until enough time has passed).

Preventing Private Discrimination

A private employer may not discriminate with respect to employment if the discrimination is based solely upon the bankruptcy filing. But there are hidden ways the private sector can discriminate against you. Example: A potential employer, landlord, or service provider uses your credit history as a means to evaluate you. If you're denied a job, a place to live, or goods and services because of how your bankruptcy affected your credit report, there's not much you can do short of taking your case to court. This can be a hard case to argue, however, and perhaps the better course to take is to focus on rebuilding your financial life (and not spend the money it takes to go back to court and potentially hire a lawyer) and keep looking for employers, landlords, and service providers that ignore your bankruptcy. Note, however, that should a landlord suddenly evict you, an employer suddenly fire you, or a service provider suddenly drop you as a customer, you might have a stronger case to bring to court—if you think it's worth it.

Rebuilding Your Credit

Although a bankruptcy stays on your credit report for 10 years, you can begin the process of rebuilding your credit immediately. You may find it hard to get good credit terms or a loan soon after your bankruptcy, but you can still rebuild your credit and open yourself up to getting good credit terms and loans in the future through patience, wise use of your access to money now (think income), and careful planning. Because one's income is important in the eyes of creditors, most creditors look for steady employment and a history (since the bankruptcy) of paying for purchases on credit. So if you cannot find credit (or you don't want to use credit in fear of incurring new debts), having a steady job and saving money builds your candidacy for credit in the future. Many creditors totally disregard a bankruptcy after a period of five years.

Remember: Credit can be a useful tool for managing your finances and even building wealth. But mismanaging credit can derail your long-term plans and lead to financial difficulties. If you've already experienced such difficulties, don't leap back into cycles of credit abuse without educating yourself about how credit works and the difference between using it to your benefit versus using it to your detriment.

On the Road to Wealth

Going through the bankruptcy process forces you to look at your financial profile and learn how much you own and how much money you actually have. Once your bankruptcy is final, your first goal should be to set a realistic budget and know exactly where your money goes on a daily, weekly, and monthly basis. To do this, you'll need to scrutinize your use of money and record everything, including the times you use cash to pay for a pack of gum at a convenience store. Understanding your money entails an exercise similar to the one you did in chapter 2.

If you're old fashioned when it comes to keeping records, it's okay to use a notebook, daily planner, receipt book, or journal to keep your finances in check. How strict you can be on a monthly basis for scrutinizing and recording your finances will depend on your personality, your commitments any given month, and your ability to take time-outs for doing the work. The closer you scrutinize, the longer it takes, but the greater the reward is in terms of seeing exactly where you stand financially.

Handwritten records of your spending, check writing, depositing, and withdrawing is a bit outdated today with the impact of computer technology. If you don't trust yourself with balancing a checkbook every month, consider investing in software that will help you manage your money such as Microsoft Money or Quicken. If you have a personal computer, you might already have such money management programs installed. Check your programs folder on your machine.

Soon in your new debt-free life, you'll want to take at least one month and study your finances to the point that you record every single transaction in (income) and out (expense), down to cents on the dollar. The goal: to have a clear idea of where your money goes and where you can cut back. Keep all receipts and create receipts for items when you don't get one. Although you should keep meticulous records every month, as a lesson you'll want to try being ridiculously nitpicky for the duration of one month. This will enable you to make a realistic budget. It will also get you into the practice of managing your money successfully.

Use colored pens to distinguish between the expenses (in red ink) and the deposits (in blue ink). This allows you to review the blue versus the red at the end of the month. Categorize your expenses by giving them titles:

Shelter: rent, mortgage, insurance, furniture, repairs and maintenance, utilities

Transportation: car payments, car insurance, gas, repairs and maintenance

Food: groceries, kitchen-related expenses (example: water service); do not include eating out costs or your daily trip to the coffee shop

Health: insurance, copayments, deductibles, pharmaceuticals

Education: tuition, student loan payments, books, school supplies, uniforms, after-school activities, day care, room and board

Taxes: federal and state taxes, including property tax

Retirement planning and savings: contributions to retirement plans, savings accounts

Recreation: gym and club memberships, athletic equipment, hobby supplies, collections, travel and vacation expenses

Entertainment: eating/drinking outside the home, concerts, plays, sporting events, movies, rented videos, books, subscriptions, gourmet coffee, lunches, online computer services or memberships

Clothes: work clothes, play clothes, dry cleaning, tailoring

Communication: phone bills, cell phone bills, high-speed Internet access, answering services, pagers, phone hardware

Religious and charitable donations: cash contributions, pledges

Interest and finance charges: interest on consumer debt (you shouldn't have any now!), bank fees (including ATM fees), late fees, etc.

If you can create a spreadsheet with the above categories and drop your data into it for at least one month, you will be able to draw basic conclusions about where your money goes. And then you can take action.

According to author David Bach *(The Automatic Millionaire),* you don't need a lot of time or money to make a million dollars. If you save $5 a day, you'll be a millionaire in 41 years. If you save $10 a day, you're a millionaire in 34 years. How? It's the magic of compound interest: Money not only earns interest, but interest earns interest. Example: If you invest $1,000 and it earns 10 percent each year, after the first year your investment will be worth $1,100. In the second year, you now earn 10 percent on that $100 as well as the original $1,100, which brings your total to $1,210 and so on. If you save $25 every week for 40 years, even with just a 5 percent return, you'll have more than $165,000.

Finding that extra money to set aside every day is easier than you think. Bach calls it "eliminating the latte factor," which means getting rid of excess expenses that are not necessary for your daily living (such as designer coffee from a trendy coffee shop) but that add up to a lot of wasted money. Eating out in restaurants, buying expensive (needless) gadgets, abusing your cell phone (past your free minutes), and indulging in your shoe-buying or beer-drinking habit are typical examples.

> Compounding is the most important financial tool you can use. It's like putting two rabbits in a room and coming back to find that they've multiplied to 20. The longer you stay out of the room, the more rabbits you get.

Your public library has information about budgeting and money management techniques. You can also find worksheets online to help you establish a realistic budget and see where your money goes. David Bach's web site at www.davidbach.com is a good starting point. Other ones include www.fool.com, www.personalfinancebudgeting.com, www.kiplinger.com, www.smartmoney.com, and www.moneycentral.msn.com. In fact, you'll find dozens of sites

---

The Big 5 Learning Tips for Your Road Ahead

- Learn money managing skills by taking classes or self-teaching through books, seminars, audiotapes, even friends and contacts.
- Learn how to prioritize and cut back the nonessentials (think excess factor).
- Learn to save.
- Learn how to use credit to your benefit—not your destruction. If you cannot control your impulse to buy on credit, get a prepaid credit card. Watch out for 0% interest rates on credit cards or balance transfers.
- Learn to curb bad spending habits and how to say no.

geared toward helping you figure out a budget just by entering "personal finance" and/or "budget" into an Internet search engine.

Low-cost budget counseling services can help you analyze your income and expenses and develop a budget. Check your Yellow Pages or contact your local bank or consumer protection office for information about them. In addition, many universities, military bases, credit unions, and housing authorities operate nonprofit counseling programs. Making gradual adjustments to your lifestyle will make for lasting good money habits. Avoid radical changes; like radical diets, they never last and come back to haunt you!

Using Credit to Your Benefit

While you were insolvent and racking up debt on your high-interest credit cards, you were the quintessential customer for credit card companies. The scary part about going into debt is how quickly it can happen. Young adults, such as college students, are particularly at risk because credit card companies target them heavily. Why? The credit card companies assume that their parents will bail them out if necessary, and younger people are not used to managing credit in their life. Learning how to use credit to your advantage will be key to your success after bankruptcy. Trouble is, you learned how to spend and use credit poorly before your bankruptcy, and no one ever taught you how to use credit wisely.

You may want to avoid using credit cards right away again after your bankruptcy. If you made overspending your habit for many years, making a lifestyle change to prevent falling down that slippery slope can be as difficult as changing your diet and exercise habits to lose 20 pounds. People are creatures of habit, so think honestly about your tendencies when considering another credit card.

Are You a Target?

People with bad credit and young adults keep the credit card companies in business (while allowing those who use credit wisely to get away with great benefits, such as paying for

Being a compulsive buyer is akin to being an overeater, a gambler, an addict, and an alcoholic. But getting a handle on your spending habit can be easier than, let's say, overcoming your alcoholic tendencies. And there are programs available to help you get control of your habits. Debtors Anonymous is a nationwide 12-step program that helps you deal with your spending problem and gives you the guidance for getting control of your spending. Debtors Anonymous, whose support program works similarly to Alcoholics Anonymous, may suggest that you first build money management and spending skills using cash until you're ready to use credit and rebuild your credit. For those who've clearly abused their credit in the past and gotten into debt serious enough for bankruptcy due to their credit card debt, focusing on paying for things with cash only is a good idea. Check out www.debtorsanonymous.org for more information and to find a meeting near you. You can also dial directory assistance or request information by sending a self-addressed envelope to Debtors Anonymous, General Service Office, P.O. Box 920888, Needham, MA 02492-0009. Phone: 781-453-2743; fax: 781-453-2745. Or e-mail the office at new@debtorsanonymous.org and indicate your city, state, and proximity to larger cities. Several Debtors Anonymous meetings happen online; meeting times and access numbers change periodically. For details call 609-466-8861.

something a few weeks later and avoiding carrying around cash). When credit card companies hand young adults credit cards that increase their buying power beyond anything they've ever experienced, it's understandable that young adults tend to abuse that credit and get in over their heads. Imagine an 18-year-old who's never seen more than $350 in his bank account for mowing lawns and painting houses all summer long in between school, and then he receives a credit card with a $5,000 limit. A credit card company would love to add a young college student to its customer list and have that person paying interest for long after he or she graduates. The longer it takes for someone to pay off a credit card, the more money the credit card company makes. In essence, the credit card company is roping you in as a future customer, maybe a customer for life.

> People with bad credit are also targets of credit card companies. Because credit card companies make their money on interest, people who cannot manage their bills and don't pay them in full each month make credit card companies very rich. A credit card company will tolerate someone who always pays his or her bills in full every month so long as there are enough people who don't and those people fuel the credit card companies' bottom lines.

Turning a Blind Eye to the Ad Machines

Today's advertisers are savvy, manipulative, and sophisticated. They know how to get you to buy, and even how to get you thinking that debt isn't that bad. Billions of credit card solicitations go out to people each year with letters that look personalized to you. They make you feel special—a chosen one—so it's harder to resist the invitation. Moreover, the government pushes people to buy because it adds to the economy and protects jobs. Following 9/11 and the plunge into a recession, politicians and well-respected government leaders urged Americans to help out by going out and spending money. This trend will never end. Whenever a recession looms or the indicators of the economy point to a slowdown, the government will persuade people to renew the economy with their hard-earned money. No one will talk about saving or cutting back or even the consequences to excessive spending on an individual level. Why? The government is less concerned about individuals than it is about the masses and the power the masses have as a whole on the economy.

Nearly two-thirds of the gross national product (GNP), an indicator of the state of the economy, is a result of consumer spending. So if we're not spending money on goods and services—including goods and services we don't need to live—that GNP goes down and you hear things in the media about a weak or slow economy. During the holiday season, the media likes to cover how much people are spending in retail stores and how much profit those stores are making as an ultimate end-of-year indicator of just how well the United States is doing. Then, once New Year's is over and those credit card bills start arriving, people get the so-called holiday hangover and worry about how they will pay for those bills.

Keeping Up with the Joneses

When you're strapped for cash, credit cards are easily abused. As the saying goes, "It's un-American to pay in cash." A lot has changed since our grandparents' generation. Families who experienced the Depression were big savers, while we've become big spenders. Part of the reason Baby Boomers have had the luxury of spending a lot (and fueling the economic booms in recent decades) is because they inherited money from their parents and grandparents who saved and invested so well. But less and less is getting passed on to future generations as families spend more and save less. No one has a Depression mentality anymore; we have the opposite mentality. At the beginning of the twenty-first century, we live in a consumer culture that argues against building family money. Media and marketers encourage you to spend what money you have and some that you don't have. The money you don't have typically comes from credit cards. These cards are easily abused for the sake of living beyond one's means and keeping up with the Joneses.

Sometimes it doesn't take a medical bill or a job loss to abuse credit; overspending for luxury items, vacations, entertainment, eating out more, and buying unnecessary goods can also become abusive. People have grown so accustomed to financing their lifestyle with credit instead of cash that they will take expensive vacations or plunk a $50,000 wedding onto a card assuming they'll be able to pay for that holiday or ritzy wedding with future income. This sets up a mentality that every purchase can eventually be paid with future income. But when all those purchases add up to a lot of money, it becomes increasingly hard to visualize paying off that debt without winning the lottery or hitting it big in Hollywood.

As hard as it may seem to picture, some of the richest Americans don't look or act wealthy. They drive old cars, shop in flea markets and hunt down good buys, avoid the department stores, patronize the Costcos and Walmarts, and worry about money down to every last penny. Instead of flushing their money into depreciating assets (things that lose value over time such as a car), they make wise purchases of appreciating assets (things that increase in value over time such as a house) and they invest smartly for the long run. While they don't appear wealthy when they are walking down the street in a T-shirt and shorts, they have bank accounts that give them the security and freedom to live a long and happy life.

Become a Member of the Forty Percent Club

In your life after bankruptcy, you should aim to become part of that 40 percent club of people who pay off their bills in full each and every month. What a credit card allows you to do is pay for something conveniently and borrow time for paying the bill. Let's say your closing date (the date when your credit card bill for the month ends and you have that month's sum to pay) is the 15th of every month. You can buy a $300 television on July 16 and not have to worry about paying for that television until after August 15 when you eventually receive the bill and are asked to pay the minimum amount. While the credit card company would rather you pay less than the total balance so it reaps the rewards of charging you interest, you should choose to pay the entire bill in full.

If you find it too difficult to pay your credit card bills in full every month, try getting a credit card where you pre-pay a certain amount and cannot go over that amount or avoid credit cards entirely. The truth is, if you declared bankruptcy as a result of credit card debt, chances are you will find the shift to a new way of using credit very difficult without a lot of practice. You may want to avoid the use of credit cards and focus on paying for everything in cash or by check before venturing out again with a piece of plastic that has enormous buying power. Once you feel you are ready to use credit, start with one credit card and add more if you think it will help manage your finances.

Some find that by having more than one credit card, they can stagger their closing dates and deal with paying for those monthly bills more effectively. For example, have one credit card that closes on the 15th of every month and one that closes on the 1st of every month. That way, you receive two separate bills at different times of the month instead of getting one larger bill that you have to pay by one date.

Tip: Set aside a calendar that you use to mark down the dates your bills are due. For example, credit card bills, energy bills, phone bills, cable bills, water bills, and so on. That way, if you missed a statement in the mail, you'll know that you still need to pay it. Just because you didn't get the bill doesn't mean you're not responsible for it on time. As part of your agreement with the company providing you a good or service, it's up to you to make sure you pay your bills monthly—regardless of receipt of the actual bill. Many companies call the bills they send out reminders to pay, and not necessarily bills!

If you avoid using credit cards for a little while after your bankruptcy, at some point you'll want to reestablish yourself in the credit community in order to repair your credit score. Only then can you rebuild your credit and open yourself up to loans for larger purchases, such as a home, a car, or a small business. It's important to use credit, but you must use it wisely.

Choosing a Credit Card

When you are ready to use a credit card again, don't pick the first solicitation that comes in your mail. Do your research and find one that fits your needs. Understand the credit terms and conditions to any card you choose. Compare terms and fees before you agree to a certain card. Know how a particular credit card company calculates balances, including finance charges, transaction fees, annual percentage rates, and so on. How credit card companies compute balances when you maintain a balance over time can get confusing. Do your best to understand your statements, and if you pay every balance off each month, your statements should be easy to read. Watch out for cash advance features, as they are often costly and don't come with grace periods for payment.

Credit card companies want your business so you have more leverage than you think. You can negotiate interest rates and limits. Calling the credit card companies and talking with a representative over the phone easily accomplishes this. If you encounter trouble negotiating, hang up and try another. There are hundreds of credit card companies seeking customers. One will respond to your wishes. You can find the best credit card rate on the following web site: www.bankrate.com. And for more general information, check out www.smartmoney.com/debt.

Annual Fees. If you choose a card with an annual fee, be sure you're getting some benefit out of that fee, such as mileage points on an airline for traveling or points that have cash rewards. There are plenty of credit card companies, however, that have no annual fees attached to them and that will give you the benefits of a credit card without it costing you anything. If you

Once you have a credit card, continue to negotiate terms to its use. If you misplace a bill and fail to submit your payment in time, you can argue your finance charge. Don't be afraid to get on the phone and argue any fees you find on your bill, unless you've chosen a card that has an annual fee. Explain to them that you missed your payment by mistake and you never meant to miss that payment. If you're in good standing with the company, they should remove that charge. If they don't, you can threaten to cancel the card.

choose a no-fee card and pay your bills on time and in full, you're getting the benefits of a credit card for free.

Charge Cards vs. Credit Cards. American Express is the best example of a charge card. Charge cards have no limits and must be paid in full at the end of the month. They typically have annual fees. Credit cards, however, work differently: You assume responsibility for paying for charges in full at some point, but the credit card company allows you to finance your purchases over time and you have set limits. These limits usually are larger than any person's ability to pay off a maxed-out credit card in one month. That is, if a credit card gives you $5,000 in credit and you use all that credit in one month, you probably won't be able to pay off that bill at once. This is why credit cards can be so dangerous—credit cards give people more power than they can handle if they plan to pay off cards every month.

Unauthorized Charges. Don't pay someone else's misuse of your card. If your card is used without your permission, you can be held responsible for the first $50, but not if you report the loss before it happens. You can also dispute charges for unsatisfactory goods and services, which is why buying with a credit card affords you some security in your purchase. To do so, you must have made the purchase in your home state or within 100 miles of your current billing address, and the charge must be for more than $50.

Banking to Your Benefit

The banking industry has gotten as fierce as the credit card industry. Banks vie for people's attention as much as credit card companies do, so you have leverage when choosing a way to bank.

Find a No-Cost or Low-Cost Bank

Like credit card companies, banks make money from the fees they charge customers. If you don't pay attention to your bank statement or balance your books, you'll miss the charges that slip through unnoticed by you because your bank takes money out of your accounts. Every bank has a list of charges it can apply to your account if you break one of the rules of its banking. If you don't bother to read the fine print or remember the terms of your accounts when you set them up and begin banking, these charges and fees might surprise you. Examples include checking fees, minimum balance fees, ATM fees, returned item fees, debit fees, monthly service fees, NSF (non-sufficient fund) fees, ATM replacement card fees, and the rather sneaky currency conversion fee (which in New York State, for example, adds two percent to each debit transaction made overseas in addition to a $1.50 to $5 surcharge), and so on. You want to avoid as many fees as possible, which entails understanding all the terms to your banking agreements and occasionally fighting fees that pop up and that you think are not necessary.

For example, banks can create odd-sounding fees that you don't understand until you get slapped with the fee. Take the excess activity fee that one popular bank charges people when they do too many transactions online instead of visiting a teller or ATM or sending correspondence by snail mail. Federal electronic banking laws prohibit you from making transactions more than a couple times a month, so if you transfer money frequently (more than the allot-

Bankrate.com estimates that Americans dropped $2.2 billion in ATM charges in 2004. All those charges happen when we swipe our cards carelessly through dinky cash dispensers at a corner liquor store, our own banks, and someone else's bank. If your bank charges you $2 for the transaction, and the machine that dispenses the cash charges another $1.50, you're wasting away $3.50 every time you get that cash. How can you cut back on these fees? Limit your ATM visits to those machines in your bank's own network, and withdraw larger amounts each time to avoid limited transaction fees. Also, when you pay with your ATM card at point of sale locations, ask for cash back; it's a free service.

ted time per month), you need to be sure you keep track of your transactions and do some by phone, mail, or by walking into your local branch. This sounds ridiculous, but banks find every which way to add fees and charges. And because they do so without asking (they take the money directly from your account), it's like they have a license to steal. So you have to watch out and be very vigilant with all your accounts. Become a careful reader of your bank statements, looking for errors and knowing what every debit and deposit means. If you ever have a question, call your bank's toll-free number and ask.

Find a bank with free checking and be sure to ask about minimum balances, ATM fees, and how to avoid commonly charged transactions. Also ask if they have any protections you can use, such as overdraft, that will prevent you from draining an account while checks you've written need to be paid. Note, however, that overdraft fees can be heavy, so ask! With all the banks and options out there, you can find a bank that meets your needs and lifestyle.

High Interest Savings Accounts

Open a savings account that you mark as untouchable in your mind; this is the fund you use to get through temporary financial setbacks. You add a predetermined, set amount each month (no matter what) and let the account build. You don't intend to use this account unless an emergency comes up or you suddenly need the money for living due to a job loss or serious illness. Figure out a reasonable number you can devote each month to this account and be religious about adding that money to it. You may be able to set up an automatic transfer from your checking account to this savings account so you don't have to think about it. Plan to set aside enough money for six months worth of living expenses.

Once you have that emergency fund set up, keep adding to the account and do your best not to use the money unless absolutely necessary. It is also helpful to have a car fund to help pay for those incidentals along the way that can be big, such as maintenance, repair, and deductibles on insurance claims (more on insurance below). Costs related to your car can be sudden and unexpected, so setting aside $500 for those situations will ease any troubling situations.

You don't have to keep a savings account with the same bank as your checking, although that can be more convenient. Try shopping around for savings accounts that offer higher interest rates. Online-only banks are more competitive when it comes to higher interest rates than brick and mortar banks, so it pays to do your homework. Moreover, once you establish a decent amount in your savings account, you can find banks willing to increase that interest rate so long as you remain above the minimum required balance for a high-interest account.

Consider a Credit Union

Credit unions offer a different kind of service than regular banks. They don't offer as many options and typically have smaller ATM networks, but they have lower service fees on checking accounts and lower required minimum balances. Contact Credit Union National Association at www.cuna.org to find out if you qualify to join one of these member-owned institutions. In some instances, it boils down to location: Residents of Los Angeles County, California's East Bay Area, and the Florida Keys automatically qualify. You can also contact the Federal Credit Unions office at National Credit Union Administration, 1776 G Street, NW, Washington, DC 20456.

Investment Accounts

Beyond the emergency savings account you keep for unexpected expenses—or even to build a fund for purchasing a home—having a retirement account that you fund once a month with a minimum amount is important for your future. If your employer does not offer you a 401(k) or similar plan, open an IRA (Individual Retirement Account) with a discount brokerage house and commit to putting a certain amount into that account every month. Personal finance experts call this paying yourself first. There are different IRAs from which to choose, such as a traditional IRA, a Roth IRA, a Rollover IRA, and so on. Consult your bank or a financial advisor for help in choosing one that fits your needs. You can also learn more about these kinds of accounts online at sites like www.fool.com, www.money.cnn.com, and www.moneycentral.msn.com. These sites are comprehensive and great starting points for learning more about money. Some have life-expectancy tools for figuring out how much money you need to make before you can retire comfortably.

Tips to Managing Money Wisely

- Learn to negotiate interest rates. Yes! Even with credit card companies. They want your business.
- Learn to not keep up with the Joneses. (Move away from them!)
- Watch out during holidays, birthdays, and special occasions that taunt people to spend unwisely. It's okay to downsize your gift list, as well as your gifts.
- Scrutinize your bills every month—know what you're spending and where.
- Avoid unnecessary fees such as those from ATMs, check-writing fees, monthly service fees, overusage of cell phones, or even parking tickets.
- Balance your checkbook. Search for errors between your records and your bank's.
- Pay bills on time.
- Go online to pay bills if you don't like sitting down and writing checks.
- Consider money management software to track your expenses and deposits.
- Use a calendar to mark dates bills are due.
- Use a no-fees or low-fees bank.
- Set up automatic deposits into a savings and/or investment account that you don't touch.
- Avoid payday-in-advance shops.

The National Foundation for Consumer Credit (NFCC), founded in 1951, is the umbrella group for the only national network of nonprofit counseling organizations providing education and counseling services on budgeting and credit face-to-face, by telephone, by mail, and online. All members receive confidential services for free or a nominal amount. To locate the closest NFCC member office, call 800-388-2227 or visit the NFCC web site at www.nfcc.org.

- Avoid excess expenses every month.
- Check your credit report at least once a year.
- If anything seems too good to be true in terms of a deal, it probably is.

Beware of Fraud and Identity Theft

Identity theft has become the fastest-growing crime; more than 40 percent of all consumer complaints in the United States relate to identity theft. This crime, which cost consumers and their banks or credit card companies more than $1.4 billion in 2004, affects one in every 11 Americans now. By 2006, losses could reach $3.68 billion. ID theft happens when someone steals a piece of personal information about you and uses it to commit a fraud in your name. The thief might steal your Social Security number, name, date of birth, credit card information, bank account numbers, mother's maiden name, and so on, and use these things to do any of the following:

- Open up new accounts
- Change the mailing address on your current credit cards
- Rent apartments
- Establish services for utility companies
- Write fraudulent checks
- Steal and transfer money from a bank account
- File bankruptcy (ah-ha!)
- Obtain employment
- Establish a new identity
- Apply for a mortgage, car loan, or cell phone

Once someone assumes your identity to get credit in your name and steal from businesses, you probably won't realize it happened until months later. Debtors are classic targets for identity thieves because they are typically not good with managing money and will take longer to realize someone has stolen their identity. As an honest person recovering from a bankruptcy, the last thing you need is an identity theft problem. If your identity is stolen after your bankruptcy, your life and ability to get it back on the right track financially will be severely challenged. Your experience with bankruptcy aside, the prevalence of identity theft alone in America today is enough to require careful scrutiny of your finances.

Being good with money after your bankruptcy demands that you be wary of identity theft and take the precautions to avoid it. The two best ways to prevent ID theft are to guard your personal information, specifically your Social Security number, checks, and credit card information, and to be very careful in every transaction you make, whether it's over the Internet, a counter, a phone, or by mail.

If you become a victim of ID theft, contact the three credit bureaus to have them flag your file and contact the Federal Trade Commission (FTC) for more information. Go to www.ftc.gov for detailed advice and instructions.

Federal Trade Commission's Mission

The FTC does more than help identity theft victims. This federal agency is such a great source of information that we encourage you to use it as you work your way toward being a smarter, more financially sound consumer. The FTC protects consumers against unfair, deceptive, or fraudulent practices and enforces a variety of consumer protection laws and trade regulation rules. You can access the FTC's library of consumer publications on the web site and also contact the FTC at Consumer Response Center, Federal Trade Commission, Washington, DC 20580 or call 202-382-4357.

Scams take place every day—over the phone, e-mail, pagers, in your mailbox, at your front door—and as we've mentioned before, debtors and people who have a history of bad credit or poor money management skills are targeted (so the fact that you've filed for bankruptcy might make you a target!). As you begin your new life and practice good money management, you'll need to be extra cautious about protecting yourself and your money. The most frequent kinds of frauds and scams involve credit repair firms, telemarketers, investment opportunities, wealth-building scams, travel scams, home repair cons, funeral chasers, fake contests, and self-employment pitches. You've seen these ads before: "Earn up to $100,000 a year working from home!" and all you need to do is attend a seminar and/or purchase a kit that teaches you how to become a millionaire from the comforts of your home. Some infomercials tout easy ways to make money in real estate; others promote low-interest government loans or grants to start a new business or to go to college. These companies prey on consumers that don't do their homework and who believe that building wealth is as easy as 1-2-3. No matter how professional their ads and infomercials appear to be, or how many experts endorse the program, many of the claims made are false, misleading, or unsubstantiated. Promises of quick, easy money can be a powerful lure. But if you buy into a business opportunity at a seminar, you may find that the products and information you purchased are worthless and that your money is gone.

The following are some tips to avoid such scams:

- Be skeptical about any get-rich-quick claim.

- Be suspicious of any unidentified telephone, e-mail, or pager messages that claim to offer information about a sick or injured relative, a debt, bad credit, or prize offer. Also be wary of messages from unfamiliar sources (with weird return telephone numbers and international access codes).

- Avoid high-pressure sales pitches that require you to buy now or risk losing out on the opportunity (legitimate offers will always be there tomorrow).

- Take your time to do careful research, including asking companies for written substantiation for claims in their presentations.

- Be cautious of success stories or testimonials, because they may be paid for and not reflect the experience of most consumers.

- Check out companies with your local consumer protection agency, Better Business Bureau, and state Attorney General's office. Find out if any unresolved consumer complaints are on file.

- Before you buy anything, check out the company's refund policy and get everything in writing.

- Most important: Never let your emotions interfere with your business affairs!

Always remember: The greater the potential return, the greater the risk. And investments seldom exist without some risk involved. Never invest what you cannot afford to lose.

Resource Roundup: Web Sites

Consumer information:	www.ftc.com
Phone rates:	www.1010phonerates.com
To buy or lease a car:	www.autobytel.com
	www.smartmoney.com/autos
	www.edmunds.com
	www.kbb.com

Online calculators:

Altamira Net Worth Calculator: www.altamira.com/altamira/toolkit/net+worth+ calculator.htm

Altamira Cash Management Calculator:

www.altamira.com/altamira/toolkit/capital+builder+calculator.htm

Kiplinger Credit Calculator:

www.kiplinger.com/tools/index.html

CNN and Money Magazine Debt Calculator:

http://cgi.money.cnn.com/tools/

CreditCalc Wizard:

www.zilchworks.com/cgi-bin/calc/cardcalc.pl

Bankrate.com Credit Card Calculator:

http://aol1.bankrate.com/aol/calc/MinPayment.asp?nav=cc&page=calc_home

Using Insurance to Protect You

Insurance is not something only the rich are entitled to have. Everyone should carry some form of insurance to protect oneself from the what-ifs. If part of your bankruptcy was blamed on a judgment against you or a bill you had to pay because you didn't have insurance in place to protect you, then now is the time to buy some insurance and limit the chance of falling into bankruptcy again as a result of another judgment or whopping bill that insurance should typically cover.

There are hundreds of ways that you can be found liable (responsible) for some terrible situation, but there are only a few ways to protect yourself—legally and financially—from the consequences of rotten luck. Of course, all the insurance in the world won't protect you from every loss. The same holds true when it comes to health and the risk of illness. There are simply more claims than there are coverages. But, it's better to have some coverage. Even if you work steadily and save wisely through a long working life, legal, health or financial crises can still wipe out the money you make.

The most important types of insurance to carry are:

- Homeowners or renters
- Auto
- Health

Once you begin to amass new assets in your postbankruptcy life and learn to lead a healthy financial life, you can also consider adding a personal umbrella policy to your set of coverages. Here's why: When a court hands down a liability judgment that exhausts the limits of your homeowners or auto policy, you are responsible for the balance. This means you may have to sell your home, cash out your IRAs, or sell other assets in order to make the payment on the judgment. And, if your assets are exhausted and the judgment is still not satisfied, you may even have to dip into your future earnings to pay the remainder of the outstanding judgment. A personal umbrella policy, however, kicks in once your reach the limits of your other policies (this was how Bill Clinton paid for his legal fees in his defense against Paula Jones). Remember: One major liability case can wipe out the assets that took you a lifetime to create. Avoiding another bankruptcy is essential to your future.

Health Insurance

Buying health insurance is trickier than buying a homeowners, renters, or auto policies. You can't make one phone call or double-click your way to a good health policy. With 47 million Americans with no health insurance, the task of getting affordable insurance seems impossible. But do your best to get some coverage, and in the least, so-called catastrophic coverage, which will protect you if you land in an emergency room following a very bad accident and subsequently rack up hundreds of thousands of dollars in medical bills. If enormous medical bills were what landed you in bankruptcy court, you must do what you can to buy some health insurance.

If you cannot afford an individual policy or join a health maintenance organization, you can look into organizations or associations you can join that offer policies (think alumni organizations, guilds, unions, etc.), think about changing jobs to one that offers health coverage, or look into state-run programs that offer policies for your uninsured children. Health insurance may become a large expense in your postbankruptcy life, but it will protect you in the long-run and should not be considered an excessive expense.

Shopping for Insurance

The insurance market has become so competitive that you can shop for insurance like you shop for a car or computer. Companies typically offer discounts for people who buy more than one policy, so if you use company X for your homeowners insurance, you'll get a discount on your car insurance if you use that same company.

If you plan to start a home-based business or any type of business, look into a business owners policy (BOP) or adding some business-owners liability coverage to your existing homeowners policy.

When searching for health insurance, start by asking your friends and family members where they get their insurance. Use the Internet for research. But watch out: Avoid any health insurer that has offers too good to be true. There are plenty of unscrupulous companies out there posing as legitimate health insurers that will take your money and never help you out when you need them most—in the ER or at the doctor's office. Stick to health carriers you've heard of. Get some referrals. Make sure they are well respected. A good web site for researching insurance companies is www.jdpower.com. (J. D. Power and Associates is a private company that conducts research used by a variety of industries to improve product quality and customer satisfaction. It bases research solely on responses from millions of consumers and business customers worldwide. J. D. Power gives consumers free access to its library of research online.)

> Remember: You can't protect yourself from every bad thing that can happen, but you can minimize the risk you live with every day by using insurance. Think of insurance as a shield against some of the perils you might encounter.

More Tips for Watching Your Wallet

- Avoid impulse buying. Set a rule, such as the 48-hour policy, whereby you go home and think about making a purchase that you hadn't planned.
- Avoid sales. Everything is always on sale and for sale. Buying a $200 watch that was originally $400 didn't save you $200—it cost you $200!
- Avoid anything that obligates you to make a large fixed monthly payment.
- Avoid cosigning a loan or agreement.
- Avoid joint obligations with people who don't have good spending habits or credit.
- Avoid high-risk investments.
- Avoid accessing credit card cash advances, payday cash advances, or any advances that tack on expensive interest.
- Avoid banking on future income
- Avoid forgetting about your budget.

Set Financial Goals

Don't organize your finances, start afresh in your new debt-free life, and forget to set financial goals. Whether it's next month, next year, five years or 20 years down the road, setting financial goals is a way of planning for your future. And by planning what you want to accomplish, you'll be likely to reach those goals and have the money to support you.

Keep a notebook where you write down your goals. Divide the notebook up into sections labeled short-term, long-term, and very long-term goals. Short-term goals include things you would like to do soon, or within the next couple of years. Examples: finish school, buy a car, take a vacation, run a marathon, find a better job, plan a wedding. Long-term goals include things you want to accomplish in five, 10, even 20 years. Examples: buy a home, start a business, start a family, fund accounts for retirement and children's education. Very long terms goals include retiring, sending children to college, and having money to support your medical needs later in life.

By developing a budget you'll be able to set realistic financial goals. So long as you plan well and save accordingly, there is no limit to the goals you can reach and the rewards you can achieve.

Conclusion

We've given you a wealth of information in this chapter. Just when you thought the work was all done once the court sent you the final notice of your discharge, you must really start working hard to prevent yourself from bankruptcy again and doing what you can to build wealth. It's easier than you think.

Once you have your fresh start, speaking with experts who can assist you in organizing and maintaining your financial health is beneficial. If you cannot afford any assistance, do your own homework with the resources you do have, such as the Internet, library, friends and family, and community centers that offer free courses or seminars on how to manage money.

Below is a list of resources for if and when you want to hire someone to assist you in your new life. Never hire a financial advisor without checking out his or her background. Remember: Knowledge is power and these people can extend a great deal of power to you through their services.

The Financial Planning Association
www.fpanet.org
Phone: 800-647-6340

You can search by zip code for an advisor who has qualified as a Certified Financial Planner (CFP).

National Association of Personal Financial Advisors
www.napfa.org
Phone: 800-366-2732

You can search by zip code for a financial planner who works on a fee-only basis.

Certified Financial Planner (CFP)
www.cfp-board.org
Phone: 800-282-7526

The Institute of Certified Financial Planners will provide you with referrals to CFPs in your area if you call them. It also offers a Financial Planning Resource Kit, a collection of free brochures, that will answer most of your questions about the subject.

The American Institute of Certified Public Accountants Personal Financial Planning Division
www.aicpa.org/index.htm
Phone: 888-777-7077

They can provide referrals to members who have CPA licenses as well as CFPs.

To check backgrounds, experience, and licenses, you can contact the following organizations.

National Association of Securities Dealers
www.nasdr.com
Phone: 800-289-9999

This is the best place to start. This site lists just about everything you could ever need to know about a financial advisor, including where they went to school, where they have worked, and if there are any complaints listed.

Certified Financial Planner Board of Standards

www.cfp-board.org

Phone: 888-237-6275

This group sets and enforces the standards advisors must meet in order to call themselves certified financial planners. This site allows you to check the status of a CFP-registered advisor.

North American Securities Administration Association

www.nasaa.org

Organized in 1919, this organization is devoted to investor protection. This site is dedicated to helping investors protect themselves against securities fraud and can provide you with additional information on this topic.

National Association of Insurance Commissioners

www.naic.org

Phone: 816-842-3600

This group is an organization of state insurance regulators. Through its online National Insurance Producer Registry (NIPR), you can find information on more than 2.5 million insurance agents and brokers, including their licensing status and disciplinary history.

CHAPTER 8

Frequently Asked Questions

This chapter is dedicated entirely to answering the most frequently asked questions. We've organized the chapter according to topic, so you can easily locate a set of questions that pertains to one part of the process.

Customers who enter our stores are full of questions when they first contemplate bankruptcy. They are starving for answers and sometimes feel embarrassed that they have to ask for them. There's nothing to be embarrassed about, however. No one gets a lengthy course in bankruptcy unless you go to law school and study it in particular. Bankruptcy is not a subject in high school, or even an elective in college. People who don't deal with bankruptcies in their daily lives do not know what it's about. And it's typically not knowledge you pick up along the way the same way you do about buying a house or balancing your checkbook. Even lawyers who don't deal with bankruptcies have questions!

Please note: Generally speaking, there are many exceptions to the various rules. Many questions can be hard to answer in one manner because options may exist depending on state law. Always check your local court's rules and don't ever hesitate to call your local court's clerk and ask specific questions.

Thinking about Bankruptcy

What is bankruptcy?

Bankruptcy is a constitutional right for people or businesses who owe more money than they can pay to either work out a plan to repay the money over a certain time period (Chapter 13), or discharge most of their bills (Chapter 7).

What are the types of bankruptcy?

There are four common types of bankruptcy.

Chapter 7: This is the so-called straight bankruptcy for individuals and companies that want to discharge (wipe out) their debts in exchange for giving up assets that cannot be excluded from the bankruptcy using allowable exemptions. In Chapter 7, most of your debts are discharged. Businesses that file under Chapter 7 do not intend to stay in business.

Chapter 13: This is the so-called reorganization Chapter. In a Chapter 13 case you file a plan showing how you will pay off some of your past-due and current debts over three to five years. A Chapter 13 costs you more money than a Chapter 7, but it allows you to keep valuable assets, such as your home and car, that would otherwise be lost in a Chapter 7.

Chapter 11: This is a type of reorganization used by businesses and a few individual debtors whose debts are very large. Chapter 11 is very complicated and expensive—best left to huge corporations and lawyers!

Chapter 12: This is the Chapter for family farmers.

Who can file a bankruptcy?

Any person, partnership or corporation may file a bankruptcy. If the person or entity who owes the money files a petition to start the bankruptcy, it is called a voluntary bankruptcy. Voluntary cases can be filed under Chapters 7 and 13 (Chapter 12 is also voluntary for farmers).

Will I go to jail if I don't pay my debts?

No, debtor's prisons are illegal. You can go to jail for acts related to bankruptcy, but you cannot be put in jail simply because you owe money. Situations that can put you in jail include tax fraud or being held in contempt of the court. For example, if a judge orders you to appear in court or to go to a deposition to answer questions related to a debt (example: child support) and you fail to appear, you may face jail time for disobeying the judge. Tax fraud can land you in jail, but you won't go to jail for merely being unable to pay taxes.

I am divorced or getting a divorce; how will that affect me?

Just like a cosigner, a spouse or ex-spouse may be jointly liable on a debt. Your bankruptcy protects you, but it does not protect your spouse or ex-spouse. If you are contemplating bankruptcy while getting a divorce, seek the advice of an attorney. You cannot get divorce while your bankruptcy case is pending unless you ask the bankruptcy court to lift the automatic stay. This can get complicated, so consult with a lawyer who can advise you how to proceed.

How much do I have to owe before I can file bankruptcy?

There is no set monetary amount establishing entitlement to seek relief in bankruptcy. The Bankruptcy Code requires the case to be filed in good faith.

Do I need a lawyer?

You don't need a lawyer to file for bankruptcy. You need to fill out the proper forms, file them with the clerk at your local bankruptcy court, attend your creditors' meeting and await the court's discharge of your debts. You can always hire an attorney, however, to assist you in your bankruptcy proceeding. You can also employ the services of a bankruptcy petition preparer such as We The People to help you type your documents.

What property can I keep?

Individual debtors can exempt (keep) some real, personal, or intangible property. Exempt assets are protected by state law from distribution to your creditors. In some states, debtors have the right to choose whether to claim state exemptions or federal exemptions. In some cases, federal exemptions allow a debtor more protection than state exemptions. If a state allows federal exemptions as an option, you must choose one or the other, you cannot pick and choose between them.

Will I lose my house or apartment?

It depends on the amount of equity in your home and the homestead exemption in your state. One of the biggest worries you may face in considering filing for bankruptcy is the possible loss of your home. Though there are a few situations where you may lose your home, keep in mind that bankruptcy is not designed to put you out on the street.

If you are behind on your mortgage payments, you face a greater risk of losing your house in a Chapter 7 bankruptcy—unless you can work a deal with your lender (which includes repaying what you owe to get up to speed). Your mortgage lender will ask the bankruptcy court to lift the automatic stay to begin or resume foreclosure proceedings. In a Chapter 13 bankruptcy, you will not lose your house if you immediately resume making the regular payments called for under your agreement and repay your missed mortgage payments through your plan.

If you are current on your mortgage payments, you will not lose your house if you file for Chapter 13 bankruptcy, as long as you continue to make your mortgage payments. In Chapter 7 bankruptcy, whether you will lose your house depends on the amount of equity you have in the property (the value of your home minus what you owe on it) and the amount of any homestead exemption (which varies state-to-state) to which you are entitled. If you are a renter and are current on your rent payments and file for bankruptcy, it's unlikely your landlord would ever find out. But if you are behind on your rent, there's a good chance that your landlord will begin eviction proceedings to get you out. Your inclination may be to file for bankruptcy just to get the automatic stay in place to stop the eviction. This will work, but not for very long. Expect your landlord to come into court to have the stay lifted, which is likely to be granted.

Will I lose my car?

It depends on the amount of equity in your car and the motor vehicle exemption in your state.

Can my car loan debt become discharged by my debt so I can keep my car?

No. A bankruptcy cannot discharge your secured debts. Secured assets—assets for which you have a debt attached—can be repossessed or foreclosed on if you fail to make payments. So if you still owe money on your car, a bankruptcy will not eliminate that debt and allow you to keep your car. Your car will be repossessed unless you negotiate other ways of keeping it, such as by using a reaffirmation agreement. One exception to this rule: Certain nonpurchase money security interest loans can be voided by exempting the debt. This happens if, for example, you secure a loan by using your car title or household furniture that you already own outright. Technically, the lender has a secured interest in your assets that you used as collateral for the loan, but in bankruptcy cases these types of debts are either reduced or voided.

How often can I file bankruptcy?

You may file a bankruptcy every six to seven years depending on dates of filing and discharge.

What does it cost to file bankruptcy?

The court filing fee is $209 for Chapter 7 and $194 for Chapter 13.

Will I have to go to court?

In most cases you will not have to go to court. However, you must attend the 341 meeting (meeting of the creditors) where you will meet with the bankruptcy trustee and any listed creditors who wish to attend. This is an informal meeting where the trustee asks you questions about your petition.

Who is the bankruptcy trustee?

Upon filing your petition for bankruptcy, the court appoints a trustee—generally an attorney—to manage your assets. A bankruptcy trustee is responsible for administering each Chapter 7 or Chapter 13 bankruptcy. The trustee is not a government employee, but he or she is hired by the U.S. Trustee to handle the cases for the government. Trustees represent the interests of the creditors. In a Chapter 7, your trustee determines whether you have any nonexempt assets he or she can take away from you to sell in order to get money for the creditors. In a Chapter 13, your trustee takes your monthly payments and distributes the money to the creditors.

What happens to my credit rating?

If you need to file for bankruptcy, chances are your credit rating isn't very good anyway and a bankruptcy filing probably won't make it worse. Bankruptcies remain on credit reports for 10 years.

What about cosigners on my loans?

Cosigners are responsible for any debt that you file on.

Will filing for bankruptcy negatively impact my job or my ability to get one?

Employers cannot discriminate merely because you have sought relief in bankruptcy. Similarly, your employer cannot fire you solely because you have filed for bankruptcy.

Can I lose my job because I filed bankruptcy?

No. Your employer cannot discriminate against you solely based on your bankruptcy filing.

Will my boss find out I filed bankruptcy?

Possibly. In most cases the trustee will contact your employer to verify employment and salary.

What if I do nothing? Can I be put in jail for not paying my bills?

Debtor's prisons are illegal. If you do nothing and your debt becomes serious enough, your creditors will force you into bankruptcy by instigating legal action. Incarceration is a risk only if you have acted fraudulently regarding the bankruptcy case or have incurred debt through criminal means.

Will bankruptcy get rid of all my debts?

No. Some debts are not dischargeable, for instance: (1) money owed for child support or alimony, fines, and some taxes; (2) debts not listed on your bankruptcy petition; (3) loans you got by knowingly giving false information to a creditor, who reasonably relied on it in making you the loan; (4) debts resulting from willful and malicious harm; (5) student loans owed to a school or government body, except if the court decides that payment would be an undue hardship; and (6) mortgages and other liens that are not paid in the bankruptcy case (but bankruptcy will end your obligation to pay any additional money if the property is sold by the creditor).

Will bankruptcy stop a wage garnishment?

Yes, in most cases.

Will bankruptcy stop a foreclosure?

Temporarily, yes, but the bank may move forward with the foreclosure after the discharge or earlier by obtaining the court's approval.

Will bankruptcy stop an eviction?

Temporarily, yes, but the owner is entitled to possession of the property, and your landlord can move forward with the eviction after the discharge or earlier with the court's approval.

Will bankruptcy stop a judgment?

Yes. Most collection actions are stopped by bankruptcy. However, there are some exceptions: Criminal cases can usually go forward if you've been charged with a crime.

Will a bankruptcy remove a lien?

Certain liens may be removed, but this requires a motion to be filed with the court.

What if I owe money on my car, boat, or such? Can I still keep it or will I have to give it back?

The Bankruptcy Code provides that you may reaffirm secured property, but having too much equity in any asset may cause the trustee to take it. If the payments on such secured property are current, reaffirmation may not be required.

Where can I get a copy of the Federal Rules of Bankruptcy Procedure?

A copy of the Federal Rules of Bankruptcy Procedure (Bankruptcy Rules) are available for review in any clerk's office location and in law libraries. You can usually access the bankruptcy rules—especially your local rules—by logging on the Internet and finding your local court's web site. Start at www.uscourts.gov.

Does a married person's spouse also have to file bankruptcy?

No. In some cases where only one spouse has debts or where one spouse has debts that are not dischargeable, it might be advisable to have only one spouse file.

Will bankruptcy discharge my obligation to pay community debts after a divorce?

With a few exceptions you may be discharged from all dischargeable community debts. In some circumstances you may still be liable to your spouse if he or she pays the debt, or files a complaint against you in bankruptcy court.

Are pension plans, 401(k) plans, and IRA accounts exempt?

Generally speaking, 401(k) plans and other ERISA-qualified plans are generally excluded from the bankruptcy estate. But IRA accounts are not ERISA-qualified plans and are only exempt to the extent necessary for the support of the debtor and his or her dependents. State laws may vary on this question, so consult a local bankruptcy attorney if you have concerns about these plans in your state.

May I transfer my assets to a friend or family member before filing bankruptcy?

Don't transfer your assets to friends, family, or anyone else to protect the assets from your creditors. The transfer may very well be considered a fraudulent transfer. If it is, you may lose both the property and your right to a bankruptcy discharge.

Choosing Which Type of Bankruptcy

Why choose Chapter 13 over Chapter 7 bankruptcy?

Although the overwhelming numbers of people who file for bankruptcy choose Chapter 7, there are several reasons you may prefer to select Chapter 13:

- You cannot file for Chapter 7 bankruptcy if you received a Chapter 7 or Chapter 13 discharge within the previous six years (unless you paid off at least 70 percent of your unsecured debts in a Chapter 13 bankruptcy). On the other hand, you can file for Chapter 13 bankruptcy at any time.

- You have valuable nonexempt property.

- You're behind on your mortgage or car loan. In Chapter 7, you'll have to give up the property or pay for it in full during your bankruptcy case. In Chapter 13, you can repay the arrears through your plan and keep the property by making the payments required under the contract.

- You have debts that cannot be discharged in Chapter 7.

- You have codebtors on personal (non-business) loans. In Chapter 7, the creditors will go after your codebtors for payment. In Chapter 13, the creditors may not seek payment from your codebtors for the duration of your case.

Filing a Chapter 7 Bankruptcy

How long does the bankruptcy process take?

Approximately one to two months from the date of filing, the 341A meeting (creditors' meeting) will occur. Without extraordinary motions, hearings, or proceedings, the Notice of Discharge is entered approximately 90 days after the date of filing.

Where do I file my bankruptcy case?

A bankruptcy is filed in a federal court in the bankruptcy district where you have lived the greater part of the past 180 days.

How much money can I have in my checking/savings account when I file?

You can exempt cash to a certain amount, so having a few hundred dollars in your account is okay. Avoid having no cash or closed accounts when you file, as this may look like fraud to the bankruptcy court.

What if a check hasn't cleared when I file?

Any money in your checking account at the time of filing that is over your exemption limit (and wildcard if you can use one) can be taken by the trustee and used to pay your debts.

Can I pay off a loan to a family member before I file?

No. Be careful how you transfer money before filing for bankruptcy. Transfers made before filing can be considered as either preferential or fraudulent. If you pay a large sum of money to a family member or friend—a preferential transfer to a creditor you'd rather pay back first—the trustee may recover that payment. One of the purposes of bankruptcy law is to ensure equal treatment of creditors. You cannot choose to pay the creditors you like, such as your father, then discharge the credit cards in bankruptcy. Worse than a preferential transfer is the fraudulent transfer. A fraudulent transfer is where you give your assets away, sell them for less than they are worth, or put them in someone else's name to try to hide your assets from your creditors. This is always a bad idea.

Are there any creditors that I should continue to pay?

Yes. Creditors such as landlords, secured creditors (if you want to keep the collateral securing the debt), and some utilities should be paid under most circumstances.

What if I do not list a creditor on the bankruptcy papers?

You are required to list all creditors. If you intentionally omit a creditor from your schedules, it is perjury and you may lose your bankruptcy discharge. However, if a creditor is not known to exist at the time the schedules are filed, you may amend your schedules at any time the case is open to add an additional creditor.

What does the case number tell me?

A bankruptcy case number consists of the year of filing, five additional digits, and the initials of the judge assigned to the case. Example: 05-XXXXX-LAK is a case filed in 2005, followed by a five-digit case number, assigned to the Honorable Lauren A. Kent.

What is an automatic stay?

The automatic stay is a provision under the Bankruptcy Code that freezes the ability of a creditor to continue foreclosures, lawsuits, garnishments, and other judicial procedures during administration of the Bankruptcy Code.

How do I stop the constant calls from creditors?

Creditors must comply with the Fair Debt Collection Practices Act. They are supposed to call a reasonable number of times and at reasonable hours. Arguing with some creditors encourages them to call more often. The automatic stay is not in force until your petition is filed with the court, at which point the calls must stop. If they continue to call, you can take legal action against them.

Do I have to notify all my creditors personally?

The mailing matrix is used by the bankruptcy court to notify creditors of the pending case, date of the creditors' meeting, and other pertinent information. Because the court can take a week to notify your creditors, you may want to inform problematic creditors immediately after you file.

What should I do if I get a letter from an attorney suing me?

If you have already filed your petition, you do not have to do anything. The automatic stay prevents any action on the part of a creditor for recovery.

What if my wages are being garnished?

The automatic stay stops a garnishment. However, you may have to contact your employer and provide information about your bankruptcy—case number, date of filing, creditors' meeting date, etc.

What is a joint petition?

A joint petition is the filing of a single petition by an individual and the individual's spouse. Only people who are married on the date they file may file a joint petition. Unmarried persons, corporations, and partnerships must each file a separate case.

What happens during the time from after I file my petition to the creditors' meeting?

Payments to secured creditors are usually required if you wish to keep the collateral. Monthly living expenses should also be made. Payments should be discontinued regarding debts that are being sought for discharge.

I have options for claiming exemptions. Which ones do I use?

If you live in California, you have to pick one of two systems of exemptions. System 1 is typically best for homeowners. If you live in a state that allows you to pick between your state's exemptions and the federal ones, you have to pick which set of exemptions best protects your assets. You cannot mix and match, however, between two systems; you must pick only one system. A good way to choose a set of exemptions is to study each set of exemptions and figure out how your most important assets can be saved from each set. Pick the one that covers most of your important assets. For people who live in a state that does not allow you to use anything but the state's exemptions, then you have nothing to decide. You must use your state's exemptions.

Do I have to disclose all of my assets?

Yes. If you knowingly and fraudulently conceal an asset from the court you have committed a felony and can be fined up to $5,000 or imprisoned for up to five years or both.

What is a mailing matrix?

The mailing matrix is the master address list containing the names and addresses of the debtor, attorney (if used), U.S. Trustee, creditors, and cosigners. It is extremely important to list every creditor.

What do I tell people who call me, such as creditors, collection agencies, attorneys, etc.?

If representing yourself, you should respond to creditor inquiries regarding factual information about your case, such as filing date, case number, creditors' meeting date, reaffirmation date, and so on.

How do I stop money being taken out of my paycheck?

Upon filing the bankruptcy and supplying your payroll person with a copy of the face page of the petition, the deductions should cease with the next pay period.

Can the bank come and take my car?

If you are not current on your payments, your bank may have the right to go to court and ask permission to repossess the car.

Will I have to pay any court fees later besides my filing fees?

In a Chapter 7 case, the court-filing fee of $209 is the only cost involved, unless you have to make changes to your petition and file amendments. This filing fee includes a $155 filing fee, a $39 miscellaneous fee, and a $15 trustee fee. Every court has a fee schedule, which includes other miscellaneous clerk fees that your local court can charge for any services performed by clerks. Examples of fees beyond your initial filing fee include fees for converting from one Chapter to another, reopening a case, amending schedules or the master mailing list, filing certain motions, certifying documents, and asking for copies of documents. Your bankruptcy court should be able to provide a list of fees it can charge. Bankruptcy judges can waive some of these fees, and most can be paid in installments upon request.

My mother left me some money in an inheritance. Do I need to list this in the bankruptcy?

All assets must be disclosed in the bankruptcy schedules.

My house, which was a gift from my grandmother, is fully paid. Will it be taken in the bankruptcy?

If the house falls within the allowable exemptions, you may claim it as exempt. Generally, it must also be your homestead (your principle place of residence).

What is an insider?

An insider is every officer and director of a corporation and any person, including a relative or a friend, who owns more than 10 percent of the stock in that corporation.

What is the difference between a secured debt and an unsecured debt?

A secured debt is backed by property. For example, most loans for homes and automobiles are secured debts. This means that the lender has the right to take the home or car if the borrower fails to make payments on the loan. An unsecured debt is one where you have promised to pay someone a sum of money at a particular time and you have not pledged any property to secure that debt. Examples of unsecured debts include credit cards and medical bills.

What does reaffirming a debt mean?

A debtor can arrange with a secured creditor to continue paying on a particular debt such as a car or bedroom set. Upon receiving a notice about your bankruptcy, secured creditors will contact you, asking you if you want to reaffirm your debt. You must be current on your payments to reaffirm, and if you're filing without an attorney, a judge must approve the reaffirmation.

What does redeeming a debt mean?

Some secured debts may be redeemed by paying the creditor an amount equal to the current value of the property—not what you originally paid or what you owe now.

Should I reaffirm a credit card?

The court generally disfavors reaffirmation of unsecured credit cards. Paying on debts that should be discharged defeats the purpose of bankruptcy. If your card has a zero balance on it upon your filing, you do not list that card in your paperwork because it is not a debt. You cannot use bankruptcy to wipe out a certain card's balances, and then continue to use that card. Your credit card company likely will terminate your account.

How should I handle my tax refund?

If you are filing your bankruptcy between the months of January and May, you should plan your filing based on the possibility of a federal or state income tax refund. Income tax refunds that have not been received and spent by you are nonexempt property. If you are expecting a substantial refund, the trustee will most likely arrange for you to turn the check over to their office when you receive it. One planning tip is to prepare your paperwork, but delay filing the bankruptcy until you have received your refund and spent it on necessities like food, rent, utilities, and so on. This is permitted under law.

I am surrendering secured property. How do I get it to my creditors?

You don't have to worry about delivering secured assets to your creditors. They will notify you and make arrangements with you for pick-up.

Can any civil or criminal fines be discharged, such as traffic tickets or a DUI?

No. Any fines, penalties, or restitution that a federal, state, or local government has imposed on you for violating the law are not dischargeable. This includes traffic and parking tickets.

Will my student loans be discharged?

Student loans usually cannot be discharged in bankruptcy unless you can successfully prove that they cause a severe financial hardship to you. This can be difficult to prove without an attorney, so it's best to assume that your loans are not dischargeable from the start.

Can I get another student loan?

Yes. An employer or government agency cannot discriminate against you because you have filed for bankruptcy. This includes student loan agencies.

What is excess income?

When completing your paperwork, you will need to list all of your monthly income from any source, as well as your expenses. The trustee will determine whether you have excess income available to pay some of your debts. You need to be honest in your answer, but make sure that you list all expenses in your budget (you are entitled to some recreation and entertainment in your life). Your expenses (after your debts are discharged) should be close to or more than your income. If there is considerable excess income each month, the trustee can require you to convert your case into a Chapter 13. What is considered excess income can differ from trustee to trustee, but an amount of $350 or more per month may be enough. Make sure that you include every possible expense in your budget.

Attending Your Creditors' Meeting

When is the meeting of the creditors?

Usually 20 to 40 days after you file the petition.

Can creditors fight my bankruptcy?

Yes, but they cannot use the meeting of the creditors as a forum for arguing their side of the story against you. Creditors can challenge your bankruptcy by filing a motion with the court if they believe that they have a claim against secured property or an objection to the discharge of their debt.

How long do creditors' meetings take?

These meetings are routine and very businesslike. They typically take only three to five minutes. And in busy courts, your time with your trustee may only take 90 seconds. Most of your time in a creditors' meeting is spent waiting your turn, so set aside two hours for this meeting. By the time you attend your meeting, most of the paperwork is done, and if changes or amendments need to be made, they will happen outside of this meeting.

What if the trustee asks me a question to which I don't know the answer?

You are required to respond to the trustee's questions truthfully and to the best of your ability. You are not required to guess at answers. Respond directly to the questions as best you can. Your case will not be dismissed unless you are dishonest or conceal information and a proceeding is brought to dismiss the case.

What if a creditor shows up at the creditors' meeting and accuses me of purchasing something on credit knowing I was going to file bankruptcy?

Purchases should not be made when you are reasonably certain you are going to file bankruptcy. If the accusation is incorrect, say so.

Can the trustee and I negotiate on certain things?

If you are filing without an attorney and you have property that is nonexempt or exceeds allowable exemptions, you may negotiate with the trustee and select which property you desire to claim as exempt, and if necessary, you can bid to purchase the property from the bankruptcy estate.

What if I sold my secured property?

Truthfully answer questions posed to you. Assets should not be sold, transferred, or disposed of in contemplation of bankruptcy. The burden will be on the creditor to pursue any further court proceedings.

What if I forget to list a debt?

Generally, all dischargeable debts are discharged in a bankruptcy. However, your creditor may be unaware that you filed and attempt to contest the debt. It is important to list all debts on your bankruptcy schedules.

Life after Bankruptcy

If I have one credit card I want to keep after the bankruptcy, can I do so?

All creditors are required to be listed in the bankruptcy schedules. To exclude a credit card from the bankruptcy filing, the account should have a zero balance at the time of filing. The creditor may decide not to continue the card regardless of the debt or any offer to reaffirm the debt.

Can I get a new credit card?

That depends. Some credit card agencies will issue a credit card a year or two after a bankruptcy. However, there are often restrictions, and you probably won't qualify for a low interest rate. Many credit card issuers have special programs for bankruptcy filers, called secured credit cards. You deposit $500 with the card issuer and you get a card and a line of credit of $600 or so. Similarly, cell phone companies can offer such programs.

How many people will know of my bankruptcy?

Generally, only creditors and interested parties care about your bankruptcy case. It is, however, a matter of public record and can be viewed upon inquiry at the bankruptcy court. It will remain on your credit report for up to 10 years.

How can I reestablish credit after bankruptcy?

Managing money well and having steady employment are the two most important factors in your life postbankruptcy. You may be able to obtain a secured credit card, a card where you deposit money to establish the credit limit. Using the card will help to establish credit as will paying your bills timely. When credit cards begin soliciting you again (sooner than you'd think), proving you can manage your money and bills wisely will be essential to reestablishing your credit.

Should I use a credit repair service to fix my credit report after bankruptcy?

Be very cautious about credit repair services. The Federal Trade Commission, the agency that investigates credit services, has never found a legitimate credit repair service. There are two main types of credit repair: 1) using the Fair Credit Reporting Act (FCRA) to challenge credit information on your credit history; and 2) using illegal maneuvers to create new identities for people with bad credit, thus wiping out their old identities and the bad credit that was attached to those identities. There is nothing a credit repair service can do for you legally—using the FCRA—that you cannot do yourself. Neither a credit repair service nor you can remove bad, but accurate, information on your credit report. So using a credit repair service is usually a waste of money. You are much better off using the money you have toward essentials and working hard at rebuilding your credit-worthiness. If you truly have problems with your credit report showing false or erroneous information, you can file the appropriate paperwork with the credit bureaus and do your own credit repair.

What if someone sues me after I file bankruptcy?

If someone sues you for a debt discharged in the bankruptcy, you must answer the suit and tell the judge that you have filed bankruptcy. If you do not answer the suit, a valid judgment may be entered against you even though you filed bankruptcy. Bankruptcy does not affect lawsuits for debt incurred after you file your bankruptcy.

Can I own anything after bankruptcy?

Of course! Don't wrongly assume that you cannot own anything for a long period of time after filing for bankruptcy. You can keep your exempt property and anything you obtain after the bankruptcy is filed. However, if you receive an inheritance, a property settlement, or life insurance benefits within 180 days after filing for bankruptcy, that money or property may have to be paid to your creditors if the property or money is not exempt.

Can I get a house or car loan immediately after filing bankruptcy?

That depends. You will pay a higher interest rate than someone with perfect credit and may have to make a bigger down payment, but it's not true that having a bankruptcy on your record means you cannot get a home or car loan for 10 years. For example, you are eligible to apply for a FHA home loan two years after a bankruptcy. Creditors and lenders do exist to help people who have gone through bankruptcy. Choose them carefully.

Odds and Ends to Bankruptcy

What is a motion?

A motion is a request for a hearing before a judge where you ask the court for something. It's a formal written statement in which the party who is requesting an action sets forth the request, together with his or her grounds for the action requested. In most cases, if you want an order from the court regarding your case, or if you want the court to act on your case (example: schedule a hearing), you must file a motion.

Motions are court documents; they are the vehicles by which you ask the court to do something or respond to you. You cannot write a personal letter to the court and expect the court to respond in a legal manner.

What is a certificate of service?

A certificate of service is another document that must be filed alongside any motion (formal, written request) to the court. It gives the court proof that you have mailed something or done something required of you. A certificate of service is simply your written statement that you have provided a copy of the pleading, which is the subject of the certificate of service to the respondent and other interested parties in your case. A certificate of service must list the name and address of each person and attorney being served with the motion and also the name of the party (or parties) that an attorney represents. You should also indicate by what means you forwarded a copy of the pleadings to the other parties, for example, via first class postage prepaid mail, facsimile, and so on. Even when you file a document by facsimile transmission, you must still submit a certificate of service with the pleading. A proof of mail is a certificate of service.

What should I do if I cannot make my Chapter 13 payment?

If you have filed a Chapter 13 bankruptcy and cannot make a payment on time according to the terms of your confirmed plan, you should contact your trustee and explain the problem.

If your situation is temporary and you expect to make up the payments, explain to your trustee how and when that will happen. Significant changes in your circumstances may require that your plan be formally modified. If your situation calls for an end to your plan, your trustee may request that the court dismiss the case or convert it to a case under another chapter.

What if I don't agree with an order entered in a case?

You may file a notice of appeal after an order or judgment has been entered in a case. When an appeal is filed, the matter is referred to the Bankruptcy Appellate Panel (BAP) or to the United States District Court if requested. You must file the required filing fee when you file a notice of appeal. At various points in the appellate proceedings, you are required to file certain additional documents. Appealing a judgment can be tricky, so consulting a bankruptcy attorney can help you.

I have filed for bankruptcy in the past. Can I do it again?

You cannot file for Chapter 7 bankruptcy if you've filed for a Chapter 7 or 13 within the past six years and have received a discharge. If you've paid at least 70 percent of your debts in a Chapter 13 case, the six-year bar does not apply. You also cannot file for Chapter 7 if your previous Chapter 7 or 13 case was dismissed within the past 180 days for reasons of court violations or your request for a dismissal upon a creditor's objection.

How do I get information about my past bankruptcy filing?

All bankruptcies are public information. You can obtain information about a past bankruptcy filing by contacting the court where you filed and asking about past records. Each bankruptcy district has its own archiving and record-keeping procedure. You may be able to obtain your past case number right over the phone, or you may have to visit the Records department where files are kept. Start by calling the court where you filed.

CHAPTER 9

Definition of Terms

The following is an alphabetical list of terms you're likely to encounter during your bankruptcy process. When filling out your forms, you may find referring to this list useful. Most of these terms have already been defined and described throughout the book.

Abandon. To leave alone, referring to assets you have that are nonexempt. Your trustee abandons assets that are not worth selling or that would be too hard to sell to raise money for creditors. You get to keep abandoned assets.

Adversary Proceeding. This is a lawsuit that is filed by a creditor who says your debt to that creditor should not be discharged.

Assets. Your stuff. Specifically, any real property (your house), personal property (your car), or intellectual property (your patent rights to an invention) in which you own an interest (a legal share). Money owed to you and portions of property (such as half of a house you share with your wife) are also examples of assets.

Automatic Stay (STOP!) Provision (or Order). An automatic and instant relief from your creditors' attempts to collect from you; a court order that takes effect when the bankruptcy petition is filed. It prohibits a broad range of activities against the debtor, property of the debtor, and property of the bankruptcy estate. The automatic stay lasts from the day you file to the day the court either dismisses your case or grants you a discharge.

Bankruptcy. A legal procedure for dealing with debt problems of an individual or company where a discharge or an adjustment of certain debts is requested.

Chapter 7. The most common type of bankruptcy. Chapter 7 is a liquidation (discharge) of most of your debts.

Chapter 13. A repayment plan for individuals. A type of bankruptcy whereby you pay back a portion of your debts in a court-supervised plan over a certain period of time, usually 36 months.

Claims. "I claim you owe me money." In the broadest sense, a claim is any right to payment held by a person or company against you. You can often think of claim as debt. A claim does not have to be past due but can include sums that will come due in the future. In filling out the Schedules, you should include any debts owed, whether they are already due or will become due only in the future.

Claims Objections. You are entitled to object to any claim filed in your bankruptcy case if you believe the debt is not owed or if you believe the claim misrepresents the amount or kind of debt (such as whether a debt is secured or priority) you owe. In some circumstances, an objection to a claim can be initiated by filing an objection to the claim in the bankruptcy court; in other circumstances, it must be initiated by filing an adversary proceeding (like a lawsuit in your bankruptcy case). Because claims objections can be complicated and time sensitive, advice from an attorney is helpful.

Codebtor. If you share a debt with someone else, you are a codebtor. A husband and wife filing one petition are codebtors.

Collateral. An asset used as security (a pledge or promise) for repayment of a loan. Many people use large assets like homes, cars, and home furniture as collateral for loans. Example: Your car is collateral on the car loan. Your house is collateral you've used to secure a business loan from a bank.

Community Property. A form of property ownership solely between a husband and wife recognized in only a few states. Those states are Alaska (with an agreement), Arizona, California, Idaho, Louisiana, Nevada, New Mexico, Puerto Rico, Texas, Washington, and Wisconsin. Specific community property laws differ greatly among the states, but they all share a defining feature: All assets acquired during the marriage by either spouse are automatically split, so that each spouse owns a separate, undivided one-half interest.

Contingent Claim. A debt that has not materialized yet, because it relies on a future event that may or may not occur. Example: You've cosigned a loan for a friend; you will not become liable for that debt unless your friend defaults on payment.

Creditor. The person to whom you owe money or who claims you owe money.

Creditors' Meeting (341A Meeting). A meeting that takes place three to six weeks after the bankruptcy petition is filed, at which time the debtor may be asked questions by the court-appointed trustee and the debtor's creditors have the opportunity to ask about information provided by the debtor on the bankruptcy petition.

Debt. Something owed, an obligation to pay.

Debtor. The person who owes a debt. A person who has filed a petition for relief under the bankruptcy laws.

Deed of Trust. A document that pledges real property to secure a loan. The state of Georgia calls these documents a Deed to Secure Debt. The property is deeded by the title holder (trustor) to a trustee (often a title or escrow company), which holds the title in trust for the beneficiary (the lender of the money).

Discharge. The legal elimination of a debt through a bankruptcy case. To dismiss or release from obligation to pay, such as your debts. When a bankruptcy discharges your debts, you are no longer responsible for paying those debts—ever again. This word can also be used as a noun: a discharge is a release of obligation to pay. Hence, the court discharges your debts, and you receive a discharge.

Disclosure Statement. A written document prepared by the Chapter 11 debtor or their plan proponent that is designed to provide adequate information to creditors to enable them to evaluate the Chapter 11 plan of reorganization.

Dismissal. The cancellation of your bankruptcy filing by the court for reasons such as fraud, failure to abide by the bankruptcy court's rules, or voluntary dismissal (by your request).

Disputed Claim. A debt that you and your creditor disagree to in terms of amount and/or the existence of the debt. Example: Someone gave you money on a promissory note, and your understanding of that loan is different from that of the person holding the promissory note.

Equity. The monetary value of your property, such as a home, that does not include the lender's portion of the value. Example: Your home is worth $250,000. When you bought it for $230,000, a bank loaned you the money in a mortgage. You've paid $40,000 against the principal of your loan (this excludes any interest on your loan), so your equity is roughly $60,000 ($40,000 + the increase in the home's value of $20,000). Another example: Your car has a value of $4,000 but there is a $3,500 lien on it (you owe someone money because you've used your car as collateral for a loan), so your car now has an equity value of only $500. This $500 would be the amount subject to exemption.

Executory Contracts/Unexpired Leases. Contracts that remain in force and under which the parties to the agreements remain obligated to perform according to the contracts' provisions. Examples: rental/home leases, car leases, business leases, time-shares, business or service contracts, copyright and patent licenses, insurance contracts, boat slip leases.

Exempt. The ability to avoid the lien of certain nonpurchase money security interests in personal property so as to be able to keep the property and also discharge the debt. See Lien.

Exemption. The rules that allow you to keep some of your assets in your bankruptcy. There are state exemptions and federal exemptions. In some states you can choose one set over the other; but in most states you have to use your own state's specific exemptions. (In California, two systems of exemption exist.)

Expenses. What you spend, or the money that you need, to pay for monthly expenses, such as food, rent, etc.

Foreclosure. The forced sale of real estate to pay off a loan on which the owner of the property has defaulted.

Homestead. Your primary residence that is not subject to the claims of creditors. Homestead exemptions allow you to exempt certain equity in your home in attempts to keep it.

Income. How much you make from all sources, or the amount that appears on your pay stubs.

Insider. Every officer and director of a corporation and any person, including a relative or a friend, who owns more than 10 percent of the stock in that corporation.

Insolvency. The state of being unable to pay your debts because you owe more than you have. If your debts exceed the sum of your assets, you are said to be insolvent.

Interest. Your financial right, title, or legal share in something, such as a piece of land or a business. Example: You and your wife own a home in a community property state. You have 50 percent interest in your house.

Joint Tenancy. A term that relates to the ownership of real property, which provides that each party owns an undivided interest in the entire parcel, with both having the right to use all of it and usually the right of survivorship, which means that upon the death of one joint tenant, the other has title to it all. Example: You are your wife share joint tenancy in your home.

Lien. A charge upon specific property designed to secure payment of a debt. Any official claim or charge against property or funds for payment of a debt or an amount owed for services rendered. Example: You've placed your home up as collateral for a small business loan. The lender has a lien against your home. A mortgage or a deed of trust is a form of a lien, and any lien against real property must be recorded with the County Recorder to be enforceable. Security interest liens can play a large role in a bankruptcy proceeding. These refer to debts that you incurred by pledging assets (usually voluntarily) you own as collateral to secure a loan. The company or person who gives you the loan is said to have a security interest in your asset. Agreements with such lenders typically give the lender the right to take the asset if you miss a payment. A few more specifics follow.

If you have a debt that resulted from the purchase of the asset, such as a home, car, or large furniture, the lien is referred to as a *purchase-money security interest.*

If you have a debt that resulted from a loan that was not for the purchase of the collateral, as in the case of refinancing a home, getting a home equity loan, or securing a loan from a finance company, the lien is referred to as a *nonpossessory nonpurchase-money security interest.* Another way to look at this kind of lien: If you pledge an asset that you already own outright in order to borrow money (secure a loan) from a lending company or credit union, the loan is called *nonpossessory.* If you have a debt that resulted from your pledging property to a pawnshop, the lien is referred to as a *possessory nonpurchase-money security interest.*

Other than the mortgage or deeds of trust liens you have as a result of the purchase of your home and subsequent refinances, home equity loans, and so on, there are numerous other types of liens including: a *mechanic's lien* against the real property upon which a workman, contractor, or supplier has provided work or materials; an *attorney's lien* for fees to be paid from funds recovered by his or her efforts; a *medical lien* for medical bills to be paid from funds recovered for an injury; a *landlord's lien* against a tenant's assets for unpaid rent or damages; a *tax lien* to enforce the government's claim of unpaid taxes; a *judgment lien* for money you owe as a result of a lawsuit against you; a *child support lien* for money you owe to your child's other parent.

Life Estate. The right to use or occupy real property during your lifetime but never own it. Example: A life estate set up by your late husband allows you to live in your home for the rest of your life, at which point the home goes to your daughter.

Liquidate. To sell your assets in an attempt to repay some of your debts. Your trustee will liquidate any nonexempt assets you have once you file. For the majority of Chapter 7 filers, there are no assets worth selling so the trustee has nothing to liquidate. When you see the word "liquidate," think of "to pay off," "to get rid of," or even "to kill." When you liquidate your debt, you get rid of it! This is accomplished by selling your assets and giving any proceeds to your creditors. Note: Liquid assets refer to cash or items that can be converted easily and quickly to cash, such as a money market account, stocks, Treasury bills, and bank accounts.

Mailing Matrix. A master list of names and addresses of the debtor, attorney (if used), U.S. Trustee, creditors, and cosigners. A creditor mailing matrix is the names and addresses of your creditors only.

Market Value. The price for which an asset would sell if sold in the ordinary course of business. Market values for homes are easily obtained by conducting some research of real estate in your area. When evaluating other assets, think "quick sale," or what your assets would go for if sold in a pawn shop or yard sale.

Meeting of the Creditors. See Creditors' Meeting.

Nonexempt Assets. Assets that cannot be kept and that you risk losing to your trustee.

Personal Property. All personal assets that do not include real property (home). Examples: cars, furniture, clothing, books, jewelry, money, bank accounts, paintings, etc.

Petition. A formal written request (asking the court for something). A bankruptcy petition is your request to the court to discharge your debts. Your bankruptcy petition consists of various forms and schedules that make up your entire petition. However, the first two pages of your entire petition are specifically called the Voluntary Petition and can initiate a bankruptcy case alongside your mailing matrix, with your other documents following within 15 days.

Priority Claim. Debts granted special status by the bankruptcy law, such as debts to a government agency. A priority debt is paid before unsecured nonpriority debts and after secured debts. It cannot be wiped out in bankruptcy. Examples: certain taxes, child support, student loans.

Pro Se/Pro Per. To represent yourself in court without an attorney.

Proof of Claim. The written statement filed in a bankruptcy case setting forth a creditor's claim. Proofs of claim usually include a copy of the documents on which the claim is based; if the claim is secured, the proof of claim also includes evidence of the secured status of the debt. With limited exceptions, a creditor (other than a governmental unit) in a Chapter 7, 12, or 13 case must file a proof of claim within 90 days after the first date set for the meeting of creditors. If a creditor files a claim after the specified deadline, the debtor may object to the claim as being untimely filed.

Proof of Service by Mail. A document that you sign telling the court that you mailed something and to whom you mailed it. It is a certificate of service.

Reaffirm. An agreement by a Chapter 7 debtor to continue paying a dischargeable debt after the bankruptcy. This is usually done for the purpose of keeping an asset that could be subject to repossession. A *reaffirmation agreement* is a written agreement between a debtor and a creditor in which the debtor promises to pay a debt that is dischargeable. Such agreements are commonly used where the debt is secured by a lien on personal property, which a debtor owns (for example, where the creditor has a lien on the debtor's car to secure payment of a car loan). So you can reaffirm property that can be taken away by either the trustee or a secured creditor, if you promise to continue making the proper payments. You must be current on your payments at the time you reaffirm an asset.

Real Property/Real Estate. Land and things permanently attached to the land.

Redeem. Agree to buy the debt at fair market value, probably less than what you owe. Example: You buy your car at current market value. If your car is worth less than what you still owe on it, redeeming it allows you to keep it and pay it off for less than what you would have paid if you reaffirmed the debt.

Redemption. The right of the debtor in bankruptcy to purchase certain types of collateral from secured creditors by paying the value of the collateral rather than the total secured debt. You redeem assets through a *redemption agreement.*

Reorganization. A Chapter 11 or 13 plan describing the terms by which the debtor intends to repay his debts, usually over a three-year to five-year period.

Residence. A place where a person lives primarily. That place can be a house, a mobile home, or a boat. Not a vacation or second home.

Schedules. Lists that you must provide as part of your bankruptcy filing, such as a list of your real estate property (Schedule A), a list of your personal property (Schedule B), a list of your exempt property (Schedule C), and so on.

Secured Debt. Debts where the assets securing the debt can be repossessed or foreclosed on, such as your home mortgage, car loan, rented furniture, and so on. A secured creditor is one who holds an item of yours as security for the debt. The bank that loaned you the money to buy your house holds a mortgage or trust deed lien on your house as security for the loan; therefore, the mortgage company is a *secured creditor.*

Security Interest. A generic term for the property rights of a lender or creditor whose right to collect a debt is secured by property or asset. Example: Your mortgage company has a security interest in your home.

Single Asset Real Estate. The term is defined as "a single property or project, other than residential real property with fewer than four residential units, which generates substantially all of the gross income of a debtor and on which no substantial business is being conducted by a debtor other than operating the real property and which has aggregate non-contingent liquidated secured debts of no more than $4,000,000."

Statement of Financial Affairs. An official form in your petition that provides information about you, such as how much you earned this year to date, how much you earned last year and the year before, and who helped you prepare your petition. This statement is a series of questions you must answer in writing concerning sources of income, transfers of property, lawsuits by creditors, and so on.

Surrender. Agree to give up the debt and let the trustee do what he or she wants with the asset (the collateral you've used to secure the debt). Example: You let your trustee take your car, sell it, and distribute the proceeds to creditors after the car lender is paid off. If you owe more on your car than your car is currently worth, let the trustee take it. You can purchase a cheaper vehicle.

Trustee. An impartial person appointed to oversee the case of a person who has filed for bankruptcy protection. Your trustee takes possession of all your nonexempt assets, reduces them to cash, and makes distributions to creditors (subject to your right to retain some exempt property and the rights of secured creditors). Your trustee's job is to make sure that your documents are complete and to review your list of assets for items that are not protected by law. In no-asset cases, where you don't have assets worth selling for money to pay creditors, your trustee gets only a flat fee to manage your case. Your trustee is a fair and impartial participant in your bankruptcy. The *U.S. Trustee* is the bankruptcy arm of the Justice Department.

Unliquidated Claim. A debt with an uncertain amount or an amount that has yet to be determined. Example: You are involved in a lawsuit whose outcome is uncertain. You may have to pay as a result of losing your case or pay attorneys' fees. This is an unliquidated claim.

Unsecured Debt. A debt that is not tied to any asset. Credit card debts are classic unsecured debts. Others include personal loans or medical bills. An *unsecured creditor* is one who holds no security or collateral for a loan. In other words, your credit card company cannot reclaim the things you've purchased on the card to help pay for the money it is owed. Unsecured debts generally are characterized as those debts for which credit was extended based solely on the creditor's assessment of your future ability to pay.

Voluntary Petition. The first two pages of your bankruptcy petition. Together with a creditor mailing matrix, this part of your petition can be used to initiate your bankruptcy proceeding—and trigger the automatic stay—as an emergency filing.

Wildcard Exemption. An exemption available in some states that allows you to exempt a portion of any assets of your choice. Some states do not allow you to apply a wildcard to real estate. In almost all states, you can apply the wildcard to nonexempt property or use it to increase the amount of an exemption to an asset.

LIST OF APPENDICES

Appendix A: Worksheets A and B
Appendix B: List of Bankruptcy Court Addresses
Appendix C: List of We The People Store Addresses

To access official forms and exemptions tables, go to *www.wethepeopleforms.com* and enter your password: **WTPBK.** These forms can also be found at *www.wiley.com/go/ wethepeopleforms*. Among the forms you'll find on the site, the most important ones to complete your filing include the following:

Form 1
Schedule A—Real Property
Schedule B—Personal Property
Schedule C—Property Claimed as Exempt
Schedule D—Creditors Holding Secured Claims
Schedule E—Creditors Holding Unsecured Priority Claims
Schedule F—Creditors Holding Unsecured Nonpriority Claims
Schedule G—Executory Contracts and Unexpired Leases
Schedule H—Codebtors
Schedule I—Current Income of Individual Debtor(s)
Schedule J—Current Expenditures of Individual Debtor(s)
Form 6—Summary of Schedules
Form 6(cont'd)—Declaration Concerning Debtor's Schedules
Form 7—Statement of Financial Affairs
Form 8—Statement of Intention
Form 21—Statement of Social Security Number

Other forms you may or may not need include:

Exhibit A
Exhibit C
Application to Pay Fee in Installments
Motion

For information on local court forms, contact your local court or access your local bankruptcy court's official site. Start by going to *www.uscourts.gov* and click on "U.S. Bankruptcy Courts," then click on "U.S. Bankruptcy Court Web Sites" in the lower left-hand corner. Navigating your way to your local court's site is easy. If you have questions, call you local court directly using the contact information in Appendix B.

Worksheets A and B

WORKSHEET A:
TAKING INVENTORY OF YOUR FINANCES

CATEGORY 1: Monthly Expenses

EXPENSE	MONTHLY PAYMENT
Rent	$
Mortgage	
Electric	
Gas	
Phone	
Water/sewer	
Home maintenance	
Cable TV/internet access	
Phone/cell	
Food	
Clothing	
Car payments	
Gasoline/transportation costs	
Entertainment/newspapers	
Incidentals—gifts, laundry	
Medical and dental	
Taxes not deducted from paycheck	
Miscellaneous	
Installment payments Car	_____
Furniture	_____
Other _____	_____
TOTAL	$

CATEGORY 2: Credit Card Balances

CREDIT CARD	BALANCE
	$
TOTAL	$

CATEGORY 3: Other debts

DEBT	BALANCE
	$
TOTAL	$

CATEGORY 4: Property/Assets (What You Own)

ASSET	QUICK SALE VALUE*
Home(s)**	
Cash	
Checking, savings, CDs	
Security deposits held by utilities or landlord	
Household goods/furniture/electronics/appliances	
Books/pictures/art objects	
Clothing	
Furs/Jewelry	
Sports/hobby equipment/firearms/gadgets	
Cash value in insurance policies	
Annuities	
Interest in pension or profit sharing plans	
Stocks and interests in incorporated business	
Interest in partnerships/joint ventures	
Bonds	
Accounts receivable	
Alimony or family support to which you are entitled	
Tax refunds	
Equitable or future interests or life estates	
Interest in estate of descendent or life ins plan	
Other liquidated debts owed to you (claims, funds due you, benefits)	
Patents, copyrights	
Licenses and franchises	
Car(s) ***	
Boats/motors & accessories	
Aircraft and accessories	
Office equipment & supplies	
Machinery/fixtures	
Inventory (business)	
Stocks and interests in incorporated/unincorporated business	
Interest in partnerships/joint ventures;	
Animals, crop, farm supplies, etc (for farmers)	
TOTAL	

* A quick sale value is what you think your assets would sell for if sold quickly. Consider how much your assets would sell for in a pawnshop or at a garage or yard sale.

** If you have a mortgage on your home, list any home equity loans and liens you have here:

        Total liens and mortgages   = _____

        Total ownership equity

        (Home value less total liens/mortgages)   = _____

*** Use the current value of your car today if you tried to sell it quickly.

WORKSHEET B
ATTACHMENT TO SCHEDULE J

Monthly business income

Total: $_____ Source: _____

Monthly business expenses

EXPENSE	MONTHLY PAYMENT
Rent/mortgage	
Repair/upkeep	
Electricity/ heating fuel	
water and sewer	
Telephone	
Garbage	
Security	
Other utilities	
Taxes	
Installment payments on equipment	
Rental/lease payments	
Maintenance of equipment	
Advertising	
Bank service charges	
Interest	
Depreciation	
Office expenses	
Dues and publications	
Laundry or cleaning	
Supplies and materials	
Freight	
Travel and Entertainment	
Wages and Salaries	
Commissions	
Employee benefit programs	
Pensions/profit sharing plans	
Production costs	
Other expenses	
TOTAL MONTHLY EXPENSES	
EXCESS INCOME OVER EXPENSES	

Bankruptcy Court Addresses

UNITED STATES BANKRUPTCY COURTS

Bankruptcy court addresses and phone numbers are always subject to change. Before you visit your local bankruptcy court or mail in your petition, call the court clerk to verify the address. Also note that actual mailing addresses may differ from the physical location of the court. The web sites to the courts are updated frequently, so you can start on a court's specific site and verify all information. For sites that change their web address, start by going to www.uscourts.gov and click your way to your local courthouse.

ALABAMA
www.alnb.uscourts.gov

Middle District of ALABAMA,
    Montgomery Division
Post Office Box 1248
One Court Square
Suite 127 Lee Street
Montgomery, AL 36102
Telephone: 1–334–206–6300

Northern District of ALABAMA,
    Birmingham Division
1800 5th Avenue North
Birmingham, AL 35203
Telephone: 1–205–714–4000

Northern District of ALABAMA, Eastern Division
103 U.S. Courthouse
12th and Noble Streets
Anniston, AL 36201
Telephone: 1–205–237–5631

Northern District of ALABAMA, Northern Division
P.O. Box 1289 (35602)
400 Wells Avenue
Decatur, AL 35601
Telephone: 1–205–353–2817

Northern District of ALABAMA, Western Division
P.O. Box 3226
Federal Courthouse, Rm. 348
1118 Greensboro Avenue
Tuscaloosa, AL 35403
Telephone: 1–205–752–0426

Southern District of ALABAMA
P.O. Box 2865 (36652)
201 St. Louis Street
Mobile, AL 36602
Telephone: 1–334–441–5391

ALASKA
www.akb.uscourts.gov

District of ALASKA
Historical Courthouse
605 West 4th Avenue, Rm. 138
Anchorage, AK 99501–2296
Telephone: 1–907–271–2655

District of ALASKA, Fairbanks Division
Historical Courthouse
605 West 4th Avenue, Rm. 138
Anchorage, AK 99501–2296
Telephone: 1–907–271–2655

District of ALASKA, Ketchikan Division
Historical Courthouse
605 West 4th Avenue, Rm. 138
Anchorage, AK 99501–2296
Telephone: 1–907–271–2655

District of ALASKA, Juneau Division
Historical Courthouse
605 West 4th Avenue, Rm. 138
Anchorage, AK 99501–2296
Telephone: 1–907–271–2655

District of ALASKA, Nome Division
Front Street
P.O. Box 130
Nome, AK 99762
Phone 907–443–5216

ARIZONA
www.azb.uscourts.gov

District of ARIZONA, Phoenix
U.S. Bankruptcy Court
230 North 1st Avenue
Phoenix, AZ 85025
Mailing Address: 230 North 1st Avenue, Ste. 101
Phoenix, AZ 85025
602–682–4000

District of ARIZONA, Prescott Valley
3001 N. Main Street, Ste. 2E,
Prescott Valley, AZ

District of ARIZONA, Tucson
U.S. Bankruptcy Court
110 S. Church Ave., Ste 8112
Tucson, AZ 85701
520–620–7500

District of ARIZONA, Yuma
U.S. Bankruptcy Court
325 W 19th St., Suite D
Yuma, AZ 85364
Mailing Address: P.O. Box 13011
Yuma, AZ 85366
928–783–2288

ARKANSAS
www.arb.uscourts.gov

Eastern District of Arkansas
District of ARKANSAS
P.O. Drawer 3777
300 W. 2nd
Little Rock, AR 72201
Telephone: 1–501–918–5500

CALIFORNIA
Central District of CALIFORNIA,
  Los Angeles Division
300 N. Los Angeles Street, 1st Floor
Los Angeles, CA 90012
Telephone: 1–213–894–3118
www.cacb.uscourts.gov

Central District of CALIFORNIA,
  San Fernando Division
21041 Burbank Boulevard
Woodland Hills, CA 91367
Telephone: 1–818–587–2900
www.cacb.uscourts.gov

Central District of CALIFORNIA,
  Riverside Division
3420 Twelfth Street
Riverside, CA 92501
Telephone: 1–951–774–1000
www.cacb.uscourts.gov

Central District of CALIFORNIA,
  Santa Ana Division
Ronald Reagan Federal Building and
  United States Courthouse
411 West Fourth Street
Santa Ana, CA 92701–4593
Telephone: 1–714–338–5300
www.cacb.uscourts.gov

Central District of CALIFORNIA,
  Santa Barbara Division
1415 State Street
Santa Barbara, CA 93101
Telephone: 1–805–884–4800
www.cacb.uscourts.gov

Eastern District of CALIFORNIA,
  Sacramento Division 8308
501 I Street, Suite 3–200
Sacramento, California 95814
Telephone: 1–916–930–4400
www.caeb.uscourts.gov

Eastern District of CALIFORNIA,
  Fresno Division
1130 "O" Street, Rm. 2656
Fresno, CA 93721
Telephone: 1–559–498–7217
www.caeb.uscourts.gov

Eastern District of CALIFORNIA,
   Modesto Division
P.O. Box 5276 (95352)
1130 12th Street, Rm. C
Modesto, CA 95354
Telephone: 1–209–521–5160
www.caeb.uscourts.gov

Northern District of CALIFORNIA,
   San Francisco Division
P.O. Box 7341 (94120–7341)
235 Pine Street, 19th Floor
San Francisco, CA 94104
Telephone: 1–415–268–2300
www.canb.uscourts.gov

Northern District of CALIFORNIA,
   San Jose Division
280 S. First Street, Rm. 3035
San Jose, CA 95113–3099
Telephone: 1–408–535–5118
www.canb.uscourts.gov

Northern District of CALIFORNIA,
   Santa Rosa Division
99 South E Street
Santa Rosa, CA 95404
Telephone: 1–707–525–8539
www.canb.uscourts.gov

Northern District of CALIFORNIA,
   Oakland Division
P.O. Box 2070
1300 Clay Street, Rm. 300
Oakland, CA 94604
Telephone: 1–510 2879–3600
www.canb.uscourts.gov

[Northern District of CALIFORNIA,
   Salinas Courthouse (not a division)]
1000 South Main, Room 214
Salinas, CA 93901
Telephone: 1–831–757–7420

[Northern District of CALIFORNIA,
   Eureka Courthouse (not a division)]
The Eureka Post Office & Courthouse
Fifth & H Street
Eureka, CA 95501
Telephone: 1–707–443–9061

Southern District of CALIFORNIA
Jacob Weinberger U.S. Courthouse
325 West F Street
San Diego, CA 92101
Telephone: 1–619–557–5620
www.casb.uscourts.gov

COLORADO
www.cob.uscourts.gov

District of COLORADO
721 19th Street
Denver, CO 80202–2508
Telephone: 1–303–844–4045

CONNECTICUT
www.ctb.uscourts.gov

District of CONNECTICUT, Bridgeport Division
915 Lafayette Boulevard
Bridgeport, CT 06604
Telephone: 1–203–579–5808

District of CONNECTICUT, Hartford Division
450 Main Street
Hartford, CT 06103
Telephone: 1–860–240–3675

District of CONNECTICUT, New Haven Division
157 Church Street, 18th Floor
New Haven, CT 06510
Telephone: 203–773–2009

DELAWARE
www.deb.uscourts.gov

District of DELAWARE
824 Market St., 3rd Floor
Wilmington, DE 19801
Telephone: 1–302–252–2900

DISTRICT OF COLUMBIA, D.C.
www.dcb.uscourts.gov

District of COLUMBIA, D.C. Division
333 Constitution Ave., N.W. Room 4400
Washington, D.C. 20001
Telephone: 1–202–565–2500

FLORIDA

Northern District of FLORIDA, Tallahassee
110 East Park Avenue, Suite 100
Tallahassee, FL 32301
Telephone: (850) 521–5001
www.flnb.uscourts.gov

Northern District of FLORIDA, Pensacola
220 West Garden Street, Suite 700
Pensacola, FL 32502–5745
Phone: (850) 435–8475
www.flnb.uscourts.gov

Middle District of FLORIDA, Tampa Division
Sam M. Gibbons United States Courthouse
801 N. Florida Avenue
Tampa, Florida 33602
(813) 301–5065
www.flmb.uscourts.gov

Middle District of FLORIDA, Jacksonville Division
300 North Hogan Street, Suite 3–350
Jacksonville, FL 32202
Telephone: 1–904–301–6490
www.flmb.uscourts.gov

Middle District of FLORIDA, Orlando Division
135 West Central Boulevard, Ste. 950
Orlando, FL 32801
(407) 648–6365
www.flmb.uscourts.gov

Middle District of FLORIDA, Ft. Meyers Division
United States Courthouse
2110 First Street
Fort Myers, Florida 33901
(Ft. Myers cases are filed and maintained in the
    Tampa Division courthouse.)
www.flmb.uscourts.gov

Middle District of FLORIDA, Viera Division
Moore Justice Center
2825 Judge Fran Jamieson Way
Viera, Florida 32940
(Viera cases are filed and maintained in the Orlando
    Division courthouse.)
www.flmb.uscourts.gov

Southern District of FLORIDA, Miami Division
Claude Pepper Federal Building
51 S.W. 1st Avenue, Room 1517
Miami, FL 33130
Telephone No. (305) 714–1800
www.flsb.uscourts.gov

Southern District of FLORIDA, Fort Lauderdale
U.S. Courthouse
299 E. Broward Blvd., Room 112
Fort Lauderdale, FL 33301
Telephone No. (954) 769–5700
www.flsb.uscourts.gov

Southern District of FLORIDA,
    West Palm Beach Division
Paul G. Rogers Federal Building
701 Clematis Street, Room 202,
West Palm Beach, FL 33401
Telephone No. (561) 514–4100
www.flsb.uscourts.gov

GEORGIA

Middle District of GEORGIA, Macon
433 Cherry Street
P.O. Box 1957
Macon, GA 31202
Phone: (478) 752–3506
www.gamb.uscourts.gov

Northern District of GEORGIA, Atlanta
1340 Richard B. Russell Bldg.
75 Spring Street, S.W.
Atlanta, GA 30303
Telephone: 404–215–1000
www.ganb.uscourts.gov

Northern District of GEORGIA, Newnan Division
18 Greenville Street
Newnan, GA 30264
Telephone: 678–423–3000
www.ganb.uscourts.gov

Northern District of GEORGIA, Rome Division
600 E. 1st Street, Rm. 339
Rome, GA 30161
Telephone: 706–378–4000
www.ganb.uscourts.gov

Southern District of GEORGIA, Savannah
P.O. Box 8347
Savannah, Georgia 31412
125 Bull Street, Room 213
Savannah, Georgia 31401
(912) 650–4100
www.gasb.uscourts.gov

Southern District of GEORGIA, Augusta Division
P.O. Box 1487
Augusta, Georgia 30903
933 Broad Street, 3rd floor
Augusta, Georgia 30901
Telephone: (706) 724–2421
www.gasb.uscourts.gov

GUAM

U.S. DISTRICT COURT OF GUAM
238 Archbishop Flores Street 6th Floor
Agana, Guam 96910

HAWAII

www.hib.uscourts.gov

Hawaii District Court
District of HAWAII
1132 Bishop Street, Ste. 250-L
Honolulu, HI 96813
Main (808) 522–8100

IDAHO

www.id.uscourts.gov

District of IDAHO, Southern Division
550 W. Fort Street
Boise, ID 83724
(208) 334–1074

District of IDAHO, Northern Division
205 N. 4th Street
Coeur D'Alene, ID 83814
Telephone: (208) 664–4925

District of IDAHO, Northern Division
220 E 5th St, Rm 304
Moscow, ID 83843
(208) 882–7612

District of IDAHO, Eastern Division
801 E Sherman St, Rm 119
Pocatello, ID 83201
(208) 478–4123

ILLINOIS

Central District of ILLINOIS
2nd Floor, Room 226
600 E. Monroe Street
Springfield, IL 62701
Phone: (217) 492–4551
www.ilcb.uscourts.gov

Central District of ILLINOIS, Danville Division
1st Floor, Room 130
201 N. Vermillion Street
Danville, IL 61832
Phone: (217) 431–4820
www.ilcb.uscourts.gov

Central District of ILLINOIS, Peoria Division
2nd Floor, Room 216
100 N.E. Monroe Street
Peoria, IL 61602
Phone: (309) 671–7035
www.ilcb.uscourts.gov

Northern District of ILLINOIS, Eastern Division
219 S. Dearborn, Rm. 710
Chicago, IL 60604
Tel (312) 435–5694
www.ilnb.uscourts.gov

Northern District of ILLINOIS, Rockford Division
211 South Court St., Rm. 110
Rockford, IL 61101
Tel (815) 987–4350
www.ilnb.uscourts.gov

Southern District of ILLINOIS
750 Missouri Avenue
East St. Louis, IL 62201
(618) 482–9400
www.ilsb.uscourts.gov

Southern District of ILLINOIS
United States Bankruptcy Court
Federal Courthouse
301 West Main Street
Benton, IL 62812
(618) 435–2200
www.ilsb.uscourts.gov

INDIANA

Southern District of INDIANA,
  Indianapolis Division
Mailing Address: P.O. BOX 44978
Indianapolis, IN 46244
Street Address: 116 U.S. Courthouse
46 E. Ohio St.
Indianapolis, IN 46204
Phone: (317) 229–3800
www.insb.uscourts.gov

Southern District of INDIANA,
  NEW ALBANY Division
Mailing Address: 110 U.S. Courthouse
121 West Spring Street
New Albany, IN 47150
(812) 542–4540
www.insb.uscourts.gov

Southern District of INDIANA,
  EVANSVILLE Division
Mailing Address: 352 Federal Bldg.
101 Northwest Martin L. King Boulevard
Evansville, IN 47708
(812) 434–6470
www.insb.uscourts.gov

Southern District of INDIANA,
  TERRE HAUTE Division
Mailing Address: Federal Building
30 N. 7th Street
Terre Haute, IN 47808
(812) 238–1550
www.insb.uscourts.gov

Northern Division, FT. WAYNE Division
Mailing Address: United States Bankruptcy Court
Northern District of Indiana
Post Office Box 2547
Fort Wayne, Indiana 46801–2547
Street Address: United States Bankruptcy Court
Northern District of Indiana
E. Ross Adair Federal Building and United States
  Courthouse
1300 South Harrison Street
Fort Wayne, Indiana 46802
(260) 420–5100
www.innb.uscourts.gov

Northern Division, HAMMOND Division
Mailing Address: United States Bankruptcy Court
Northern District of Indiana
5400 Federal Plaza
Hammond, Indiana 46320
Street Address: United States Bankruptcy Court
Northern District of Indiana
5400 Federal Plaza
Hammond, Indiana 46320
(219) 852–3480
www.innb.uscourts.gov

Northern Division, HAMMOND
  Division at Lafayette
Mailing Address: United States Bankruptcy Court
Northern District of Indiana
Post Office Box 890
Lafayette, Indiana 47902–0890
Street Address: United States Bankruptcy Court

Northern District of Indiana
Charles A. Halleck Federal Building
230 North Fourth Street
Lafayette, Indiana 47901
(765) 420–6300
www.innb.uscourts.gov

Northern Division, SOUTH BEND Division
Mailing Address: United States Bankruptcy Court
Northern District of Indiana
P.O. Box 7003
South Bend, Indiana 46634–7003
Street Address: United States Bankruptcy Court
Northern District of Indiana
Robert K. Rodibaugh United States Bankruptcy
  Courthouse
401 South Michigan Street
South Bend, Indiana 46601
(574) 968–2100
www.innb.uscourts.gov

IOWA

Northern District of Iowa, Cedar Rapids
Clerk's Office
United States Bankruptcy Court
P.O. Box 74890
Cedar Rapids, IA 52407
(319) 286–2200
www.ianb.uscourts.gov

Northern District of Iowa, Sioux City
Clerk's Office
United States Bankruptcy Court
P.O. Box 3857
Sioux City, IA 51102–3857
(712) 233–3939
www.ianb.uscourts.gov

Southern District of Iowa, Des Moines
Mailing Address: P.O. Box 9264
Des Moines, Iowa 50306–9264
Street Address: 300 U.S. Courthouse Annex
110 East Court Ave
Des Moines, Iowa 50309
(515) 284–6230
www.iasb.uscourts.gov

KANSAS

www.ksb.uscourts.gov

District of Kansas, Wichita Division
167 U.S. Courthouse
401 N. Market
Wichita, KS. 67202
(316) 269–6486

District of Kansas, Topeka Division
240 U.S. Courthouse
444 S.E. Quincy
Topeka, KS. 66683
(785) 295–2750

District of Kansas, Kansas City Division
161 U.S. Courthouse
500 State Ave.
Kansas City, KS. 66101
(913) 551–6732

KENTUCKY

Eastern District of Kentucky
Mailing Address: U.S. Bankruptcy Court
Box 1111
Lexington, KY, 40588–1111
Street Address: U.S. Bankruptcy Court
100 E. Vine St., Suite 200
Lexington, KY 40507.
(859) 233–2608
www.kyeb.uscourts.gov

Western District of Kentucky
601 West Broadway
Snyder Courthouse
Louisville, Kentucky 40202
Telephone. (502) 627–5700
www.kywb.uscourts.gov

LOUISIANA

Western District of Louisiana
United States Bankruptcy Court
300 Jackson Street, Suite 116
Alexandria, Louisiana 71301
318–445–1890
www.lawb.uscourts.gov

Western District of Louisiana
United States Bankruptcy Court
231 South Union Street
Second Floor
Opelousas, Louisiana 70570
337–948–3451
www.lawb.uscourts.gov

Western District of Louisiana
United States Bankruptcy Court
300 Fannin Street
Suite 2201
Shreveport, Louisiana 71101
318–676–4267
www.lawb.uscourts.gov

Middle District of Louisiana
707 Florida Street, Room 119
Baton Rouge, LA 70801
(225) 389–0211
www.lamb.uscourts.gov

Eastern District of Louisiana
U.S. Bankruptcy Court
Hale Boggs Federal Building
500 Poydras Street, Suite B-601
New Orleans, LA 70130
(504) 589–7878
www.laeb.uscourts.gov

MAINE

www.meb.uscourts.gov

District of MAINE
537 Congress Street, 2nd floor
Portland, ME 04101–3318
Phone: (207) 780–3482

District of MAINE
P.O. Box 1109 (04402)
300 U.S. Courthouse
202 Harlow Street, 3rd floor
Bangor, ME 04401
Phone: (207) 945–0348

MARYLAND

www.mdb.uscourts.gov

District of Maryland, Baltimore Division
Garmatz Federal Courthouse
101 West Lombard Street, Suite 8308
Baltimore, MD 21201
(410) 962–2688

District of Maryland, Greenbelt Division
6500 Cherrywood Lane
Suite 300
Greenbelt, MD 20770
(301) 344–8018

MASSACHUSETTS
www.mab.uscourts.gov

District of MASSACHUSETTS, Eastern Division
United States Bankruptcy Court
1101 Thomas P. O'Neill, Jr. Federal Building
10 Causeway Street
Boston, MA 02222–1074
Phone: (617) 565–8950

District of MASSACHUSETTS, Western Division
United States Bankruptcy Court
Donahue Federal Building
595 Main Street, Room 211
Worcester, MA 01608–2076
Phone: (508) 770–8900

District of MASSACHUSETTS, Hyannis
Barnstable Town Hall
376 Main Street
Hyannis, MA 02601–3917
(617) 565–6073
(The Hyannis location does not accept pleadings for
    filing. Pleadings should be filed in the Boston
    Court.)

District of MASSACHUSETTS, Springfield
United States Bankruptcy Court
Federal Building and Courthouse
1550 Main Street
Springfield, MA 01103
(508) 770–8936
(The Springfield Court does not accept pleadings for
    filing. Pleadings should be filed in the
    Worcester Court.)

MICHIGAN

Eastern District of MICHIGAN, Detroit Division
211 West Fort Street
Detroit, Michigan 48226
(313) 234–0065
www.mieb.uscourts.gov

Eastern District of MICHIGAN, Bay City Division
P.O. Box 911 (48707)
111 First Street
Bay City, Michigan 48708
(989) 894–8840
www.mieb.uscourts.gov

Eastern District of MICHIGAN, Flint Division
226 West Second Street
Flint, Michigan 48502
(810) 235–4126
www.mieb.uscourts.gov

Western District of MICHIGAN
Gerald R. Ford Federal Building
110 Michigan Street NW, Room # 299
Grand Rapids, MI 49503
Mailing Address: P.O. Box 3310
Grand Rapids, MI 49501
Phone: (616) 456–2693
www.miwb.uscourts.gov

Western District of MICHIGAN,
    Marquette Division
Post Office and Federal Courthouse
202 West Washington Street, 3rd Floor
Marquette, MI 49855
Mailing Address: P.O. Box 909
Marquette, MI 49855
Phone: (906) 226–2117
www.miwb.uscourts.gov

MINNESOTA
www.mnb.uscourts.gov

District of MINNESOTA
301 U.S. Courthouse
300 S. 4th Street
Minneapolis, MN 55415
(612) 664–5200

District of MINNESOTA, Duluth Division
416 U.S. Courthouse
515 W. 1st Street
Duluth, MN 55802
(218) 529–3600

District of MINNESOTA, Fergus Falls Division
204 U.S. Courthouse
118 South Mill Street
Fergus Falls, MN 56537
(218) 739–4671

District of MINNESOTA, St. Paul Division
200 Federal Building
316 North Robert Street
St. Paul, MN 55101
(651)-848-1000

MISSISSIPPI

Northern District of MISSISSIPPI
Mailing Address: United States Bankruptcy Court
P.O. Drawer 867
Aberdeen, MS 39730
Street: United States Bankruptcy Court
205 Federal Building
301 West Commerce Street
Aberdeen, MS 39730
(662) 369–2596
www.msnb.uscourts.gov

Southern District of MISSISSIPPI
P.O. Drawer 2448 (39225)
100 East Capitol Street
Jackson, MS 39201
Telephone: (601) 965–5301
www.mssb.uscourts.gov

Southern District of MISSISSIPPI
Dan M. Russell, Jr. U. S. Courthouse
2012 15th Street, Suite 244
Gulfport, MS 39501
(228) 563–1790
www.mssb.uscourts.gov

MISSOURI

Eastern District of MISSOURI, St. Louis
Eastern Division
Thomas F. Eagleton U.S. Courthouse
111 South Tenth St, Fourth Floor
St. Louis, MO. 63102
314–244–4500
www.moeb.uscourts.gov

Eastern District of MISSOURI, Hannibal
Northern Division
801 Broadway
Hannibal, MO
(573) 221–0757
www.moeb.uscourts.gov

Eastern District of MISSOURI, Cape Girardeau
Southeastern Division
339 Broadway
Cape Girardeau, MO 63701
(573) 334–6391
www.moeb.uscourts.gov

Western Division of MISSOURI, Kansas City
Charles Evans Whittaker Courthouse
400 E. 9th Street
Kansas City, Missouri 64106
(816) 512–1800
www.mow.uscourts.gov

MONTANA
www.mtb.uscourts.gov

District of MONTANA
273 Federal Building
400 North Main Street
Butte, MT 59701
406–782–3354
Clerk: 406–782–3354 ext. 1243

NEBRASKA
www.neb.uscourts.gov

District of NEBRASKA, Lincoln
460 Federal Building
100 Centennial Mall North
Lincoln, NE 68508
Telephone: (402) 437–5100

District of NEBRASKA, Omaha
111 South 18th Plaza, Suite 1152
Omaha, NE 68102
Telephone: (402) 661–7350

NEVADA
www.nvb.uscourts.gov

District of NEVADA
U.S. Bankruptcy Court
Foley Federal Building
300 Las Vegas Boulevard South
Las Vegas, NV 89101
Phone: (702) 388–6709

District of NEVADA
U.S. Bankruptcy Court
300 Booth Street, Room 1109
Reno, NV 89509
Phone: (775) 784–5559

NEW HAMPSHIRE
www.nhb.uscourts.gov

District of NEW HAMPSHIRE
1000 Elm Street, Suite 1001
Manchester, NH 03101–1708
(603) 222–2600

NEW JERSEY
www.njb.uscourts.gov

District of NEW JERSEY, Camden Division
Federal Building
401 Market Street
Second Floor
Camden, NJ 08101
Telephone: (856) 757–5485

District of NEW JERSEY, Newark Division
U.S. Bankruptcy Court
50 Walnut St. 3rd Floor
Newark, NJ 07102
Telephone: (973) 645–2630

District of NEW JERSEY, Trenton Division
Clark S. Fisher U.S. Courthouse
402 East State Street
Trenton, NJ 08608
(609) 989–2200

NEW MEXICO
http://www.nmcourt.fed.us/web/BCDOCS/bcindex
.html

District of NEW MEXICO
Dennis Chavez Federal Building & U.S. Courthouse
500 Gold Avenue SW, Tenth Floor
Albuquerque, NM 87102
(505) 348–2500

NEW YORK
www.nyeb.uscourts.gov

Eastern District of NEW YORK
U.S. Courthouse
75 Clinton Street
Brooklyn, NY 11201
Telephone: (718) 330–2188

Long Island Federal Court House
290 Federal Plaza
Central Islip, NY 11722
Telephone: (631) 712–6200

www.nysb.uscourts.gov
Southern District of NEW YORK
Alexander Hamilton Custom House
One Bowling Green
New York, NY 10004–1408
Telephone: (212) 668–2870

www.nynb.uscourts.gov
Northern District of NEW YORK, Albany Division
U.S. Bankruptcy Court
James T. Foley U.S. Court House
445 Broadway, Ste. 330
Albany, NY 12207
Telephone: (518) 257–1661

Northern District of NEW YORK, Utica Division
U.S. Bankruptcy Court
Alexander Pirnie U.S. Court House
10 Broad Street, Room 230
Utica, NY 13502
Telephone: (315) 793–8101

www.nysb.uscourts.gov
Southern District of NEW YORK,
    Poughkeepsie Division
176 Church Street
Poughkeepsie, NY 12601
Telephone: (845) 452–4200

Southern District of NEW YORK,
    White Plains Division
300 Quarropas Street
White Plains, NY 10601
Telephone: (914) 390–4060

www.nywb.uscourts.gov
Western District of NEW YORK, Buffalo Division
Olympic Towers
300 Pearl Street, Suite 250
Buffalo, NY 14202
Telephone: (716) 551–4130

Western District of NEW YORK,
    Rochester Division
1220 U.S. Courthouse
100 State Street
Rochester, NY 14614
Telephone: (585) 613–4200

NORTH CAROLINA
www.nceb.uscourts.gov

Eastern District of NORTH CAROLINA,
    Wilson Division
U.S. Bankruptcy Court
P.O. Drawer 2807
1760 Parkwood Blvd.
Wilson, NC 27894–2807
Telephone: (252) 237–0248

Eastern District of NORTH CAROLINA,
  Raleigh Division
U.S. Bankruptcy Court
P.O. Box 1441
300 Fayetteville, NC 27602–1441
Telephone: (919) 856–4752

www.ncmb.uscourts.gov
Middle District of NORTH CAROLINA,
  Greensboro Division
101 S. Edgeworth Street
Greensboro, NC 27401
Mailing Address: P.O. Box 26100
Greensboro, NC 27420–6100
Telephone: 1–910–333–5647

Middle District of NORTH CAROLINA,
  Winston-Salem Division
226 S. Liberty Street
Winston-Salem, NC 27101
Telephone: (336) 631–5340

www.ncwb.uscourts.gov
Western District of NORTH CAROLINA,
  Charlotte Division
401 West Trade Street, Room 111
Charlotte, NC 28202
Telephone: (704) 350–7500

NORTH DAKOTA

www.ndb.uscourts.gov
District of NORTH DAKOTA
Quentin N. Burdick United States Courthouse
655 First Avenue North, Suite 210
Fargo, ND 58102–4932
(701) 297–7100

OHIO

www.ohnb.uscourts.gov

Northern District of OHIO
Key Tower, Room 3001
127 Public Square
Cleveland, OH 44114–1309
Telephone: (216) 522–4373

Northern District of OHIO, Akron Division
455 U.S. Courthouse
2 South Main Street
Akron, OH 44308
Telephone: (330) 375–5840

Northern District of OHIO, Canton Division
Frank T. Bow Building
201 Cleveland Avenue, S.W.
Canton, OH 44702
Telephone: (330) 489–4426

Northern District of OHIO, Toledo Division
411 U.S. Courthouse
1716 Spielbusch Avenue
Toledo, OH 43624
Telephone: 1–419–259–6440

Northern District of OHIO, Youngstown Division
Nathaniel R. Jones Federal Building & US
  Courthouse
10 East Commerce Street
Youngstown, OH 44503–1621
Telephone: (330) 746–7027

Southern District of OHIO, Columbus Division
170 N. High Street
Columbus, OH 43215
Telephone: (614) 469–6638

Southern District of OHIO, Cincinnati Division
221 East Fourth Street
Atrium II, Ste. 800
Cincinnati, OH 45202
Telephone: (513) 684–2572

Southern District of OHIO, Dayton Division
120 W. 3rd Street
Dayton, OH 45402
Telephone: (937) 225–2516

OKLAHOMA
www.okeb.uscourts.gov

Eastern District of OKLAHOMA,
  Okmulgee Division
111 West 4th Street
Okmulgee, OK 74447
Telephone: (918) 758–0126

www.oknb.uscourts.gov
Northern District of OKLAHOMA
224 S. Boulder
Tulsa, OK 74103
Telephone: (918) 699–4000

www.okwb.uscourts.gov
Western District of OKLAHOMA
215 Dean A. McGee Avenue
Oklahoma City, OK 73102
Telephone: (405) 609–5700

OREGON
www.orb.uscourts.gov

District of OREGON, Portland Division
1001 S.W. Fifth Ave., #700
Portland, OR 97204
Telephone: (503) 326–2231

District of OREGON, Eugene Division
151 W. 7th Avenue #300
Eugene, OR 97401
Telephone: (541) 465–6448

PENNSYLVANIA
www.paeb.uscourts.gov

Eastern District of PENNSYLVANIA,
    Philadelphia Division
Robert N.C. Nix, Sr. Federal Courthouse
900 Market Street, Ste. 400
Philadelphia, PA 19107
Telephone: (215) 408–2800

Eastern District of PENNSYLVANIA,
    Reading Division
The Madison Building
400 Washington Street
Reading, PA 19601
Telephone: (610) 320–5255

www.pamb.uscourts.gov
Middle District of PENNSYLVANIA,
    Harrisburg Division
P.O. Box 908
320 Federal Building
228 Walnut Street
Harrisburg, PA 17101
Telephone: (717) 901–2800

Middle District of PENNSYLVANIA,
    Wilkes-Barre Division
274 Max Rosenn U.S. Courthouse
197 South Main Street
Wilkes-Barre, PA 18701
Telephone: (570) 826–6450

Western District of PENNSYLVANIA,
    Pittsburgh Division
5414 U.S. Steel Tower
1000 Liberty Avenue
600 Grant Street
Pittsburgh, PA 15219
Telephone: (412) 644–2700

Western District of PENNSYLVANIA, Erie Division
U.S. Courthouse, Room B160
17 South Park Row
Erie, PA 16501
Telephone: (814) 464–9740

PUERTO RICO
www.prb.uscourts.gov

District of PUERTO RICO
US Post Office and Courthouse Building
300 Recinto Sur, Suite 109
San Juan, Puerto Rico 00901
(787) 977–6000

RHODE ISLAND
www.rib.uscourts.gov

District of RHODE ISLAND
380 Westminster Street, 6th Floor, Suite 615
Providence, RI 02903
(401) 528–4477

SOUTH CAROLINA
www.scb.uscourts.gov

District of SOUTH CAROLINA
1100 Laurel Street
Columbia, SC 29202
(803) 765–5436

SOUTH DAKOTA
www.sdb.uscourts.gov

District of SOUTH DAKOTA, Southern Division
U.S. Courthouse
400 S. Phillips Ave., Room 104
P.O. Box 5060
Sioux Falls, SD 57117–5060
(605) 330–4541

District of SOUTH DAKOTA, Northern Division
Federal Building & U.S. Courthouse
225 South Pierre Street, Rm. 203
Pierre, SD 57501
(605) 224–6013

TENNESSEE
www.tneb.uscourts.gov

Eastern District of TENNESSEE,
    Southern and Winchester Division
31 East 11th Street
Chattanooga, TN 37402
Telephone: 1–423–752–5163

Eastern District of TENNESSEE, Northern Division
Howard H. Baker Jr. U.S. Courthouse
800 Market Street, Suite 330
Knoxville, TN 37902
(865) 545–4279

Eastern District of TENNESSEE,
    Northeastern Division
US Bankruptcy Court
James H. Quellen US Courthouse
220 West Depot Street
Greenville, TN 37743–4924
(423) 787–0113

www.tnmb.uscourts.gov
Middle District of TENNESSEE
Second Floor, Customs House
701 Broadway
Nashville, TN 37203
(615) 736–5584

Western District of TENNESSEE, Eastern Division
111 South Highland, Rm. 342
Jackson, TN 38305
Telephone: (731) 421–9300

Western District of TENNESSEE, Western Division
200 Jefferson Avenue, Suite 413
Memphis, TN 38103
(901) 328–3500

TEXAS

www.txeb.uscourts.gov

Eastern District of TEXAS, Tyler Division
110 North College Avenue, 9th Floor
Tyler, TX 75702
Telephone: 1–903–590–3200

Eastern District of TEXAS, Plano Division
660 N. Central Expressway, Suite 300B
Plano, TX 75074
(972) 509–1240

www.txnb.uscourts.gov
Northern District of TEXAS
Earl Cabell Building U.S. Courthouse
1100 Commerce Street, Room 1254
Dallas, TX 75242
Telephone: 1–214–753–2000

Northern District of TEXAS, Amarillo Division
624 S. Polk Suite 100
Amarillo, TX 79101–2389
(806) 324–2302

Northern District of TEXAS, Fort Worth Division
501 W. 10th Street
Fort Worth, TX 76102 -3643
(817) 333–6000

Northern District of TEXAS, Lubbock Division
306 Federal Building
1205 Texas Avenue
Lubbock, TX 79401 -4002
(806) 472–5000

www.txsb.uscourts.gov
Southern District of TEXAS
Bob Casey United States Courthouse
515 Rusk Street
Houston, TX 77002
(713) 250–5500

Southern District of TEXAS, Corpus Christi
    Division
1133 North Shoreline Blvd.
Corpus Christi, TX 78407
(361) 888–3483

www.txwb.uscourts.gov
Western District of TEXAS
Old Post Office Building
615 East Houston Street, Room 137
San Antonio, TX 78205
(212) 472–5196

Western District of TEXAS
US Post Office Annex
100 East Wall Street, Room P-163
Midland, TX 79701
(432) 683–1643

Western District of TEXAS
United States Bankruptcy Court
8515 Lockhead
El Paso, TX 79925
(915) 779–7362

Western District of TEXAS
800 Franklin Avenue, Suite 140
Waco, TX 76701
(254) 750–1513

Western District of TEXAS, Austin Division
Homer J. Thornberry Federal Judicial Building
903 San Jacinto, Ste. 322
Austin, TX 78701
(512) 916–5237

UTAH

www.utb.uscourts.gov

District of UTAH
Frank E. Moss U.S. Courthouse
350 South Main Street #301
Salt Lake City, UT 84101
(801) 524–6687

VERMONT

www.vtb.uscourts.gov

District of Vermont
U.S. Bankruptcy Court
67 Merchants Row
Rutland, VT 05702–6648
(802) 776–2000

VIRGIN ISLANDS

www.vid.uscourts.gov

District of VIRGIN ISLANDS
5500 Ventrans Drive, Room 301
St. Thomas, VI 00802
(340) 774–0640

VIRGINIA

www.vaeb.uscourts.gov

Eastern District of VIRGINIA, Alexandria Division
200 South Washington
Alexandria, VA 22314
(703) 258–1200

Eastern District of VIRGINIA, Norfolk Division
US Bankruptcy Court
600 Granby Street, 4th Floor
Norfolk, VA 23510
(757) 222–7500

Eastern District of VIRGINIA, Richmond Division
U.S. Bankruptcy Court
1100 East Main Street, Room 301
Richmond, VA 23219
(804) 916–2400

www.vawb.uscourts.gov
Western District of VIRGINIA,
   Harrisonburg Division
116 N. Main, Rm. 223
Harrisonburg, VA 22802
(540) 434–8327

Western District of VIRGINIA, Lynchburg Division
1100 Main Street, Room 226
Lynchburg, VA 24505
(434) 845–0317

Western District of VIRGINIA, Roanoke Division
P.O. Box 2390
210 Church Ave., S.W., Rm. 200
Roanoke, VA 24011
(540) 857–2391

WASHINGTON

www.waeb.uscourts.gov

Eastern District of WASHINGTON
904 West Riverside Avenue Ste. 304
Spokane, WA 99201–2164
(509) 353–2404

Eastern District of WASHINGTON
402 E. Yakima Avenue Suite 200
Yakima, WA 98901
(509) 454–5660

www.wawb.uscourts.gov
Western District of WASHINGTON,
   Seattle Division
United States Courthouse
700 Stewart Street, Room 6301
Seattle, WA 98101
(206) 370–5200

Western District of WASHINGTON,
   Tacoma Division
Union Station
1717 Pacific Avenue, Rm. 2100
Tacoma, WA 98402–3233
(253) 593–6310

WEST VIRGINIA

www.wvnb.uscourts.gov

Northern District of WEST VIRGINIA
U.S. Federal Building
12th and Chapline Streets, Ste. 300
Wheeling, WV 26003
(304) 233–1655

www.wvsb.uscourts.gov
Southern District of WEST VIRGINIA,
   Bluefield Division
601 Federal Street
Bluefield, WV 24701
(304) 327–9798

Southern District of WEST VIRGINIA,
Charleston Division
Robert C. Byrd U.S. Courthouse
300 Virginia Street, East
Charleston, WV 25301
(304) 347–3000

Southern District of WEST VIRGINIA,
Huntington Division
Sydney L. Christie Federal Building
845 Fifth Avenue
Huntington, WV 25701
(304) 529–5588

Southern District of WEST VIRGINIA,
Beckley Division
110 North Herber Street
Beckley, WV 25801
(304) 253–7481

Southern District of WEST VIRGINIA,
Parkersburg Division
425 Juliana Street
Parkersburg, WV 26102
(304) 420–6490

WISCONSIN
www.wieb.uscourts.gov

Eastern District of WISCONSIN, Milwaukee Division
U.S. Bankruptcy Court
517 East Wisconsin Avenue, Ste. 126
Milwaukee, WI 53202
(414) 297–3291

www.wiw.uscourts.gov
Western District of WISCONSIN, Madison Division
120 N. Henry Street, Rm. 340
Madison, WI 53701
(608) 264–5178

Western District of WISCONSIN, Eau Claire Division
500 South Barstow Street
Eau Claire, WI 54701
(715) 839–2980

WYOMING
www.wyb.uscourts.gov

District of WYOMING
2120 Capitol Avenue, Suite 6004
Cheyenne, WY 82001
(307) 433–2200

District of WYOMING
111 S. Wolcott
Casper, WY 82601
(307) 232–2650

We the People Store Addresses

ALASKA

545 E Northern Lights Blvd.
Anchorage, Alaska 99503
(907) 276–3006

ARIZONA

15224 No. 59th Ave.
Glendale, AZ 95306
(602) 942–6777

2815 So. Alma School Rd.
Mesa, AZ 85210
(480) 456- 1412

2524 Indian School Rd.
Phoenix, AZ 85016
(602) 340–0290

3329 E. Bell Rd., Ste. 18
Phoenix, AZ 85032
(602) 953–4063

2545 E. Speedway Blvd.
Tucson, AZ 85716
(520) 318–4987

CALIFORNIA

27064 South La Paz Rd.
Aliso Viejo, CA 92656
(949) 425–0630

1137 W. Valley Blvd.
Alhambra, CA 91803
(626) 300–8011

1665 W. Katella Ave.
Anaheim, CA 92802–3021
(714) 772–0449

6332 Beach Blvd.
Buena Park, CA 90621
(714) 523–5000

1172 San Pablo Ave.
Berkeley, CA 94705
(510) 559–3456

649 W. Imperial Hwy.
Brea, CA 92821
(714) 255–9110

356 E. Olive, #101
Burbank, CA 91502
(818) 848–4421

528 Myrtlewood Dr.
Calimesa, CA 92320–1505
(909) 446–1778

21722 Devonshire St.
Chatsworth, CA 91311
(818) 882–7622

4474 Treat Blvd.
Concord, CA 94521
(925) 246–0370

1909 Harbor Blvd.
Costa Mesa, CA 92627–2666
(949) 574–8880

7603A Amador Valley Rd.
Dublin, CA 94568–2301
(925) 479–9600

345 No. 2nd St.
El Cajon, CA 92021
(619) 442–4599

18044 Ventura Blvd.
Encino, CA 91316
(818) 774–1966

1107 4th St.
Eureka, CA 95501
(707) 442–0162

1600 Travis Blvd., Ste. B
Fairfield, CA 94533
(707) 428–9871

12752 Valley View St.
Garden Grove, CA 92845
(714) 934–8382

1415 E. Colorado Blvd.
Glendale, CA 91205
(818) 546–1787

17818 Chatsworth St.
Granada Hills, CA 91344
(818) 363–5837

22551 Foothill Blvd.
Hayward, CA 94541
(510) 728–7600

4479 Hollywood Blvd.
Hollywood, CA 90027
(323) 666–8200

17131 Beach Blvd.
Huntington Beach, CA 92648
(714) 843–6229

698 S. Vermont Ave. #105
(Koreatown)
Los Angeles, CA 90005
(213) 389–2200

1826 W. Ave. J
Lancaster, CA 93534
(661) 726–7646

2115 Bellflower Blvd.
Long Beach, CA 90815
(562) 985–1101

729 W. 7th St.
Los Angeles, CA 90017
(213) 489–1980

5324 Wilshire Blvd.
Los Angeles, CA 90036
(323) 937–2311

2496 Lincoln Blvd.
Marina Del Rey, CA
90291–5041
(310) 577–8333

2400 Alicia Parkway #1A
Mission Viejo, CA 92691
(949) 951–4411

1347 McHenry Ave.
Modesto, CA 95350
(209) 523–8227

11369 Riverside Dr.
North Hollywood, CA 91602
(818) 762–8647

11755 Imperial Hwy., Ste. 200
Norwalk , CA 90652
(562) 863–1991

3753 Mission Ave.
Oceanside, CA 92054
(760) 754–9059

244 Grand Ave.
Oakland, CA 94610
(510) 452–2324

595 The City Dr. #200
Orange, CA 92868
(714) 634–4885

2400 Saviers Rd.
Oxnard, CA 93033
(805) 487–1210

73121 Country Club Dr.
Palm Desert, CA 92260
(760) 346–7074

2127 El Camino Real
Palo Alto, CA 94306
(650) 324–3800

762 E. Colorado Blvd.
Pasadena, CA 91101
(626) 535–0100

135 Keller St., Ste. C
Petaluma, CA 94952
(707) 769–1639

9030 Foothill Blvd., Ste. 112
Rancho Cucamonga, CA 91730
(909) 466–4500

2968 Churn Creek Rd.
Redding, CA 96002
(530) 222–8747

6519 Magnolia Ave.
Riverside, CA 92506
(951) 369–3591

4211 B Arden Way
Sacramento, CA 95864
(916) 679–6780

517 So. Main St., Ste. 101
Salinas, CA 93901
(831) 771–2029

1435 University Ave.
San Diego, CA 92103
(619) 725–0996

209 North Maclay
San Fernando, CA 91340–2908
(818) 838–3900

411 Divisadero St.
San Francisco, CA 94117
(415) 701–9800

441A Marsh St.
San Luis Obispo, CA 93401
(805) 596–0100

903B Irwin St.
San Rafael, CA 94901–3317
(415) 457–3773

1501 State St.
Santa Barbara, CA 93101
(805) 962–4100

500 Soquel Ave., Ste. B
Santa Cruz, CA 95062
(831) 458–5155

920 South Broadway
Santa Maria, CA 93454
(805) 928- 9700

2922 Wilshire Blvd.
Santa Monica, CA 90403
(310) 264–0517

13565 Ventura Blvd.
Sherman Oaks, CA 91423
(818) 906–0086

4360 Cochran St.
Simi Valley, CA 93065
(805) 526–7351

22933 Soledad Canyon Rd.
Saugus, CA 91350
(661) 255–8488

800 E. Thousand Oaks Blvd.
Thousand Oaks, CA 91360
(805) 371–7575

4727 Torrance Blvd.
Torrance, CA 90503
(310) 370–8399

13732 Newport Ave., Ste. 1
Tustin, CA 92780
(714) 730–5196

7219 Balboa Blvd.
Van Nuys, CA 91406
(818) 989–7431

2827 E. Thompson Blvd.
Ventura, CA 93003
(805) 641–2010

1830 Hacienda Dr. #5
Vista, CA 92081
(760) 941–1604

2061 MT. Diablo Blvd.
Walnut Creek, CA 94596
(925) 407–1010

21904 Ventura Blvd.
Woodland Hills, CA 91367
(818) 704–9394

1648 Westwood Blvd.
W. Los Angeles, CA 90024
(310) 441–5400

COLORADO

3125 28th St.
Boulder, CO 80304
(303) 544–1066

14 N. Main St.
Brighton, CO 80601
(303) 654–9983

62 E. Arapahoe Rd.
(Arapahoe)
Centennial, CO 80122
(303) 991–3651

1806 A Dominion Way
Colorado Springs, CO 80918
(719) 590–7779

7115 E. Hampden Ave.
Denver, CO 80224
(303) 302–1000

2454 Hwy. 6 & 50
Grand Junction, CO 81505
(970) 263–9191

3489 W. 10th St. #C
Greeley, CO 80634
(970) 352–5444

3355 So. Wadsworth Blvd.
Lakewood, CO 80227
(303) 984–2101

62 E. Arapahoe Rd.
Littleton, CO 80122
(303) 991–3651

7330 W. 88th Ave., Ste. E
Westminster, CO 80021
(303) 421–0367

CONNECTICUT

1100 Main St.
Newington, CT 06111–2910
(860) 665–0540

165 Bank St.
New London, CT 06320
(860) 447–9984

281 Connecticut Ave.
Norwalk, CT 06854
(203) 852–7006

163 Post Rd.
Orange, CT 06477
(203) 795–9978

FLORIDA

1701 No. Federal Hwy
Boca Raton, FL 33432
(561) 347–5340

1722 Del Prado Blvd.
Cape Coral, FL 33990
(239) 573–7311

101 E. Commercial Blvd.
Fort Lauderdale, FL 33334
(954) 491–2990

16050 So. Tamiani Trail
Fort Myers, FL 33908
(239) 267–9955

320 Osceola Ave.
Jacksonville Beach, FL 32250
(904) 241–2533

3003 So. Tamiami Trail
Sarasota, FL 34239
(941) 366–8896

GEORGIA

1524 Church
Decatur, GA 30030
(404) 270–9199

561 Forest Parkway
Forest Park, GA 30297
(404) 608–0566

HAWAII

564 South St.
Honolulu, HI 96813
(808) 548–0379

IDAHO

7974 Fairview Ave.
Boise, ID 83704
(208) 658–1745

1587 E. 17th
Idaho Falls, ID 93404
(208) 522–5176

ILLINOIS

6218 W. Cermak
Berwyn, IL
(708) 484–9200

2411 Ashland
Chicago, IL 60614
(773) 529–9900

3210 W. 95th
Evergreen Park, IL 60805
708–422–2000

801 E. Ogden Ave.
Naperville, IL 60563
(630) 778–9770

KANSAS

7620 Metcalf Ave., Ste. H
Overland Park, KS 66204
(913) 383–0505

2243 North Tyler, Ste. 107
(West Wichita)
Wichita, KS 67220
(316) 773–2400

410 North Hillside, Ste. 900
(College Hill)
Wichita, KS 67214
(316) 685–5759

KENTUCKY

3126 Dixie Hwy
Erlanger, KY 41018
(859)727–6900

MARYLAND

511-C Eastern Blvd.
Essex, MD 21221
(410) 780–7084

507 Reisterstown Rd.
Pikesville, MD 21208–5303
(410) 580–2036

MICHIGAN

2841 Breton Rd.
Grand Rapids, MI 49512
(616) 245–7008

29961 Gratiot Ave.
(Detroit)
Roseville, **MI** 48066
(586) 774–5188

MINNESOTA

2002 Lyndale Ave., So.
Minneapolis, **MN** 55404
(612) 333–3777

MISSISSIPPI

1553 County Line Rd., Ste. 200
Jackson, **MS** 39211
(601) 206–9980

MISSOURI

2722 S. Brentwood Blvd.
Brentwood, **MO** 63144
(314) 963–0600

NEBRASKA

709 No. 48th St.
Lincoln, **NE** 68504
(402) 464–2200

9207 Maple St.
Omaha, **NE** 68134
(402) 502–9898

NEVADA

2300 South Carson St., Ste. 4
Carson City, **NV** 89701
(775) 888–6830

4850 W. Flamingo Rd.
Las Vegas, **NV** 89103
(702) 222–0414

6405–2 So. Virginia St.
Reno, **NV** 89511
(775) 853–4400

NEW JERSEY

107 Broadway
Elmwood Park, **NJ** 07407
(201) 794–6491

534 Bloomfield Ave.
Verona, **NJ** 07044
(973) 857–0057

NEW MEXICO

2828 Carlisle Blvd. N.E.
Albuquerque, **NM** 87110
(505) 889–8900

NEW YORK

133 Wolf Rd.
Albany, **NY** 12205
(518) 435–9110

42–38 Bell Blvd.
Bayside, **NY** 11361
(718) 224–8704

1508 86th St.
Bay Ridge, **NY** 11228
(718) 259–8181

2349 Arthur Ave.
(Belmont)
Bronx, **NY** 10458
(718) 295–5700

92 Willoughby St.
(Downtown Brooklyn)
Brooklyn, **NY** 11201
(718) 855–8585

116–28 Queens Blvd.
Forest Hills, **NY** 11375
(718) 793–4400

1986 Ralph Ave.
(Georgetown)
Brooklyn, **NY** *11234*
(718) 968–0022

423B 2nd Ave.
Grammercy Park, **NY** 10010
(212) 213–2700

788 A. Manhattan Ave.
(Greenpoint)
Brooklyn, **NY** 11222
(718) 609–0900

3658 Broadway
Hamilton Heights, **NY** 10031
(212) 281–4800

377 West 125th St.
Harlem, **NY** 10027
(212) 280–3100

519B 207th St.
(Inwood)
New York, **NY** 10034
(212) 942–1600

5661 Broadway
(Kingsbridge)
Bronx, **NY** 10463
(718) 543–5800

796 Ulster Ave.
Kingston, **NY** 12401
(845) 331–5833

470 Hawkins Ave.
Lake Ronkonkoma, **NY** 11779
(631) 467–2667

45–01 Northern Blvd.
Long Island City, **NY** 11101
(718) 392–4300

447 Mamaroneck Ave.
Mamaroneck, **NY** 10543
(914) 835–7800

250 East Houston St.
New York, **NY** 10002
(212) 979–6100

239 W. 72nd St.
New York, **NY** 10023
(212) 501–7700

3478 Jerome Ave.
(Norwood)
Bronx, **NY** 10463
(718) 994–6400

105–28 Cross Bay Blvd.
Ozone Park, **NY** 11417
(718) 845–8300

514 5th Ave.
(Park Slope)
Brooklyn, **NY** *11215*
(718) 965–2228

211–36 Hillside Ave.
Queens Village, **NY** 11427
(718) 217–1500

3715 Nostrand
Sheepshead Bay, **NY** 11235
(718) 332–5600

861 Montauk Hwy. #3
Shirley, NY 11967
(631) 281–2212

2175 Hylan Blvd.
Staten Island, NY 10306
(718) 351–1200

46–14 Queens Blvd.
Sunnyside, NY 11104
(718) 472–3800

3427 East Tremont Ave.
(Throgs Neck)
Bronx, NY 10465
(718) 863–2200

554 West 181st St.
(Washington Heights)
New York, NY 10033
(212) 928–8000

127 Post Ave.
Westbury, NY 11590
(516) 333–3306

49 Westchester Sq.
Westchester Square, NY
(718) 931–7500

148 Mamaroneck Ave.
White Plains, NY 10601
(914) 683–5105

NORTH CAROLINA

624 Tyvola Rd., Ste. 101
Charlotte, NC 28217
(704) 665–6353

302-b SE Greenville Blvd.
Greenville, NC 27858
(252) 355–8107

4940-C Capital Blvd.
Raleigh, NC 27616
(919) 713–0339

OHIO

794 Main St.
Milford, OH 45150
(513) 831–3380

OKLAHOMA

3747-B South Harvard
Tulsa, OK 74135
(918) 794–0305

OREGON

400 NW Walnut Blvd. #200
Corvallis, OR 97330
(541) 738–9872

377 Coburg Rd., Ste. C
Eugene, OR 97401
(541) 345–1128

520 S.E. 10TH Ave.
Hillsboro, OR 97123
(503) 693–8885

PENNSYLVANIA

718 Market St.
(Center City)
Philadelphia, PA 19106
(215) 238–8809

2836 Cottman Ave.
Philadelphia, PA 19149
(215) 333–8281

34 West Lancaster Ave.
Shillington, PA 19607
(610) 796–1250

301 W. Baltimore Pike
Springfield, PA 19018
(610) 626–4141

RHODE ISLAND

298 Atwells Ave.
Providence, RI 02903
(401) 521–4700

TENNESSEE

8161 Kingston Pike
Knoxville, TN 37919
(865) 560–2221

86 Thompson Lane
Nashville, TN 37211
(615) 445–3611

TEXAS

13729 Research Blvd., Ste. 850
Austin, TX 78759
(512) 996–8558

7726 Forest Lane
Dallas, TX 75230
(214) 265–8800

2672 No. Belt Line Rd.
Irving, TX 75062
(972) 570–4800

WISCONSIN

4210 E. Washington Ave.
Madison, WI 53704
(608) 245–5003

INDEX